מסורה

ArtScroll Series®

Rabbi Nosson Scherman / Rabbi Meir Zlotowitz
General Editors

BEING

&

Published by

Mesorah Publications, ltd

Becoming

A guide for better living,
parenting and teaching
by a veteran educator and therapist.

Dr. Jacob Mermelstien

FIRST EDITION
First Impression ... April 2000

Published and Distributed by
MESORAH PUBLICATIONS, LTD.
4401 Second Avenue / Brooklyn, N.Y 11232

Distributed in Europe by
J. LEHMANN HEBREW BOOKSELLERS
20 Cambridge Terrace
Gateshead, Tyne and Wear
England NE8 1RP

Distributed in Israel by
SIFRIATI / A. GITLER
10 Hashomer Street
Bnei Brak 51361

Distributed in Australia and New Zealand by
GOLDS BOOK & GIFT SHOP
36 William Street
Balaclava 3183, Vic., Australia

Distributed in South Africa by
KOLLEL BOOKSHOP
Shop 8A Norwood Hypermarket
Norwood 2196, Johannesburg, South Africa

ARTSCROLL SERIES®
BEING AND BECOMING
© Copyright 2000, by MESORAH PUBLICATIONS, Ltd.
4401 Second Avenue / Brooklyn, N.Y. 11232 / (718) 921-9000 / www.artscroll.com

---

ISBN:
1-57819-504-7 (hard cover)
1-57819-505-5 (paperback)

Typography by CompuScribe at ArtScroll Studios, Ltd.
Printed in the United States of America by Noble Book Press Corp.
Bound by Sefercraft, Quality Bookbinders, Ltd., Brooklyn N.Y. 11232

Preface

It is self-evident that while modern man is winning the war on physical illness, and to a large extent the war on poverty, modern man is not doing well in battling emotional distress and general unhappiness. The proliferation of psychotropic drugs, medically prescribed as well as illegal ones, the many "self-prescribed" addictions man uses to "feel good," the popularity of psychotherapy, and the many "how to" books and articles that are meant to help people cope emotionally, should convince us that there is something wrong here, and that all these remedies are just not doing the job.

Various reasons for this sad state of affairs have been advanced. Yet a simple reading of Torah as it describes the nature of man tells it all. The Torah states: "It is not good for man to be alone."[1] The remedy then, obviously, is for man to connect with another. To prove this point, one may view psychotherapy as doing, besides whatever it does analytically, just that – namely, creating in an individual a feeling of having someone who cares, one who tries to understand, one who has a genuine interest without personal motives (such as those a parent or spouse has), and one who *is* oneself genuine – or at least tries to be so. More than 40 years of practice in clinical psychology have convinced me that this is so.

Now, obviously, the *Ribbono Shel Olam* has not created man with such a "deficiency," with a lifelong need of therapy. (Neither do I buy, except in rare instances, the notion of "chemical imbalance".) No, G-d's creation is perfect. Moreover, man is born to parents, is helpless enough for a considerable period of time, and thus becomes a recipient of caring and loving. He then goes on to live in a society and theoretically never, ever, needs to feel alone. So what goes wrong?

We hypothesize that society today fails the individual by its inability to make individuals feel that others care. Worse yet, all too frequently, when intervention does take place, it crowds or crushes. Lost is the art of being there for another while giving the other space and dignity to grow oneself. The machine and technol-

---

1. *Bereishis* 2:18

ogy have displaced man from center stage. Technology is "superior" to man. It does things more speedily, it is free of human error, and, with miniaturization, takes up less space. It does things better and faster. Thus, one corresponds with machines, transacts business with machines, even plays with machines and is medically treated by machines (or chemicals). The one thing machines cannot do is to relate. And the one thing that cannot be speeded up or miniaturized is relating, caring, feeling. "More" time or interaction is not wasted – it is better. Obviously, not everyone is in need of "clinical" therapy. There is, and must be available to man, a more natural source for therapy, namely, the psychotherapist within every one of us: the *feeling* we have naturally for our fellows, and the *thinking* that should tell us what to say, when to say it, and how to say it. All of this would help our fellow man create a better feeling or mood, a feeling of not being alone, and a feeling of hope or security to displace feelings of despair or anxiety.

This book is an attempt to have individuals realize that because of their intrinsic humanity, they are therapeutic agents to begin with. By growing the Torah way, they can become better people and better therapists. And by stopping and thinking, they can learn what to say and when to say it, what to do, and what not to do.

The first psychotherapist known to us was *Aharon HaKohen*, the High Priest Aharon. Though our sages describe some of his techniques,[2] the *mishnah* in *Avos* directs us, rather, to study his being, his *middos*, his traits.[3] I propose that in this directive lies the secret, the key, to universal help for emotional distress. What emotional "heroism" do we see in *Aharon HaKohen?* The Torah testifies that Aharon, the elder of the two brothers, truly rejoiced in the glory enjoyed by Moshe, his younger brother.[4] He felt neither jealousy nor envy, but joy in another's well-being.

---

2. *Avos d'Rabbi Nosson* 12:3
3. "Hillel says: 'Be among the disciples of Aharon, loving peace and pursuing peace, loving people and bringing them closer to Torah' " (*Avos* 1:12). I suggest that Aharon's love for people, his need to reach out and relate with them, was the key to his success in reaching people and bringing them closer to the Torah way – that is peace, loving-kindness and genuinely loving interpersonal relationships. His loving, reaching-out personality – that is, his *being* – was far more crucial than his *doings*.
See also Anthony Storr, *The Art of Psychotherapy* (New York: Methuen, 1980), pp. 164-185.
4. See *Shemos* 4:14; see also *Midrash Rabbah, Shemos* 3:17.

Let us linger for a moment and consider how our world would look should every human being shelve his own negative feelings – losses, disappointments, shortcomings, or jealousies – and supplant them with the joy of feeling for others and caring for others. Technique would be secondary. Primary would be the therapeutic personality all of us possess, that is, the ability to feel for another, and share in both his pain and in his joy.

At first glance, the notion of possessing such feelings of empathy towards others implies selfless nobility at one's own expense. This seems difficult to achieve. How is one to forgo one's own needs ("What's in it for me?"), and attend to others?

Yet, hard as it seems, every one of us is already doing it – and at a great gain, not a loss at all. The parent who, because of his/her love for the child, tolerates the natural "disorder" created by the arrival of the child and has patience for the child, does not lose or give up anything at all. To the contrary, the parent grows. By *being* tolerant or patient for the child, the parent becomes a better person, a more patient and tolerant one, and becomes ever more loving. So it is with one's spouse, parents, siblings, neighbors – virtually all of mankind. One grows by being there for his fellow in several ways.

To begin with, such behavior distracts a person from his own unhappiness, preventing him from wallowing in depression or generating ever more frustration or anger. Thereafter, by caring for the other and becoming patient and tolerant, he becomes himself a better person, with greater tolerance for his own troubles, and more patience and love for others. And as a bonus, a network of reciprocal helpful relationships is formed.

We return for a moment to *Aharon HaKohen*, to study his traits which enabled him to feel that powerfully for another. He loved peace, he needed peace – an absence of conflict, a sense of well-being within himself, within others, *and* between others. So he pursued it. But how? By loving people and thus caring for them. Consequently (and, I suggest, automatically), this loving and caring, combined with his personal need to do something about it, was *mekarev* them (drew them closer) to Torah. It enveloped them with *his* beliefs, *his* opinions, and *his* attachment to Torah and the Torah way of sweetness and gentility, the Torah way of forgiving, of loving, and of emotional attachment between man and his fellow man.

From a behavioral-science point of view, when psychotherapists realize that the most powerful tool in their possession is the ability to feel for others, the ability that G-d has implanted into every human being, they will worry less about technique. They will concern themselves with being genuinely caring, genuine in their own conduct, and most importantly, genuine in dealing with their patients. Thus we find successes and failures, regardless of the therapist's orientation. To be sure, there are techniques, there are useful theories, there is learning, and there is experience. Yet equally, or more importantly so, there is something basic that all of us possess, the universal "man making man," the caring, the reaching out to care for, to relate to, our fellow man. Psychotherapists, because they choose this profession, should be individuals already programmed to reach out to others and to care. As they practice this reaching out, they become ever more caring, developing a very special relationship which is genuine and unaffected by the clinician's personal biases or interests. Furthermore, they will add what they have learned scientifically, but not discard this basic tool of being genuine – in caring, in personal conduct, and in relating to their patients.

If we truly understand this basic undercurrent of genuine caring that facilitates therapy, we will understand why therapists cannot agree on what, exactly, therapy is. Nor can they conceptualize and describe what takes place during the "talking cure." Fortunately, there are voices in the profession that do speak of therapists being an example for the patient, of reaching the patient, and of caring.[5]

In closing, I ask the reader not to consider this book as a "how to" guide. Life is too varied, and there are many, many nuances which makes every situation unique. Nor is this a *"mussar shmuess,"* a lecture in being *"gut and frum,"* and certainly not an-

---

5. For further reading on this theme, and on how Torah, *menschlichkeit, mussar, tochachah,* and psychotherapy complement one another to make individuals grow and create loving interpersonal relationships, see Jacob Mermelstein in "Reply," in *Intercom* (a publication of the American Association of Orthodox Jewish Scientists) (New York: April 1978), vol. 17, no. 1, pp. 31-36.

other opportunity to make the reader fault him/herself for having been an imperfect parent or spouse. For we are not robots, and it is our imperfections that make us into unique humans. I do hope and trust, however, that my words will help the reader to stop and think – and understand his/her fellow, particularly the spouse and the child, as feeling human beings, who have adapted to life on the basis of *their* experiences and *their* pains and losses. Consequently, they behave and act in ways other than those of the observer. To the observer – parent, spouse, or friend – such feelings and behavior may seem to be maladaptive, but they somehow make sense to the other. In order to help the spouse, child, or friend, the observer must first make an attempt to understand the other person's behaviors and feelings, and only afterwards can this individual be helped to modify or adjust his or her behavior. Not all "misbehavior" comes about because of sheer willfulness or rebelliousness. As the saying goes, "There are no villains, only victims." While certainly not totally true, there is enough there to help us become ever more tolerant and understanding for those whom we label "maladjusted," "disturbed," or simply just "different."

Acknowledgments

From childhood on, I have been taught — and have practiced — to say "Thank you." Thank you, *Ribbono Shel Olam*, and thank you, my fellow humans. With the publication of this book, additional and specific "thank yous" are in order. Here they come.

Man is at any given moment a composite of what he has learned from others – thoughts and ideas, as well as feelings and emotions. Thus, anything one is able to contribute to the fund of human knowledge, as well as ways and means of helping others, is no more than the proverbial midget sitting on the shoulders of the giant. This is a fact, not a display of false humility.

I thank the *Ribbono Shel Olam* who has enabled me to learn from others, true giants, each of whom had some "specialty" which I hope to have incorporated into my psyche – a mode of learning, a way of relating, a view of Torah, of a *ben Torah*, and much more. Among them were the *geonim, zichronam livrachah, HaRav* Shlomo Heiman, *HaRav* Yaakov Kamenetsky, *HaRav* Reuven Grozovsky, *HaRav* Gedalya Schorr, *HaRav* Shraga Feivel Mendelowitz, and the *Admorim* of the Kapitznishe dynasty, *zechusam yagen aleinu*.

Additionally, during my stint as a yeshivah principal and teacher, I had the invaluable benefit of the guidance of *HaGaon HaRav* Aharon Kotler, *z"tl*, concerning Torah education and how to deal with those less committed without compromising Torah principles. I consider myself equally fortunate in enjoying the guidance of present-day *gedolim*, as well as their trust in the work I do.

My mother, *a"h*, a direct descendant of *HaGaon* R' Yaakov M'Lissa, who was herself an amateur therapist par excellence, taught me the invaluable lesson of *b'sever panim yafos*, the utility of a genuine smile in communicating with others, in spite of one's own problems or general shyness. My father, *a"h*, taught me the art of "stretching" by placing me in grades higher than my age would warrant. Additionally, he would exhort me to associate with those who knew more – yet to learn from everyone, including from those who were less proficient.

In this respect, I have learned more from my patients over the 40-odd years of practicing psychology than I have from my own studies, from my teaching of first grade through graduate school, from heading a college psychology department, or from research. Similarly do my *talmidim/chaveirim* for whom I say a daily *Daf Yomi shiur*, themselves true *bnei Torah*, keep me on my toes and help me glean ever more insights from Torah.

Most of the chapters in this book first appeared in *The Jewish Parent*, a publication of Torah Umesorah. I am grateful to *HaRav* Dr. Joseph Kaminetsky, *a"h*, the former National Director of Torah Umesorah, who encouraged my writing, and, *yibadel l'chaim*, *HaRav* Joshua Fishman, its Executive Vice President, as well as to Mrs. Bernice Brandt, Director of National Society of Hebrew Day School-PTAs. Other chapters had their genesis as articles in *The Jewish Observer*, for which I thank *HaRav* Nissan Wolpin. I find that the beliefs and opinions which I expressed in the original articles are equally applicable today, with only minor updating.

The "father" of this project is *HaRav* Nosson Scherman, who was the first to suggest compiling all of these writings into a book. His recommendation of Mrs. Nina Indig as the book's editor was most fortunate; she is a true professional whose suggestions, criticisms, and ideas were invaluable. Finally, a heartfelt *yasher kochachem* is due to the staff at ArtScroll, — Avrohom Biderman, Avrohom Kay, Mrs. Mindy Stern, Mrs. Rivkah Hamaoui, Mrs. Esther Feierstein, Hindy Goldner, and Gitty Perlstein — who put it all together.

Needless to say, my children – on whom I "practiced" – continue to validate my ideas on parenting by being my joy and *nachas*. Their choices of spouses, who are now my children as well, additionally encourage me in my mode of dealing with others. Thank you for being my friends in addition to – or in spite of – our relatedness. The same holds true for my grandchildren, grandchild-in-law and great-grandchildren, *baruch Hashem*.

Last but not least, *achronah achronah chavivah*, it is time to thank my wife, herself the daughter of the known *baal chesed*, R' Mendel Weitman, *a"h*, the founder of the Boyaner *Gemilas Chesed*, and his wife, Alta Bracha, *a"h*. I will refrain from citing the usual virtues of an *aishes chayil*, a woman of valor, in order to highlight the greatest gift a woman can bestow upon her husband, by describing a trait at which she excels.

People continue doing what they do because of "reinforcement." For children, this may come in the form of gold stars, chocolate bars, or grades. What about the adult? What reinforcer can a man hope for, on which he can rely without developing an addiction for approval or applause? It is the effect one's doings have on others, particularly one's loved ones. This effect a man notices in the glow of pleasure radiating from his wife's eyes, and her ever-present support and encouragement, resulting in the feeling that he is not alone. She does not prod, nor push; neither is she a "*mashgiach*" to tell him what to do. She does not steal his thunder by being a martyr or taking credit. No, she does none of these. What she does do – and powerfully so – is project a small, still voice, saying, "You can do it. We are in this together. I hold your hand. You are not alone."

Thank you, Renee.

And thank you all.

Table of Contents

Learning to Live and Learning to Learn

Emotional Climate in the Home / First Aid for Emotional Stress / Modifying Habits

Causes / The Positive Use of Authority / The Disciplined Jew in a Compulsive Society / Deprogramming the Compulsive

Chapter One

Teaching and Learning, and "the Need to Be Me"

The Need to Teach and the Need to Learn

o teach our young is a universal phenomenon observable in all societies, from the most primitive to the most highly advanced. All parents teach their children to master their environment, to acquire the necessary skills in order to sustain themselves, and to develop the know-how to function socially within the group. Dependent upon each society's value system, the child's lessons will differ in content and in character, and may be formal or informal, dispensed in the home, in the school, or in a combination of the two. In any case, the fact that all parents do teach permits us to label this teaching behavior as an instinctual parental behavior pattern — *a need to teach*. A similar phenomenon observable in the animal world confirms that this trait is indeed innate, reflexive, and instinctual.

Concurrently, one observes behavior in infants and children that clearly demonstrates *a need to learn.* Almost from the moment of birth, the child observes and takes in — first with his eyes and mouth, and then with his limbs and fingers — stimuli and things in his environment in order to master and to learn. Long before the mother deludes herself into thinking that she has "taught" the child, our tot has learned all by himself many tasks that are and will be vital to him in order to function as a human. The infant inspects his body and his crib — and learns that he is an identity separate and apart from his environment. He observes colors and shapes. When able, he moves things about and propels his body — and thus begins to master himself and his environment. Playing peek-a-boo, he learns that he can "make" things appear and disappear, and that things exist even when they are not in his field of vision. The game of dropping things and having mother pick them up, that so frustrates his elders, is another way of showing that there is power and mastery within him. His babbling, and the parental response to it, show him that *his* vocal productions make others respond, and thus becomes the precursor of language.

When older, the child asks questions endlessly (and thus annoys us), explores things (and thus gets in our way), and attempts to imitate his elders. All of this is instinctual learning behavior — the child learns because he has a need to master, a need to learn.

One would then logically expect that the parent's need to teach, and the child's need to learn, should combine and jointly enhance the learning process. All too frequently this is not the case at all, and parental efforts impede rather than facilitate. Consequently, of all the parent-child conflicts that upset us, the child's learning behavior ranks high on the list of serious family problems. This apparent puzzle then deserves our careful attention, since its analysis may hold the key to motivating the child in his striving to learn.

"The Need to Be Me"

An important need of the child in the process of growing up is his need to become independent — to do things because he chooses, rather than because he must. The wonderful nature of things makes it so that the child is quite helpless during infancy — more so than any other living organism. Because of this, there is an extended period of time during which his parents have the opportunity to teach him. Equally important is that as he matures, this dependence and helplessness be replaced with independence and ability. This independence, of course, must be learned. As is true with all instinctual behavior patterns, the striving for independence is present in the matrix of what is to be at the earliest period of life. Thus we are faced with a dilemma: The child must be taught (to be taught means to be told and to be dependent), which, in turn, is incongruent with his need to learn and become independent (his "need to be me").

The examples of speech development and learning proper toilet habits should suffice to demonstrate how teaching can hinder learning rather than facilitate it.

Children master the art of speaking because they have an instinct to speak. They learn to speak faultlessly and grammatically, abstracting and generalizing, classifying and ordering, all by themselves. All they need is an environment (other humans to imitate), and the neuropsychological apparatus (the intellectual-physical ability), and they speak. Their innate need to learn facilitates all this, and the fact that speaking furthers their striving for independence spurs them on. When parents "teach" their child to speak, overly correcting and criticizing him, frustrating both his need to learn (by himself) and his striving towards independence, stuttering or stammering may set in. The parents' teaching has worked against the child's need to learn.

Because children have the need to learn and imitate, one can expect that they will learn proper toilet habits, and they do — all by themselves. All that is necessary is a mature sphincter to enable the child to "hold" or "give," general physical maturity to enable him to inhibit motility and "sit," and the information (intelligence) of knowing where the toilet is and what it is for. Successful toilet training is done by the child, not by the parent, because enhancing the need to learn is the need to master and become independent. To "give" and to "hold" is mastery and independence. When parents do attempt to force toilet training, they at best prolong the process, and at worst, may develop a significant parent-child conflict, setting the stage for emotional problems in the parent-child relationship. Toilet training is particularly crucial because it is usually the earliest battle of wills, and because "giving" and "holding in" parallels so closely the notion of independence — "I do how I want to and when I want to."

To be sure, approval and reinforcement are essential and further the learning process. Children want to please their parents and do what parents think is right. However, it is vital not to steal the child's show, not to have him feel taught. Rather, it is the child who has mastered. It is he who has chosen to master and to conquer his environment.

There are, furthermore, certain critical periods when "being told" is particularly distressing to the child. One of these occurs at the time the child first begins to master his environment, the "terrible twos." Here the child has just mastered speech and walking about, and his notion of independence is being challenged by the teachings and directives of his parents. Thus there are the endless nos, the contrary behavior, and the temper tantrums.

Another such period is when mastery and independence are about to be completed — the age of adolescence. At this time, the need for independence is so great that the young adult may verily work against his own interests in order to be "himself." He may destroy himself and his future in the world of reality, in order to survive psychologically, "to be me."

These are but two of the critical periods in the life of the child where the teaching/learning, dependence/independence dilemma is at its height. Moreover, its role at all stages of development cannot be overemphasized, and may well be the determinant for success or failure whenever parent and child, or teacher and student, interact.

Teaching to "Learn"

Assuming, then, that all children have an innate need to learn, the role of the teacher-parent demands clear definition in order that it complement the child's native desire rather than supplant it. We can begin by suggesting what is *not* "teaching to learn."

The effective teacher-parent is not a coercer who "makes" the child learn. To do so automatically generates a negative reaction — for it robs him of his will, his need for independence, his power to do as he pleases. The teacher-parent is not a reservoir who fills an emptiness in the child; rather, the "hollow" within the child has a sponge-like consistency that absorbs learning all by itself.

The teacher-parent is not simply an animate text who predigests learning for the student. Writers of texts have the time and resources to carefully select material, grade it, and present it in exact dosages for effective learning. The teacher-parent can rarely duplicate this exacting structure of the textbook. Structure or rigidity are not desirable in the teacher, because they suggest a mold into which children's minds are poured, and connote a demanding and exacting attitude.

The effective teacher-parent is exceedingly careful not to rob the child of his learning experiences by making them his own, by overly basking in the light of the child's success or being shattered by his failure, and thus vicariously becoming the real beneficiary of the learning that takes place. This is a trap that must be avoided at all costs because initially, although success may come about as a result of the adult's strong involvement, in time such involvement frequently leads to failure. The child may be well motivated, he may have the ability — but he *must* drop out because his learning is not his own. Rather, he realizes that to learn is to capitulate, to give up independence and to learn for — and "be" — the parent, and not "be me." In addition, because of the parent's intense involvement, learning becomes the arena for the parent-child struggle, the marketplace for blackmail, and the weapon of spite. Or, to please the parent, the child may become "hooked" on scholastic success at the expense of social-emotional development. Additionally, there is the danger of the need to be the "best" scholastically, with possible overwhelming stress, anxiety, and chronic frustration. The "perfect" learning child then becomes a very unhappy child.

The teacher-parent who teaches to learn creates an environment that makes the child want to learn on his own and make learning his own thing. She does not serve the material but offers it, ever careful that it is the child who is learning, not the adult who is teaching. This teacher-parent's ingenuity lies in her ability to select material that is meaningful to the child here and now, and will thus make the child want to learn — and yet have utility in the child's total education. The learning environment is fashioned by an attitude that teachers and students are not adversaries but partners, and an expectation that children will learn. Playacting or lofty proclamations will not do the trick — for children read us well. Teachers who approach the classroom either fearing the students or prepared to control them have lost before they begin. The pupils will sense instantly that the teacher has come to *teach* by force or effort — and learning is thwarted. It is then the teacher's "thing," not their own.

Teachers cannot be satisfied to be just another book or resource — even one that moves or speaks. The teacher who teaches to learn is not a purveyor of facts or skills. He provides the human element and creates the intangible but vital classroom atmosphere. Concepts that come to mind here are excitement, enthusiasm, feeling, warmth, relationship, and love. The teacher puts life into the inanimate book and creates excitement and enthusiasm by virtue of his being human. Because of his feeling and warmth, a proper relationship is created; and through the partnership of love, learning takes place — truly the child's thing, for all children want excitement, warmth, love, and learning.

Parents may, and indeed should, show an interest in the child's learning, but they should not have the child learn for the parent's sake, nor should they vicariously go back to school with him. The parent offers the child — be it food or learning; the child is grateful — and eats or learns because it is his own thing. When, however, the child is coerced to eat or learn, he then uses this activity to thwart the parent in order to gain independence, or as a weapon in the parent-child power struggle.

The child's innate need to learn, and the parent's need to teach, do not automatically combine. There is a third, and crucial, element — the "need to be me." Teaching that is coercive thwarts this need for independence and thus impedes the learning process. Learning opportunities must be offered, and the child will learn by himself. The human element, the warmth, feeling, sympathy, and "oneness" is the bridge between the teacher-parent and pupil-child along which effective learning travels.

Chapter Two

To Be a Teacher

hat does it mean to be a "teacher"? How does one act, function, or behave, and what are the essential qualities and traits one possesses that make him or her worthy of this appellation? To act as a teacher is certainly not simply to dispense knowledge or skills, for there are far better instruments to do just that, such as scientifically designed texts and learning programs, high-tech computers and ingenious software, that dissect material and individualize instruction. Nor is the teacher a manipulator of human minds, for minds that are bent and coerced resist, and make the learning-teaching process a struggle. A teacher, furthermore, never simply conveys facts or skills to the learner. There are always overtones, side-effects — positive or negative — in terms of attitudes toward learning, human behavior, and personality development. Effective teachers have always left an aftertaste, whether sour or sweet, and thus a legacy for a lifetime, a heritage of traits and attitudes toward learning and living — thereby frequently making or breaking the student. A teacher, then, is an individual who, through his behavior and innate qualities, influences another human being in a most potent fashion, intentionally or unintentionally, to learn that which he teaches, as well as to learn about life — to mature and to grow. Thus we have the student who not only thinks as his teacher does, but learns — and verily acts, talks, walks, and gestures — as he does.

How is this done? How does such teaching take place? Most important, to whom should we entrust our precious young, and upon whom do we bestow the title "teacher," one who effects in another learning, growth, maturation, and all that is positive in human behavior? The bankruptcy of our educational institutions testifies to the inadequacy inherent in the modern models of "teaching" and "teacher." Fortunately, our holy Torah provides for us a prototype of teaching, and a model for the teacher.

The Teacher

Whom does the Torah entitle "teacher"?

There is, for example, only *one* Avraham *Avinu*, only *one* Yosef *HaTzaddik*, and *one* David *HaMelech*. There is also only *one* Moshe *Rabbeinu*, the teacher par excellence. Moshe is the model, the prototype, the ultimate — *the* teacher.

We rush to our modern texts, our teacher-rating scales and studies to compare notes as to what makes one a good teacher. An interesting conclusion emerges. If we try to rate *our* teacher, the great Moshe *Rabbeinu*, using just a few of what are considered "desirable" traits in modern teachers — enthusiasm, cooperation, clarity of language, experience — we draw a total blank.

Enthusiasm and cooperation? What does Moshe *Rabbeinu* say? *"Shlach na beyad tishlach* — Choose anyone but me!"[1] Experience? Moshe *Rabbeinu* pleads, *"Lo ish devarim anochi, gam mismol, gam mishilshom* — I cannot speak, I am totally inexperienced."[2] As to command of language, he begs off justifiably: *"Ki chvad peh uchvad lashon anochi* — I am handicapped of speech."[3] Yet Moshe was *the* teacher, the one and only one deserving the title "teacher"!

---

1. *Shemos* 4:13.
2. Ibid. v. 10.
3. Ibid.

Moreover, the A-mighty assures Moshe as he is about to give his first lecture: *"V'sham'oo lekolecha* — They will surely hearken to your words."[4] What a wonderful promise! Imagine going into a classroom with prior assurance that one will speak and the students will learn. *Rashi* adds: *"Mei'aleihem* — by themselves. [They will listen by themselves, without coercion, without oratory, without your experience or training, even without your enthusiasm or cooperation.]" *Rashi* goes on and explains how this will be: *"Shetomar lahem lashon zeh* — because you will use these words ...," and further elaborates that the words Moshe was to use, *"pakod pakadeti,"* are the words Yosef used, *"Pakod yifkod Elokim eschem,"* as well as the language Yaakov employed.

What is the magic in the word *"pakod"*? What is the power of this formula? Surely it is not the word *"pakod"* itself. Furthermore, the commentaries correctly question, nowhere has this word been used by Yaakov. Yet *Rashi* insists that it is *"pakod,"* the proven formula Yosef *and* Yaakov used, that will now serve Moshe as well. *"Pakod,"* then, cannot be simply a word but a *concept,* an attitude, an intangible, a psychological "set" that works the magic. As we search the Torah for its precise definition and meaning, we find precision obscured by the word's usage in a variety of contexts. Baffling and inexplicable at first sight, we soon discover its meaning *because* of its diverse applicability. Thus we find: *"VaHashem pakad es Sarah."*[5] There, *pakad* apparently means to *remember.* *"Veyafkeid hamelech pekidim"*[6] — here it means to *appoint* officials, overseers, by the king. *"Velo nifkad mimenu ish"*[7] — there it refers to counting human losses in warfare. Finally, in, *"Vayifkod Shimshon es ishto,"*[8] it means to *cohabit* with one's wife. To remember, to appoint, to sustain a human loss, and to cohabit — what do these have in common? Obviously, then, *"pakod"* means to remember, and as a concept, much more — it means to take care of a human need; *"pakod"* means to take charge, and more — it means to take pains and exercise prudence; *"pakod"*

---

4. *Shemos* 3:18.
5. "And G-d remembered Sarah" (*Bereishis* 21:1).
6. "And the king should appoint officers" (*Esther* 2:3).
7. "And no one was lost" (*Bamidbar* 31:49).
8. "And Shimshon cohabited with his wife" (*Shoftim* 15:1).

refs to sustaining or not sustaining human loss, and more — it refers to solicitude and anxiety; and *"pakod"* means to cohabit, and more — it is regard and it is love. *"Pakod"* cannot be translated because it is intangible, but its connotation is clear: It means care, concern, regard, worry, attentiveness, vigilance, relationship, love — and more. When dealing with humans, it is the vital ingredient that transmits the human element; the intangible that envelopes the interaction with warmth, and says one cares. The magic is not in the word *"pakod,"* but in its connotation of loving and caring. It is not the explicit word, but the implicit thought that was present in Yosef and Yaakov, regardless of the precise language used, that made the difference. And it is this basic human quality of loving, caring, and attentiveness in Moshe that would assure his success as teacher par excellence.

To be a teacher, then, is to love and to care, to be attentive and to have regard for the student, to be concerned and to relate. Teaching with love assures learning with love. To extrapolate from the well-known maxim: *"Ve'ahavta lerayacha kamocha, zeh klal gadol baTorah* — To love one's fellow [the student] is the prime rule in teaching Torah, i.e., in teaching and in learning."[9] That is the insight Torah gives us — with success assured.

However, there is a catch here. The word *"pakod,"* when re-arranged slightly, becomes *"kapod,"* to be exacting. When we care, when we relate, there is the danger of overdoing, of turning caring into becoming demanding and exacting, and thus being intolerant of failure, and critical. *"Velo hakapdan melamed* — He who is exacting, demanding, and critical cannot teach successfully."[10] Learning to love brings love of learning. *"Pakod,"* to care, to love — facilitates; *"kapod,"* to demand, to be exacting — impedes.

His Teaching

When the teacher has to have a "talk" with the student, what exactly does he say? He says little and listens a great deal. As the

---

9. *Toras Kohanim* (see *Rashi* on *Vayikra* 19:18).
10. *Avos* 2:6.

Baal Haggadah (author of the Passover *Haggadah*) elaborates: "*Mah hu omer?* What does he [the child] say?" This is repeated again and yet again when discussing the Four Sons. "What does *he* say? *Ma hu omer?*" Concern yourself not with what you, the teacher, have to say — but listen to what he, the student, has to say. When he is about to learn, listen to and study *his* needs, *his* interests, *his* questions, and *his* mode of learning.

When he fails to learn, listen to *his* difficulties, *his* problems and *his* pain. When you speak to him, do not give him your "little talk," for he already knows what you have to say, and he has turned you off. But listen to what *he,* the student, has to say — "*ma hu omer.*" For then you will know where it hurts and wherein the remedy lies. You will then be his ally — not his adversary, the authority, the enforcer, the fixer.

Instead of the "little talk," instead of what *you* want the child to do, why not consider what you, the teacher, can do? Let us note what the *Baal Haggadah* has to say: "*Chacham mah hu omer?* What does the wise child say?" Regarding the wise child who has a lot of questions and sees the finer points of learning: great! Let him learn! But remember: "*Ain maftirin*" (one needs to retain the taste of the *afikoman* and avoid other foods). There must be a *taam,* a good taste, an emotional charge in learning beyond the intellectual exercise.

"*Rasha mah hu omer?* What does the wicked child say?" Wait! How can we call a mere child a *rasha,* evil and wicked? We do so because we know his future, like a *ben sorer umoreh.*[11] He says, "Why do you want this burden, this pain?" How does he know that it is a burden? Obviously, he observes this attitude in his elders. "It's too much trouble to clean for Pesach. Matzos are too expensive ... Daddy finds learning with me, or even by himself, a bore if not a chore ... My teacher is a grim fellow to whom teaching and learning are obviously burdensome." He reaches the obvious conclusion: "Why do all of this? Why burden oneself?" Sadly enough, he will be — he cannot help but become — a *rasha.*

"*Tam mah hu omer?* What does the simple child say?" The simple child, the slow learner, asks, "*Mah zos?* What is this?" For him,

---

11. "A wayward and rebellious son" (*Devarim* 21:18).

simplify the material and do not elaborate beyond his ability to understand.

"*V'she'eino yodaya lish'ol* ... And for the child unable even to ask ..." Do not excuse yourself by saying, "You can take the horse to the water, but you cannot make him drink." Not so! One never gives up on a human being. You must find some way to arouse the child's curiosity and motivate him to see, observe, and ask.

His Message

What is the major message of teacher-student communication? What signals emanate from teacher to student that promote motivation, growth, and maturation? The Talmud[12] lauds Rabbi Elazar b'Rabbi Shimon as the greatest in his generation. Yet his son had gone astray and his comportment was befitting the lowest of the low. So the *Chachamim* (Sages) searched for the errant son in order to reform him. What did they do when they found him? The *Chachamim* did not scold or chastise, nor did they lecture. They ordained and addressed him as *Rebbi*, a scholar, a saintly man. The young man returned and became an outstanding scholar, the pride of Israel.

Our great *Chachamim* knew well what laborious research would tell us 2,000 years later: Individuals live up to the expectations we have of them. A series of psychological studies have clearly demonstrated that when we expect the child to behave, he behaves; to learn, he learns; to be a *mensch*, he becomes a *mensch*. The converse is also true, unfortunately. Let us ordain our student to be a person, a *mensch*, a learner. Let us give him respect, and he will be as we expect him to be. That is the essential "message" the teacher must send the student.

The Torah Jew has always been a successful learner, for to be a Jew in its fullest sense is to be a *ben Torah*, a student, a learner. In Torah lies infinite resource for us concerning what learning and teaching are all about.

---

12. *Bava Metzia* 85a.

Chapter Three

For Love of Learning

A Matter of Us and Them

O
ne day last summer, I had forgotten my *tallis* and *tefillin* in a yeshivah where I had *davened* that morning. At 3 o'clock on that hot afternoon I finally found time to pick them up. And what did I find besides my *tallis* and *tefillin?* A crowded *beis hamidrash* (study hall) of high-school boys learning Torah. Half a block down the street there is a public school having a far, far greater number of students. And what is going on there on a typical summer day? Nothing. It's deserted. School is out! Vacation!

These yeshiva high-school boys are not unique among Torah Jews. This summer as during summers past, Torah Jews carried their learning and their *Daf Yomi* (the daily folio of Talmud) with them to wherever their vacations or their businesses took them. Torah is, *baruch Hashem* (thank G-d), found all over, and it travels — in *Shas gemaras* (complete tractates of the Talmud), in a single *maseches* volume, in user-friendly pocket-size editions, in laptop computers, and on hastily copied sheets.

And the world has noticed. The popular media has been awakened to the *Siyum HaShas*. Thus we may be tempted to pat ourselves on the back, and to bask in the sunshine of our neighbors' adulation for truly being the "people of the book." Privately, we may add, *"Re'u ma bein b'ni I'ven chami* — Behold and see the difference between my child [the Jewish child] and the child of my father-in-law [the non-Jewish child]."[1] Yes, we are different, we are students, we are thinkers, learners, and scholars.

However, there are far too many students who have difficulty learning and, in spite of adequate intelligence,[2] do not feel sufficiently motivated. Others simply do not find learning at all rewarding. Thus they fail to become Torah learners as adults.

So we have a task at hand, namely, how to have all Torah students perceive Torah learning in the very same manner as the aforementioned high-school boys, so that it is innately rewarding and self-perpetuating. Can one learn to love learning?

Fulfillment or Fun?

To begin with, one needs to set aside the notion that learning and schooling must be "fun," or, for that matter, that life should be "fun." This popular thought, generally ascribed to "modern psychology" (whatever that is), conflicts with the dictates of common sense. There is great satisfaction and meaning in meeting one's obligations, in doing a job well, in understanding things deeply, in pleasing others, in doing things in a social-emotional setting, in exchanging points of view with others, and so on. Moreover, there are few tasks, if any, that objectively are either a chore or a pleasure. Rather, it is attitude, time, place, and context that make the difference.

For example, the high-powered executive who has servants at his beck and call might enjoy personally washing and waxing his car Sunday mornings. Or the affluent fellow who can well afford to buy the very best delicacy will more greatly enjoy the common fish he has caught by rising early in the morning and braving inclement weather to go deep-sea fishing.

---

1. *Bereishis* 29:32 (*Rashi*).
2. There may be factors other than mental ability operating that interfere with learning. Those, of course, merit careful professional evaluation and intervention.

More importantly, we will attempt to demonstrate that *limud haTorah*, or study of, and involvement with, Torah, is not at all analogous with "teaching and learning" as understood in common parlance. As a practical experiment, ask your gentile neighbor's child to describe his feelings relating to the word "school." Then ask him to do so with the word "vacation." The relative positive-negative responses should be obvious. By contrast, to our boys mentioned earlier or to an adult Torah Jew, vacation is not at all the opposite of "learning." Instead, they may view vacation as providing more time to learn Torah, or at least not less.

"Limud HaTorah" and "Learning"

In a typical public school, we have teachers and students, and there is subject matter to be mastered. The teacher needs to motivate the students by either demonstrating the relevance of the subject matter, or by being an entertainer in order to capture the students' interest. To continue the process of learning, the teacher must *reinforce* it through reward and punishment, i.e., grades, awards, and diplomas.

The student, on the other hand, must overcome the ever-present resistance to the chore of learning. He rejoices when the subject matter is mastered. Now he can stop learning. He knows what he is supposed to know.[3]

Lehavdil (by contrast), we visit a Torah study hall, a *beis hamidrash* — post-high school, high school, or even elementary school.[4] What have we here? Ideally, we do not have a formal

---

3. To be sure, here and there are voices in general education speaking of the *whole* child, and of education primarily as observing, thinking, and discerning, freeing children from "deadly formalism and teaching facts and words" (e.g., Pestellozzi in Henry Barnard's *Pestellozi and His Educational System*, pp. 74-75 [Syracuse: C.W. Bardeen, 1854]). Factually, however, the public school system remains subject-oriented.

4. Children observe and learn not only what to do and how to do it, but also what is important in life, and what is less important. This importance of things is learned not by what he is told is important, but by what the child observes. Telling the child that he and the family are important, while the father unnecessarily spends most of his day in business, sends, at best, the message that this is not so — it is business and money that are important. And at worst, it becomes a confused hypocritical message, with possible neurotic consequences.

Similarly, the father who gets up at 5 o'clock in the morning to go fishing, rain or

classroom where a teacher, acting as a salesman, has to juggle a number of variables in order to "sell" a product to his students, the reluctant buyers, for learning to take place. Instead, we have excitement and discussion, a blurring of teacher and learner. The *rebbe* explains, the student argues and wins a point or loses a point, but there emerge no losers, only winners. The *gemara* is difficult, but there is triumph in its mastery, and intimate social bonds are created and continually reinforced. "Generation gap," "old fashioned," "times are different" — what are you talking about? Here are Abaye and Rava, *Rashi* and *Rabbeinu Tam*, the *K'tzos* and the *Nesivos*, the 15-year-old student and the 50-year-old *rebbe* — a team of learners and teachers reveling in spiritual delight, ensconced in mutual love and respect. Thus a foundation is laid for a lifelong love of learning.

Indeed, Torah learning continues. See the children and their parents at the Shabbos table, exchanging *divrei Torah*, Torah thoughts,[5] with the parents and children alternately teaching and learning.[6] Then there are tens or hundreds of thousands of Torah *Yidden* — singly, in pairs, or in groups — learning in homes, in the *beis hamidrash*, on commuter trains, or by telephone.

It's early morning in the Torah home. Snow falls outside; it is

---

shine, sends one message. By contrast, the father who gets up on a cold winter morning *with joy* to learn sends quite another message.

With the reader's permission, a word of *d'rush* (exegesis): The *Baal Haggadah* (author of the Passover *Haggadah*) says: "*V'es amaleinu — eilu habanim.* (Our burden refers to our children.)" To this we say: Do you want to know how your child will grow up, what will be valued by him, what will be important? Then observe "*es amaleinu,*" where *you yourself* toil, what is important enough to you, not only in doing, but also in expending extra effort and toil. Thus the parent-teacher — by the extra effort, toil, *and* the passion and joy — "teaches" the child the importance of learning, the meaningfulness, the joy, *and* the innate reward of learning for the sake of learning.

5. A worthwhile incident from my personal office files: I counseled a severely depressed young man experiencing no love from his father — only teaching, fixing, correcting, criticizing. I asked him, "Do you remember one pleasant time with your father?" After much thinking the young man replied that yes, there was one time when his father took him to a ball game. Because his father knew nothing about baseball, here the son could finally shine and explain things to his father, rather than being at the receiving end of being told and criticized. Must we have ball games for children to have a day in the sun? How beautiful for children who shine with their *d'var Torah*, their *sevara*!

6. Rabbi Betzalel Zolty, *zt"l*, the late Chief Rabbi of *Yerushalayim*, strongly urged engaging students as early as possible into *lomdus*, mental debates in learning, in order to kindle joy and excitement in them (heard at a Torah Umesorah convention).

cold. A day off? Another hour of sleep? No, our *lomdei Torah*, our *lomdei Daf Yomi*, are up and about. A quick cup of coffee is followed by the joyful plunge, with *chaveirim* (fellow learners), into the most refreshing *yam haTalmud*. Learning begins, exhilaration mounts while juggling *sevaros* (points of view), oxygenating brains — all while expanding their love of G-d, of their fellows, of our Torah.

Learning takes place formally and informally. Two men meet on a train or on a plane. They don't each reach for a drink of whiskey to calm themselves and withdraw from people into temporary oblivion or a relaxed reverie (or become emboldened to pick a fight). No, there is the potential for the excitement of a shared *d'var Torah* on today's *daf* — and the forging of another friendship, even if it lasts only the length of this particular journey. Additionally, besides the learning, such an experience of an interpersonal nature helps to make each participant into a "people person," a lover of man. This is always a most potent and beneficial prescription for mental health.

And now, behold how we gather to celebrate all of this: the joy, the love for learning, the sense of security; the love for G-d and for our fellow man — and the continuity of all this. Tens of thousands of individuals in the United States, and likely hundreds of thousands the world over, celebrated the *Siyum HaShas*, the completion of the Babylonian Talmud. There were no caps and gowns, there were no valedictorians or prizes and awards. Even the celebration of having completed *Shas* and knowing *Shas* will, in very short order, be put aside. In its place there will be the dedication to begin again, to learn, to know, to know better and know more — and to keep on learning — a celebration of dedicating ourselves to a lifetime of learning.

Learning to Love, Learning to Learn, and Learning to Love Learning

Learning as living is an ongoing, lifelong process. It is *bein adam le'atzmo*, intrapersonal; *men darf zich oisarbe'ten*, one needs to grow. It is also *bein adam lechaveiro*, interpersonal in that it involves an interaction with *chaveirim*, with others. And it is *bein adam laMakom*, spiritual, in how one relates to his Creator. Involving oneself with others in this spiritual task of learning Torah makes the man himself a lover of man and a lover of G-d, and thus a better human being.

How does one get initiated into such an experience?

"*Mipi olelim veyonkim yisadeta oz* — From the mouths of infants and sucklings You [*Ribbono Shel Olam*] have established Your might.''[7] We suggest: The infant's mouth contains a host of miracles within a miracle. The mouth learns from the moment of birth — it learns loving and it learns learning. And because learning and loving are inextricably interwoven, it follows that, well handled, one should learn to love learning.[8]

Mipi: The child enters this world fully equipped physically, but there is no outward evidence of either social-emotional or cognitive-mental-verbal functioning. There is, however, a great deal of scientific evidence that the embryo has already learned of the emotional climate while in his mother's womb. For us *Torah Yidden* there is a great deal more.

First, there is the Torah that the *malach*, the angel, learns with every embryo,[9] creating an implant wherein his future learning of Torah will be absorbed.[10] Then there is the Torah home in which his mother carried him for nine months.[11] At birth and thereafter, there is the Torah language the infant "hears," both the emotional part of parent-child interaction which is part of *darchei no'am*,[12] the sweet-

---

7. *Tehillim* 8:3. See *Targum, Bereishis* 2:7. He translates the word "man" as *ruach memalela*, "the speaking spirit." "Speaking" — which includes thinking — that is man. Compare the words of *Targum* referring to "speaking man" as *ruach memalela*, and *Rashi's* translation of *ruach Elokim* as the *kisei hakavod*, the *Ribbono Shel Olam*, organism, part of the *Tzelem Elokim, kaveyachol*, Who is similarly defined.

8. Parenthetically, pediatricians advise parents to hold their children while feeding them. Holding and cuddling children is very important, for there is a correlation between loving and learning. Clearly, children learn best when teachers are loving and caring.

9. *Niddah* 30b.

10. What is the purpose of the angel teaching the embryo Torah, when at birth all is forgotten? A word of *d'rush*: We know of tissue rejection of foreign bodies. Torah has to be *al levavecha*, internally implanted. Thus the Torah one learns is not really foreign — it is the return of one's own "tissue."

11. See *Avos* 2:8, *Bartenura*. Rabbi Yochanan ben Zakkai praised the mother of Rabbi Yehoshua ben Chananya for taking him, while still in her womb, to the *beis hamidrash* for lengths of time.

12. *Mishlei* 3:1.

ness of Torah behavior and relatedness, *and* the cognitive/verbal learning one "sees and hears" even at the most primitive level. There is *Toras imecha*,[13] the ostensibly minor doings of the mother: her sweet mannerisms, her saying a *berachah* with the child, the washing of his hands, the *Modeh Ani*, and so forth. And then — when the child begins to speak formally — there is the *Torah tzivah lanu Moshe*[14] of the father. All of this, naturally, is imparted lovingly, creating a most joyful environment of loving and learning.

Formal Schooling Versus "Learning" as a Mode of Living

The word "schooling" denotes whatever transpires in a typical classroom in the world around us. There is specific subject matter to be mastered, clearly defining the teacher and the student, a formal setting, and numerous other factors.

"Learning," on the other hand, is dedicated to a far broader activity — namely, something one does all one's life: learning about one's environment, about oneself, about others, about self-esteem and competency, how to do things and how to feel about things, and much more. The Torah Jew does all of this in a Torah manner and, additionally, continues his learning. This is *limud* — or rather, being *oseik baTorah*.

Laasok bedivrei Torah: We arise every morning, we tend to our needs, and we thank Hashem for our Torah with the *berachah "Laasok bedivrei Torah* — to occupy ourselves with the words of [also: matters of] Torah." Though we follow this *berachah* with a very brief Talmudic discourse, there will be additional learning during that day. However, there will obviously be interruptions at work and with other matters. Other *berachos* do not allow for such interruptions. Why is this permitted here? Moreover, why the verb *laasok*, "to occupy," rather than "to learn"? Thus we must say that *laasok*, to occupy ourselves with Torah, is far more than learning Torah. It includes nothing less than the full range of human function in a Torah manner. It is a totality of existence. It involves

---

13. *Mishlei* 1:8.
14. *Devarim* 33:4. See *Succah* 42a.

thinking, feeling, doing — 24 hours a day — and, one hopes, it is a continuation of what was begun much, much earlier, and a bridge to all that will continue.

The wisest of men, Shlomo *HaMelech*, compared the receiving of the Torah to one's day of marriage.[15] Simply put, one is not married for an hour or a day; there is no such thing as a part-time spouse. Similarly, to be truly a Torah Jew is a total 24-hour matter: how one eats, sleeps, greets a fellow man, and so forth. Thus one is truly *oseik*, occupied, with words and matters of Torah all day long.

In sum, schooling is an invasion of sorts, force-feeding facts to the reluctant student. By contrast, Torah learning is a natural function of living. At its ideal, it is a continuation of what takes place *in utero*, at birth, and during the years that follow. One goes to school looking forward to finishing so as to get on with life. But being a Torah Jew involves a lifetime of learning, of behaving in a certain manner, and similarly, of thinking and feeling the Torah way.

All of this comes about in the very natural setting of a Torah home where all this is learned, or rather absorbed — naturally and joyfully, with love and positive reinforcement. To the Torah Jew, then, learning Torah and being *"oseik baTorah,"* practicing Torah, is a natural, joyful experience. Additionally, because Torah learning generally involves others, it becomes also an interpersonal experience par excellence, with the *rebbe* and the *talmid*, the parent and the child, the *chaver* early in the morning or late at night, the fellow learner on the plane, the *chavrusa*, and the great group of *lomdei Shas* jointly relating and caring: *lehagdil Torah u'lehaadirah*, with a common goal for the greatness of Torah.

---

15. *"Tz'enah ur'enah bnos Tzion"*; see *Rashi* on how the day of marriage refers to the day of *Mattan Torah (Shir HaShirim* 3:11).

Chapter Four

Learning to Love Learning

Learning and Reinforcement

omewhere in New York a mother excitedly hears her infant voice the thrilling sound of "mama." She rushes to the baby's crib, beams at him and listens intently for him to emit again what she believes sounds like "mama." When he does so, she smiles at him and rewards him with a big hug and a kiss. She hastens to relate the news to Daddy and to other family members, who then join her in cooing and smiling at the infant and making a production out of this utterance, the child's first word — which "happens" to be "mama." The identical scene is repeated in every infant's home in Tel-Aviv, Israel (except that there the magic word is *ima*), and it also happens in every child's home in the world — each time with *the* word that in the particular language of the particular child's parents denotes "mother."

We know, of course, that the baby's presence in New York does not make him proficient in producing the word "mama" any more than his cousin's being in Tel-Aviv enables him to discover the word *ima.* Yet from this humble beginning our tots go on — each in his own tongue to learn *his* language, construct simple and compound sentences, manipulate words and concepts, grow, and broaden his horizons through the interaction of words, concepts, and intelligence. This ostensibly simple learning experience that practically all children master successfully should enlighten us about how all learning can come about without undue heartache or sweat.

The knowledge of facts, skills, and behavior, and the very thing we call "personality," are basically learned. Given that there is relatively little we can do about an individual's genetic endowment, the parent's task is in the area of learning — where much can, and must, be done. While it is no longer fashionable to engage in the age-old nature/nurture controversy, it is clear that even the so-called nature part in man can be modified and greatly influenced. Even innate intelligence, which is basically a genetic "given," can be "stretched" by using one's brain with stimulating learning experiences. To excuse behavior on the basis of "It's him, it's his nature," is a cop-out that has no basis in fact. Indeed, the infant's helpless state in early life as compared to other organisms, and his dependency on his parents, should indicate to us the vital role learning plays in human development.

Nature and Nurture in Human Development

Human development is always a product of (a) innate capacity, (b) a growth matrix, which is the blueprint that determines when more specific skills and behaviors mature, and (c) a predisposition to respond to environmental stimuli. This triad — capacity (genetic endowment), maturation, and the child's predisposition to undergo change and to respond to his environment — calls for parental responses in manners that make child rearing both successful and pleasurable.

The notion of a more-or-less circumscribed capacity should caution us against having expectations greater than the child's endowment warrants, or anticipating any less than he is possibly capable of. To expect too much is to experience frustration and disappointment, while to expect too little will tend to have the child produce according to such minimal expectations. Obviously, then, what is called for is a cautious, tentative attitude concerning our expectations that should be flexible and continuously modified as the child's innate capacity expresses itself in overt behavior.

Similarly, the concept of maturation governed by a growth matrix would have us adopt a pose of expectant waiting rather than indiscriminate prodding. We are all too familiar with toilet training the child before he is ready or buying a toy too mature for him, only to wind up with the child's becoming frustrated and regressing rather than progressing. Here, too, parental behavior must remain tentative and cautious — ready to respond but not really initiate.

In essence, then, there is little one can do concerning the child's endowment or his rate of maturation other than maintain a correct attitude in terms of expectations and timing — a relatively passive pose. This is not so where environmental stimuli are concerned and, more particularly, when learning is taking place.

The Method of Selective Reinforcement

Returning to our infant as he produces his first "mama," let us analyze what exactly is happening here. As a member of the human species, he is genetically endowed with the ability to utter sounds. His growth matrix has decreed that at this particular time he has matured to the stage of babbling, so that his sounds are now repeated again and again. His wise parents have expected him to do just that, but did not set a timetable nor demand the perfect enunciation of words that are intelligible and meaningful.

Now our tot babbles on, producing an endless variety of sounds fitting no specific language pattern, yet adaptable to any tongue. So our parents "approximate." Mother *thinks* she heard her child say "mama." She rushes over, repeats to the child "mama," and beams at him. The child reciprocates — and there now ensues a reverberating system from child to parent and from parent to child which consists of (a) a word: "mama," and (b) a reinforcing agent:

the smile. The word "mama" is learned simply and pleasurably.

If we now label all the irrelevant sounds as "wrong," and the sound that approximates "mama" as "correct," we can formulate the following principle for learning through selective reinforcement: Learning comes about most effectively when "wrong" responses are ignored and "correct" responses are reinforced. Indeed, intentionally or otherwise, much incidental learning comes about in this very manner. The child has learned — no problems, no heartaches, no sweat.

Unfortunately, parents become impatient and are not willing to wait and have the child emit the correct response, so they prod. Worse yet, they reverse the process by being critical and corrective, and instead of reinforcing the correct response, they reinforce (call attention to) the wrong behavior. They do not smile when the child says, "Good morning," but frown when he omits to do so.

Thus we can say that all learning is accompanied by feelings. When parents use positive reinforcement, then learning becomes pleasurable and rewarding, while when negative reinforcement — that is, criticism — is used, then learning becomes associated with emotional pain.

"Learning," furthermore, is not confined to language and similar skills. Learning encompasses far more. It includes social skills such as saying "Good morning." It is also very much involved in social-emotional matters, such as being at ease or ill at ease with others. And at its very core, it plays a vital role in learning about oneself — self-esteem. Am I wanted, am I loved? Thus learning, and particularly the emotional climate within which it is ensconced, creates man — his self-esteem, his relationship with others, and his general competency as a human being. How does all of this come about?

Unlike animals, the human infant is not born as part of a litter, but as a unique, singular individual. He is totally helpless, and remains so for an extended period of time. This time is not wasted. The child's helplessness, and the parents' instinctual need to help, create a bond that fashions an emotional life within. The infant feels loved. He learns that people exist to help; he learns to depend on others. A relationship is formed, a rudimentary beginning of social-emotional functioning. All of this depends on communication, and its primary organ, the mouth — the very beginning of emotional-cognitive-verbal functioning, a beautiful symbiosis of the primary functions of man: to think and to feel — within the context of love.

To elaborate a bit: The infant cries, the mother responds with the bottle. Communication has taken place, the mouth "works." Some time later, the infant cries again, but the bottle is still in the refrigerator. So the mother murmurs, "Yes, sweetheart, the *bottie* is coming, it has to be warmed." The child "hears" and comes to understand words. He does not yet understand the content of the message. But the soft words "mediate," they "inform" the child that his message, the cry, has been received, and his mother's comforting words tell him that help is on the way.

Thus the child learns:

(a) about himself — he is important to others, he is loved;

(b) about others — he can relate with others;

(c) about his environment — he can learn language and other skills;

(d) that he is competent; and

(e) that learning is pleasurable and rewarding.

The Critical Attitude

If there is one villain that ranks first and foremost as the creator of human misery, it is the critical attitude, even when it is euphemistically labeled as constructive. Ordinarily, there is rarely a need for overt criticism, and it certainly is never constructive. It always generates bad feelings, and by calling attention to the "wrong" behavior, actually reinforces it. Far better results are obtained by ignoring the wrong and reinforcing the correct from the very beginning. Unfortunately, once the cycle of criticism has been established, it is difficult to break.

In the adult world this sad practice is all too common. How many times do husbands tell their wives the dinner is salted correctly, and how many times that it is over- or undersalted? How many times do wives exclaim when husbands are on time — and how many times do they chide them for being late? Do employers habitually tell their workers when jobs are performed correctly, or are employees only chastised for doing wrong? Adults, of course, are children who have grown up — all too frequently victims of the "critical attitude," now continuing the sad tale with each other and with their children. Criticism then becomes a habit difficult to extinguish.

Selective reinforcement is not a utopian dream that demands unrealistic laboratory settings or limitless patience. It is a procedure that may demand a little discipline, and must be initiated at the very beginning when learning first begins — yet its returns are immeasurable in terms of effective learning and human happiness.

Chapter Five

Involvement, Intervention, and Reporting to Parents

*B*ecause the school is an agent of society and, in turn, shapes the future social system, it is obvious that the more goals of both school and home correlate, the greater the effectiveness of the educational endeavor. Thus, explicitly or implicitly, the school demands the involvement of parents in the day-to-day learning of their child, as well as agreement with, and support of, the school's broader educational philosophy. To the extent that this involvement truly furthers the child's growth, this notion is, of course, to be supported. When, however, the involvement has a deleterious effect, then the blanket assumption that the home and school should always work together needs to be reconsidered.

Much has been said concerning the woes of the school and teacher when parents are indifferent to, and uninvolved with, their child's education. Indeed, these parents explicitly or implicitly sabotage the school's efforts, primarily because of differences in value systems and in what is considered important to that home and to the school. Such parents then signal the child to ignore the school's demands. Yet there is another side to the coin. Parents can be overinvolved, and their engagement in the child's school career can deter rather than facilitate. As it is with most psychological-physical phenomena, one must look for the optimum, not necessarily the maximum.

Effective Involvement

For learning to take place in a classroom setting, the school must be assured that besides the child's mental and physical equipment, he comes to class primed with attitudes and beliefs that will make learning possible, a thing commonly called "motivation." These beliefs, traits, and attitudes have been breathed in by the child in his home atmosphere, and practiced there for a good many years. They are difficult if not impossible to simply and quickly implant now, if they have not grown and become rooted in the child's psychological makeup.

Thus, for example, there must be a commitment to books and to the value of verbal learning. The child must have mastered the ability to sit still for extended periods of time, and must be able to forgo his immediate needs and wishes and comply with the demands of others. He must be able to take turns and allow others to have their say. The child must be emotionally free of personal preoccupations in order to attend to the task at hand, and be at ease with peers and authority figures.

Not all children, of course, come thus equipped to the satisfaction of the teacher, as they do not possess the optimal mental and physical capacity or the hosts of other subtle variables that go into making learning most effective. Such "shortcomings" will then challenge the ingenuity of the teacher in assisting the students to develop certain traits, to excise others, to compensate, and to somehow cope.

Parents who want to help their child with the attitudes, traits, and beliefs vital to the learning process cannot be very helpful at this stage. Their contribution was needed much earlier — before the child was born. Children are not fed and cloaked with attitudes; they are born into an attitudinal system, an atmosphere that the child breathes, that enters the very fiber of every nerve cell. This becomes his psychological self. Attitudes and beliefs are not simply facets one attaches to personality; they are molds into which children's minds are poured.

Yet when children are deficient in positive attitudes or motivational states, and they fail to learn — or even interfere with the learning of others — there is a tendency among teachers and administrators to turn to the parent and demand that they "Do something — please! Become involved, be concerned, your child needs help!"

But how? What exactly is the parent to do, and how effective will his interference be? Moreover, will this intervention possibly confound the issue, aggravate the situation, and hinder rather than help? Such questions need careful appraisal before parents intervene, often in a vague, planless, and amorphous fashion. This is in no way meant to negate the value of a specific prescription for a parent that can be helpful indeed, be it particular help in a subject area, a tutor, a program for studying, and so forth. The problem under consideration is the blanket demands for help that all too frequently bewilder the parent, generate devastating parent-child friction, and turn the concerned parent — whether consciously or not — against the school.

Involvement for What?

It has become an accepted practice that parents are to know of their child's educational progress. To this end there are report cards, conferences, parent-teacher meetings — and "the note" that goes home when the child fails. However, just because something is being done a certain way, and this way has become the accepted one, does not prove its validity or usefulness.

The well-known story of "The Emperor's New Clothes" illustrates this point. At the risk of resembling the "ignorant child" in this fable, one asks "Why?" Why are parents told? What is the purpose of this information, what is to be done with it, and most important, has it been proved that this practice is useful? Its destructive potential is self-evident by the anger, the clashes, and the recriminations it usually produces, and the resultant deterioration of the parent-child relationship — for rarely are parents informed what, exactly, they are to do with the report they are getting. Being neither educators nor knowing the nature of the problem, and not being in the classroom — where the action really is — what can they really do? In addition, being emotionally involved with their child, their reaction is certainly going to be emotional, irrational, and all too frequently, counterproductive.

Except for relatively rare and obvious conditions, teachers do not and cannot know why children fail to learn. Vague catch words and phrases applied to the child, such as immaturity, laziness, or lack of motivation, have no functional meaning. They do not explain why the child fails, nor do they tell us what exactly is to be done to help him. Similarly, "He could do better if he tried harder," or, "She should spend more time studying" are overworked panaceas that work no better than the frequently given psychological prescription of mother-love and more attention.

To repeat the obvious: Superficial inspection of a child does not tell us his true mental capacity or functional ability. Knowing a child as a student does not reveal to us his emotional preoccupations and concerns, and much less can we know the much more subtle variables that go into the matter of motivation. Telling a child to sit still when he is unable to do so, to be patient when he is impatient, to concentrate when he cannot, to attend and to be organized when he is disorganized, are exercises in futility. The resultant feelings of helplessness then generate frustration — in the child, in the teacher, and certainly in the parent. Parents thus frustrated develop anxiety and anger that seek expression — perhaps directed at the child himself, and/or at the teacher and school who are the creators of this frustration. Or, this impossible situation creates guilt feelings within the parent. In such cases, parents "must" either deny the problem entirely, or "accept" the guilt, only to further confound and add to the emotional turmoil.

In addition, children who chronically fail to learn are, frequently, at least mildly emotionally disturbed. In such instances there is inevitably a disturbed parent-child relationship already present. Added to this now comes the helplessness, the frustration, and the anger laying the foundations of a vicious cycle — frustration generating further disturbance, which then interferes even more with learning, only to breed greater frustration — and so on.

Report Cards: How Accurate and How Useful?

At best, report cards are highly inaccurate, subjective, vague, and all too frequently vicious devices that may make the good student do better yet surely help the poor student continue on his downward trend. The child is told "what he is," what is expected of him, and he then tends to live up to these expectations. Report cards are rarely the motivators they are supposed to be. Research in learning theory has clearly demonstrated that delayed reinforcement (the report card) coming so long after learning takes place has little reinforcement value for either past or future learning. Its subjectivity is self-evident when one compares the difference in grading among teachers and schools. Parents are amazed when a child's grades indicate great improvement or marked worsening with another teacher or school, when in reality the difference was primarily due to the inaccuracies of the reporting device and the inevitable subjectivity of the grader. Experiments have shown how the very same work has been given grades ranging from superior to failing as a result of the different expectations, values, and standards inherent in the examiners. Thus, in spite of the intricate and elaborate signs and weights one sees on report cards, they are not exact measurements spewed out by highly sophisticated computers. They are rough estimates, readily affected by values, expectations, subjectivity, and a host of variables or factors which are not under the conscious control of the grader.

What do reports attempt to tell, and what do they do to the child with lesser ability? If we grade for achievement, he learns soon enough that he is a "dummy." So we grade him for effort, which only says: "Okay, so you are trying, but still stupid." Suppose, on the other hand, the child does have ability but cannot learn because of emotional preoccupations, anxiety, impatience, or other hangups. Is he to be penalized as the insane were punished during the Middle Ages? Acting out, clowning, and misbehavior in children are frequently equivalents of anxiety states and depression in adulthood. Why, then, punish the one and pity the other?

Moreover, what of some of the even subtler and more elusive variables that operate when one is constantly evaluated, tested, and measured? Prisoners in correctional institutions cry of the dehumanizing effect of total surveillance. People who deal with workmen know of the hassles that come about when workers are being constantly told, corrected, and examined. Yet children are asked to sustain the myriads of tests, quizzes, examinations, and reports that are generated in a school setting. When parents are then involved, what happens to that all-important and vital parent-child relationship? Do school and school-related problems then become the altar upon which the parent-child relationship is sacrificed?

What, Then, of Involving and Reporting to Parents?

Parents who are to be involved with their child's education — in a positive and reinforcing manner — do so by fashioning a home wherein learning is as natural as eating and sleeping. Born into such an atmosphere, the child takes learning as a natural process and interacts with his parents formally and informally in a learning-teaching dimension that is normally accepted, not a thing imposed.

When the child subsequently enters school, this parent-child learning continues, paralleling the school's efforts, overlapping, and reinforcing. The parents' natural interest then in the child's learning tells the student that school is important and the teacher is to be listened to. Thus the school's efforts, both in its broader philosophy and in its day-to-day work, are supported.

When school learning does not progress at the rate the teacher or parent expects, and parents are asked to become involved, such action needs careful consideration before it is invoked. Several vital questions must be asked: Do we know what, exactly, is the child's difficulty? Can it be resolved at all? Can the teacher handle it best on his own or in conjunction with the child? And most important, what can the parent really do? If the parent is asked to help, is the "prescription" clearly spelled out, and is the parent intellectually, educationally, and emotionally able to be of assistance? Or will such intervention set up a reverberating system of frustration and anger, involving the parent, teacher, and child, and then seriously impair the vital parent-child relationship?

Because there are no absolutes (measurement in education is always a comparison), evaluation of a child's progress is based on comparing his achievements to those of other students. Such evaluation as an accepted practice should be seriously questioned. Educationally it has little reinforcing value, and emotionally it can be catastrophic. The constant measuring, weighing, and testing would not be accepted by an adult, and it is thus unfair to impose it on a child. The poor student is then labeled early in life, and he tends to remain in this mold. Even the short-term gain to the good student is frequently offset by thus learning to view his world as overly competitive, where achievement and outdoing one's fellow man are the most important values in life.

Report cards are highly inexact devices that serve no real educational purpose. Parents who use them as a "bankbook" to swell their pride in themselves and in their offspring are *using* their child unfairly. Parents and teachers who use the report card as a stick to punish children, so that report-card time is dreaded, defeat their overall purpose to further the educational process.

Reporting to parents as we know it should be abolished. Parent-teacher conferences, if they are specific and prescriptive, can be useful. Better yet, a meeting of parent, teacher *and child* to discuss the child's progress, not in a punitive, blaming fashion but to jointly understand the situation and plan to improve it, can have a salutary effect indeed. The child can then better accept the situation without becoming defensive, take responsibility for improving it, and most important, feel that he is a somebody to be reckoned with in shaping his life, not a puppet to be manipulated by others.

The child's education must be "his thing" in which parents and teachers are ready to help him. He will then seek out their help and guidance. The child who learns in order to please his parent, or because the school demands it, will set up a defensive system which will at least partially be a negative reinforcer. Involving his parents within certain limits can be useful, but such action needs careful consideration at all times before it is invoked.

Chapter Six

Intervening Therapeutically

*J*n observing the nature of things least influenced by cultural factors — such as plant or animal life — one notes that the organism's basic pattern and rate of growth, and its final form at maturation, is determined by the organism itself. To be sure, environment facilitates, stunts, or modifies, and is indeed essential for survival. Yet the potential for growth and the striving toward maturation lie within the matrix of what is eventually to be — a plant, an animal, or a human being.

Under "normal" or usual circumstances, the demands upon the environment are relatively minimal. The tender plant needs soil, nutrients, water, and sunshine — not necessarily in optimal proportions, but within a range needed for survival. To an appreciable extent the plant can adjust and cope with less than the optimal. Even in the case of injury or assault, our plant is able to make repairs — to right itself, or send forth extra branches or roots to maintain an equilibrium — and then continue on its forward striving. Thus there is all within the organism: the potential for growth and maturation, coping mechanisms for environmental irregularities, and, within limits, reparative mechanisms to insure its survival.

Animal life is more complex and involves a good deal of nurture and parental influence. Yet here, too, the basic task remains with the organism itself. It is the infant that searches for the nipple, though the mother makes it available. The young stands up and trots towards the feeding grounds or shelter, though the parents model and lead the way. Species-determined behavior patterns are imprinted upon the young not by the parent but by the infants themselves as they copy and model themselves after the adult.

The nurture and education of our children is, of course, far more intricate, and we cannot simply transpose what we know of plant or animal life to the business of bringing up children. We can, however, abstract certain principles that should obtain in all instances of life, growth, and maturation.

Thus, we should believe that under normal and usual circumstances, all the parent or teacher should do is to create a benign environment so that the child (herself) may grow and mature. The benign environment includes the physical, emotional, and social atmosphere where basic needs are met, where there is room for self-expression, and where social learning and behavior is not taught but modeled.

In such an environment, rates of growth that do not meet parental expectations do not create undue anxiety because they are known to be built in, with maturation coming about when it is meant to. Parents do not excessively search for the perfect way because it does not exist and, more important, optimal conditions are unnecessary and possibly harmful. Instead, they aim for a range of behavior, basically positive, yet spiced with actions that are less than optimal. This will harden the "tender plant," relieve parental anxiety, and contribute to an emotionally well-balanced atmosphere. And when things do go wrong these parents will refuse to panic; they will first wait for the child's reparative mechanisms to come into play to lead her forward toward adjustment.

When Things Go Wrong

When, however, things deteriorate, and a reasonable time has elapsed for the reparative mechanisms to come into play and there is no relief, intervention is called for. But how? What is the model of intervention one should follow so that we help rather than hurt the child? What do we do to be sure that we clarify rather than confuse, support rather than knock down, and, in sum total, discover the cause of the difficulty and repair it, rather than employ patchwork procedures that appear to work, but actually only cover up the real problem?

We begin by not panicking and invoking all sorts of gimmickry, such as admonitions, prohibitions, and similar tactics. This would be analogous to treating our ailing plant (the organism) by arbitrarily dousing it with water, burning it with fertilizer, scorching it with sunshine, or rudely transplanting it. Because something *should* be done must not trap us into doing something that may or may not help at all — and may indeed do harm. To resist the temptation to do "something," it is essential to discard pet theories and beliefs concerning what makes children learn, behave, or be happy. These theories cling to us tenaciously and get in our way because they blind us to possible alternatives, and, most importantly, they bar the way for the child's reparative mechanisms to come to the fore. We must begin with humility. Unless causes for the difficulty are obvious, parents, teachers, specialists, and clinicians must commence with the assumption that they do not know. Such an attitude allows for an objective research orientation and the possible truth, and, most importantly, it facilitates and helps the child help herself.

Because the solution lies within the child does not, of course, mean that the child consciously knows the answer to her problem. Much less is she able to search for it, recognize it (if and when she finds it), or use it effectively. Indeed, the present maladjustment frequently may not be the problem itself, but rather the defenses the child has invoked in coping (ineffectively) with whatever troubles her. Thus, for example, the clowning child's problem may not be the clowning itself at all. The clowning may well be her way of coping with feelings of failure or inferiority. The maladjustment of clowning, then, is really an adjustment attempt against the primary problem of loss of self-esteem. In such cases, when maladjustments are really ineffective attempts at adjustment, the task becomes doubly difficult. The child must first give up her ineffective coping maneuver and become temporarily totally helpless, and then search for more effective ways to deal with the primary problem. In any case, the child needs help to help herself, and we must now intervene therapeutically.

The Therapeutic Intervention

The therapeutic intervention is the crucial element in the search for adjustment. Cognizant of the principle that the child herself is best able to solve her problem, intervention, then, is not something we *do*. Intervention is facilitation, the opportunity we give the child to help herself.

In searching for solutions in social living, as in any research project, one needs freedom of direction, ample time, and the privilege to make mistakes along the way. Our special brand of therapeutic intervention becomes now the unconditional relationship that allows for all these elements. This unconditional relationship is the most potent tool of the successful psychotherapist, and must be available to parents and teachers as well. To be sure, such a relationship must be genuine and the adult cannot simply act out a relationship that does not exist. We may assume, however, that "good" people who deal with children as parents or teachers, do really want to relate therapeutically. It is the many little habits, prejudices, and pet theories that have become ingrained and get in our way which need identification and surgical removal.

Basic to any relationship is mutual respect. This can come about only if we assume that children are not little devils that must be civilized from without, but individuals who have within them all the ingredients to mature into civilized human beings. Corollary to this is the notion that children are not to be pummeled into the mold of the "system," but that they may have an impact of their own on society — which will have to accommodate them and somewhat yield.

With things now evened out, both parent-teacher and child can relate with one another in a nondefensive, open, and genuine fashion in an unconditional, positive relationship. Moralizing, telling, and teaching may or may not bring a lesson across, but certainly are poison for such an unconditional relationship of mutual respect. Instead, modeling and suggesting will make the identical point without hurting the relationship. Yet the basic tool remains always genuine respect and an unconditional positive relationship.

Time, the lack of it, and the attendant impatience so typical of our civilization plays havoc with our moods and nerves. To the child, impatience is even more devastating because it engenders a feeling that to the parent time is more important that she is. It is thus essential to harness oneself in relating with the child, to be unhurried, to be exclusively attendant to her needs and to project the idea that she and her concerns come first.

With the principle before us that the child must be her own healer, the child's thoughts and words become the raw material wherein the solution lies. Provided with endless time, her mind, thoughts, and words begin to roam. Because we do not moralize, she is free to experiment and search. Since she is assured of our respect and unconditional relationship, she can test byways and dead ends — even get lost in the woods. The parent-teacher will then explain (interpret) the wrong direction and the error, being ever so careful to do this in a noncritical fashion. This the child can accept without loss of face.

Thus, within a framework of endless time, with the freedom that comes about by unconditional respect, and the support of a noncritical, nonmoralizing, and genuine listener, the solution — or at least the direction towards it — may just slip out. And even if it does not appear, the newly developed genuine relationship that now exists will allow the parent-teacher to make suggestions without the child immediately dismissing them as just another lecture. Indeed, this relationship now serves another vital function. It brings relief and support to the child, imbuing her with new optimism and allowing her to let go of behavior patterns that she has invoked as adjustive (defensive) maneuvers, but which are really maladaptive in themselves. The child who then hears the parent-teacher call to talk to her does not turn off with the idea that "here she goes again." Instead she turns on, for here comes someone who cares, someone who wants to listen, to relate and interact — not to teach, punish, moralize, lecture, or just hassle.

The human relationship is *the* powerful force that brings both supreme satisfaction and joy — and, conversely, pain, loneliness, and suffering. It is the cause of destructive wars and bloodshed — but can also make man sacrifice all in the service of a loved one. In modifying behavior, then, it can and should become the instrumentality of choice if our intervention is to be truly therapeutic.

Chapter Seven

Learning, Attitudes, and Relevance

he child learns to ride his bicycle through repeated falls and many minor frustrations — yet without any undue anxiety or anger with himself or with others. Once mastered, this skill is rarely, if ever, forgotten. Even in adulthood, after much disuse and disinterest, once the attempt is made again, bicycle riding is quickly relearned. Obviously, then, a substantial residual effect of learning this complex task remains, regardless of disuse, physical aging, and deterioration of motor facility.

Similarly, the child masters natural verbal skills through repeated stumbling — by inexact and incorrect usage of words, phrases, and concepts. Here, too, there are ordinarily few upsets in the process. Once the child has learned the language, it is never really forgotten. When physical and mental deterioration set in, language is the faculty that holds up best, and remains with the individual up to the end.

In the school setting, the child is also taught specific skills such as arithmetic, science, and literature, with much deliberation and intent. Yet only a fraction of what he is taught remains with him.

He is drilled in penmanship and spelling — and then as a business-man or professional scribbles his notes for the "expert" secretary who produces error-free documents using a high-tech computer with Spell-Check, and a publishing-quality printer.

Children are taught to appreciate music and enjoy the arts. Yet here, too, one wonders how much of this "joy" remains — and how much proclivity toward these "finer things in life" has been built into the child. Then there are the advanced-level subjects, such as geometry or poetry, which normally wind up in school graveyards, hastily and indecently buried at graduation time. Even with respect to the much heralded Ph.D. dissertation, the standard joke is that it is usually the first and last piece of good research our hero has done.

Hassles and Heartaches

All of this is achieved with a good deal of expense in terms of student time, astronomical budgets, and much intent and effort by parents, staff, and government. To these expenses we must add the intangible but certainly great costs that result from the innumerable hassles and heartaches, the broken spirits and destroyed relationships, that seem to accompany the learning process like a plague. How do we justify all of this?

Because no effective answers have been found to these problems, and schools must continue to exist, we have conjured up rationales, the clever defense mechanisms that man uses to relieve his anxiety — but that are really outright lies. Man does this to protect his ego, and institutions use them to justify their continued existence. It has been said that education is that which remains with an individual after he has forgotten all that he has learned. Funny? Maybe. But since much of the subject matter is forgotten, we should at least expect our children to "learn how to learn." Yet even this skill of "learning" becomes difficult when the material itself remains irrelevant for today.

Learning not to Learn

At first glance, having the child develop positive attitudes toward learning, and creating behavior traits that will make him a lifelong learner, are certainly laudable goals. Experience with the outcomes, however, soon disenchants us. Rather than developing positive attitudes toward learning, negativism is evinced by the child. Except for nerds and "teachers' pets," kids just don't like school. At best there are numerous dodges, procrastination, attempts to get away with things, and convenient little headaches and stomach pains. At worst there is boredom and apathy, truancy and acting out, and outright hostility toward school and its agents — the teacher and parent. Rather than "learning how to learn," our child is more apt to "learn *not* to learn." General adult attitudes — toward school, teachers, intellectuals, and the teaching profession — would indicate that this negativism toward learning is effectively conditioned and well reinforced. Thus, adults do not normally enjoy learning any more now than they did as kids.

What, then, of schools and learning? Before declaring bankruptcy by either giving up, or entrenching ourselves and defending what we are doing at all costs (rationalizing) in order to survive, let us return to our bicycle and learn how learning can take place with fewer heartaches and greater returns for our investment. Let us examine the factors operating here that can possibly be transposed, at least in part, to formal schooling.

Attitude Is Crucial

We all remember the book we were assigned to read, but somehow never touched — yet, once the course was over, it turned out to be quite interesting. The weekend do-it-yourselfer looks forward to fixing and painting, and labels his doings as hobbies, fun, and recreation. The fishing enthusiast dons shabby pants, treks for miles to discover new fishing grounds (oblivious to the dampness and cold), and is convinced that he is having fun. Conversely, the working painter or fisherman doing the very same will perceive all that as work. Obviously, then, it is not the nature of the task nor the amount of effort required that manipulate motivational forces. The crucial element is attitude: It is whether one *must* do or whether one *elects* to do. Indeed, children who are "forced" to ride their bicycle or "must" become proficient in playing ball (because of daddy's hangup) duplicate the school-learning hassle right at home or on the playground — and they usually fail.

There seems to be a fear that if we allow children (and adults) to do as they please, society would become hedonistic and lazy, and disintegrate. Yet when we examine what people do when they truly have a choice, we find that vocation and avocation do not differ that sharply. Children as well as adults want to succeed, be productive, be social, and feel worthwhile. Children do not naturally harbor destructive, lazy, or negative traits. Such characteristics are defenses and reactions against adverse environmental pressures.

Children ask and inquire, and want to know all by themselves the very things we later insist upon teaching them. Children want to read and have us read to them — with enthusiasm and joy — the very books we so crudely use later on to drill them and *make* them read. The child just loves his first schoolbag and his books, and feels proud that he is now learning to read or is given homework — only to have his attitude shattered when he is given to understand that these are not things he *elects* to do; these are chores he *must* do.

Why can we not, judo-fashion, grab this positive attitude of the child and use its strength to overcome the hurdles of learning? Why must we first bury the child's enthusiasm and will and substitute the "you have to" approach, or crudely develop unnecessary artificial motivators that the child sees right through?

So it is with the many little habits parents want to instill in their children, which turn out — quite unnecessarily — to be major hassles. Adults brush their teeth because of the refreshing feeling it gives them. They go to sleep because they are tired, and eat because they are hungry. They develop proper toilet habits because of convenience, good feelings, and the ego building it brings about.

The Child's Will

Parents are convinced that children oppose all this, and cite as evidence the fact that they have to be coerced to brush their teeth, go to sleep "on time," eat, use toilet facilities, and so forth. Such reasoning is faulty. Coercion is no proof that the child innately rebels; it simply shows that we have convinced the child that these are things he must do against his will.

Yet if we would only observe what children do when they are on their own, we would see that the child himself wills these same things. Children love their first toothbrush, though they may use it "improperly" in adult terms. They love to eat — but perhaps the "wrong" foods, and they may be inclined to sleep at the "wrong" times. And they do groom themselves — again, frequently in the "wrong" way, such as working with their hair excessively while remaining oblivious to their dirty fingernails. Thus we see their innate desire to do the things we want them to do. True, all these behaviors need shaping and perfecting, but doing this means at most adding our experience to the child's, not supplanting his will with ours.

Remembering the importance of attitudes, we should use the child's will and notion that this is something he wants to do, and ever so gently and imperceptibly add our knowledge to shape and direct his behavior into the proper mold. This is the art of teaching without the student's recognition that he is being taught, of governing well without government being noticed, and of molding in a way that does not destroy will, but uses it. We may call this the art of understanding — the use of the child's own positive attitudes to achieve the goals we set for him.

Overteaching and Underlearning

Father and son are standing in front of an exhibit. Forces of spontaneous interest and inquiry obviously are operating here. But there is also an opportunity for teaching. How can these be integrated successfully, and how can father escape the trap of lecturing and teaching his child rather than furthering the child's own learning operation? Father looks and muses, exclaiming to *himself* over a point of interest. *He* is learning and exploring — and the interest, being contagious, is caught by the child. The child, too, is looking and observing — and learning. The father, more to himself than to his son, thinks out loud, discovers a point, questions and learns. The son leans over to share and learn, now both from the object and from his father. The father drops remarks — not little lessons or lectures pushed down the child's throat, but remarks and ideas the father himself learns and incidentally shares with the child, as he would with a friend or a spouse. The outcome is that the child has primarily *learned* — he has not *been taught. Learning* took place — incidentally, and with a positive attitude, rather than *teaching,* which, from the child's perspective, would mean being told, lectured, fixed, or manipulated.

The less talented father, sensing a golden opportunity to teach his child, cannot wait to tell his child, teach him, lecture him, and thus make him into a better human being. He jumps around the exhibit, pointing out to the child the areas of interest, their importance, and all the minute facts father knows that are relevant here. There is obviously much teaching going on, but one wonders how much learning is taking place. The child is apt to turn off. There may be interest on his part, but he is tired of the many little lectures, of being told and fixed and having to learn just because father wants him to. He must protect his integrity as a person and resist coercion and manipulation. There has been too much "overteaching" and, therefore, "underlearning."

Similarly, the student who can view his teacher as an enthusiastic learner himself, can learn with him and from him. Learning then becomes an exploration the teacher undertakes, and the student is all too willing and happy to share the experience because of his own explorative inclination. Shaping, in the form of teaching, and correcting in a minor tone, can then be slipped in when necessary without harm. However, education that is primarily lecturing, correcting, fixing, and "making" the student do and perform is no different than any form of coercion that will be resisted. It is then overteaching that results in underlearning.

Thus the child on his bicycle will appreciate his father's hand steadying the machine — if the choice of activity was the child's and there was more learning than teaching in the process. A child will babble endlessly, stumble over words, ask questions, and learn language and conceptualizations — if the task is his, corrections are few in number, and failure is not a catastrophe that invites perennial parental lectures. Teaching in an undertone, or "underteaching," is most effective in all learning — at school and at home.

Learning to Live and Learning to Learn

In learning to ride a bicycle, or to use language to communicate with others, there is a "living" experience and a compactness that ties together learning, mastery, and usage. The moment the child first sits on his bicycle (or perceives language), he can already envision himself as a successful rider (or a communicating human being). The lurching and falling are minor annoyances, but because he has seen others ride, he sees himself as a (potential) rider. Learning then becomes a "living" experience and has within it the actuality of living; it is not merely a preparatory process. Learning is furthered because the child sees the fruit of success at "planting time." He is learning to live, not only learning to learn.

Once bicycle riding is mastered, the success brings along its own reward and a drive toward further attempts. The subsequent actual practice of riding then serves to make our child ever more proficient. Thus, mastery is not the end of the learning task, but really its beginning. The child learns to ride his bicycle and then keeps on riding it. He learns to speak and then keeps on speaking. He learns in order to do. And he clearly sees this connection. The focus is on usage, with learning and mastery necessary in order to make usage possible. Thus, the child is learning to live, mastering the skills necessary for living, with their relevance self-evident.

Unfortunately, the traditional school curriculum does not ordinarily lend itself to these reinforcing elements. Children cannot always see the potential fruits or their rewarding properties, and careers and future life are too distant and have little meaning or real relevance. Moreover, all too frequently the goal of learning is to pass the text, to get the "A" — and that's all.

The school is concerned with learning and mastery but, because of its very nature, provides little opportunity in real living. Thus mastery becomes an end, rather than a beginning for using that which one has mastered. Knowing something becomes then an accomplishment, a finish, something to be put aside (and forgotten).

There is no transition to usage, nor any real opportunity of putting into practice that which the child learns.

An attempt must be made to make learning a living experience rather than a preparatory one. First in order is less emphasis on marks, future careers, and distant rewards. Parents who enroll their children in first grade with a view of how this will get him into an Ivy League college later on, work against the principles of learning to live, relevancy, and a focus on doing rather than on learning. Equally so, schools that overly measure, encourage competition, and espouse future orientation do not further the learning process.

Talented teachers have always known how to break up the curriculum so that each segment encompasses learning, mastery, *and* usage. They also know how to bring excitement and relevance to the learning process and how to work with — rather than against — the child's will. All of this is, however, not enough, because of traditional school philosophy and parental attitudes concerning how children should be trained and taught.

Schools and homes must become living experiences for our young, not learning laboratories. This calls for primary orientation toward the here and now. Each learning experience may (and perhaps should) theoretically be a building block that fits into a resulting edifice at some future time, but it must also be a totality in and by itself now.

We might begin with a reconsideration of school philosophy and an understanding of learning principles — both by parents and professionals. The resulting need for relevancy and learning to live would undoubtedly demand a revision of our traditional school curriculum and methods by which parents have traditionally trained their young.

There is, however, another thought that comes to mind when we speak of relevancy, learning, and living — namely, the school and the home, and the vast but untapped possibilities of a complementary function. We have, of course, always spoken of the necessity of having the school's philosophy parallel that of the home, and of a need for close cooperation between the two. Whatever all this means may be fine, but there is more that can be gained from a joint effort in respect to our need for relevancy and living experiences. Parents must be more than enforcers, must do more than see that the child attends school, does his homework, and receives good grades. Homes can be settings where learning is applied and practiced, and where all that is theoretical in the school becomes practical and relevant.

In Torah studies, all of this is facilitated by the inherent principles in what is called "learning Torah." To begin with, the parents themselves are enthusiastic learners where learning itself is the goal — to learn is to live. Additionally, there is application, by resolving *she'eilos*, questions and doubts. And finally, because Torah learning, at every level, has some *"pilpul,"* discussions and variant points of view, it creates an interpersonal setting which furthers social living, human intimacy, and parent-child or teacher-student bonds.

The possibility of the school and the home serving complementary functions in learning and living should be explored. Such a task will need a great deal of work and will undoubtedly encounter many obstacles. Its rewards would, however, be immeasurable. To the learning process it would lend social relevance, and such a concerted effort in "learning how to live" might well produce an improved social order. This is what schools should be doing in the first place, anyhow.

Chapter Eight

Homework

Those of us who are concerned with the education of our young are said to be either "believers" in homework or "nonbelievers." Now, if the matter of homework is a belief, a "religion," then one cannot quarrel with the keepers of the faith — and homework it must be. If, however, homework is an invention of man, it must be exposed for what it is: Except for rare situations, the assignment of homework in the grades as commonly practiced is a nonproductive procedure, with side effects that are harmful, if not dangerous, on educational, psychological, philosophical, and moral grounds.

All the pro-homework arguments in the name of the need for "excellence in education," the importance of developing independent study habits in the early grades, and fulfilling the school's curriculum are nonsense when we consider the following:

(a) There is more teaching going on today than ever before in terms of time, effort, and educational know-how and equipment. However, less learning is taking place, as students remain illiterate, drop out completely, or at best remain in school, but with much frustration, anger, and a negative attitude toward learning.

(b) Any "normal" child who has been deprived of formal education due to particular circumstances beyond anyone's control can, within a surprisingly short period of time, recoup all that others have supposedly learned in years of study, augmented with loads of homework. In fact, much of high school is devoted to remedying what has (not) been learned in grade school — and so it is in college and then in graduate school.

(c) The tensions created in homes as parents become enforcers of doing homework, permanently scar both parents and children as well as the all-important relationship that exists between them.

(d) Curricula are developed by humans — men and women frequently removed from the classroom scene, who get little feedback as to what can be expected realistically and what cannot. The curriculum is an artifact that is not and cannot be tested scientifically in terms of relevance, utility, and the student ability and teacher capacity that exist in any one particular classroom situation. What can and should be done in classroom X must differ from that in classroom Y, since we are dealing with different students, teachers, needs, and relevancies. The curriculum is reminiscent of the beds in Sodom and Gomorrah which were standardized (as curricula are), and whose occupants were cut or stretched to make them fit (as our students are pressed to live up to curricular goals, or held back from creative exploring that does not "fit" curricula demands). One does not fit a child to an arbitrary curriculum — one fits the curriculum to the child.

The Psycho-Educational Issue

Suppose that a talented teacher assigns homework relevant to the work in school, on a level that allows each and every child to do it (without the parents' assistance and annoyance), then really inspects it (unlike some, whose students suspect do not bother at all), and reviews it in class for corrective learning. There are still insoluble problems that remain. For example: The student is assigned a spelling word or an arithmetic task. The student does the first example, which happens to be incorrect. There is no feedback to correct the child, and the subsequent examples simply reinforce the first error — the child learns well the incorrect spelling or inaccurate method. Learning comes about through stimulus, response, and rein-forcement. The stimulus here is present but negative, since the child is primarily stimulated to do the homework because of fear — and the reinforcement is too far removed in terms of time to be a factor. When will the assignment be corrected — if at all? Will the teacher be pleased or not? Will the reward be a pat on the head, a good grade — or a harsh spanking? Thus, no effective, immediate rein-forcement takes place, and little, if any, learning.

Realistically, moreover, can one expect teachers to be animated computers to accurately gear homework in terms of classroom ac-tivity and each individual student's ability? Should the teacher be expected to spend endless hours inspecting papers for corrective learning — spelling out clearly the errors and indicating the proper methods? Finally, is there sufficient time in class to properly review assignments to make all of this really useful?

Homework is a fossil firmly entrenched in traditional education that is perpetuated by the myth that because it has always been with us, it must continue to exist. Society has changed, and schools are looking for newer methods that will stimulate and motivate the child from within. The days of lecturing down to the child and cram-ming things down his or her throat are gone because of the futility of such approaches — and homework deserves the identical fate.

Philosophical Considerations

The matter of a "philosophy of education" — what education is supposed to be all about — has not been resolved, nor is it likely soluble as a universal and unequivocal statement of principles. As a minimum, however, we must assume that schools reflect the value system of our society and, in turn, shape — through our young — society to be. In this latter goal, the creation of society to be, we have failed miserably. While we are healthier today than ever be-fore — as well as richer, and supposedly having more fun — many of us remain either illiterate or educated in very narrow spheres, or become "intellectual giants" but social-emotional retardates. Consequently, we are today angrier, unhappier, and more malad-justed than has ever been recorded in human history.

Education is said to be concerned with preparing the child for life: to teach him more skills, to have him acquire more knowledge, and to stuff him with more of whatever learning is. The more the better. In this, education truly (and unfortunately) reflects the predominant value system of our society: more — more money, achievement, health, and beauty — and now more education as well. The attitude is that more is optimum. Thus there must be more learning with more homework, more book reports, more term papers, and more independent study — to waste not a moment of our precious time.

Deep in our innermost thoughts we know, however, that more is not necessarily better. "More" in a clinical sense is a source of (false) security, an illusion of a paradise that becomes ever more distant the more we race for it. Like a drug, the notion of "more" demands ever-increasing dosages that really fail us in the end. There is and there must be an optimum for everything, including education, that is not based simply upon "more."

Schools must not be pressure machines working with both punitive methods (the fear of failure) and reward contingencies (the promise of happiness if one learns more, knows more, and works harder). To do that is to make schools both feared and hated. The school must be a miniature society in which learning, living, exploring, and creating are integrated with satisfaction and good feelings about oneself, whether one does well or not so well.

Homework is a burden and its basic definition is simply "more learning," of which we have too much already. It is frequently the straw that breaks the camel's back because since it comes after school, homework connotes most clearly the "more" — additional, extra, a task, a burden on top of other loads.

Immorality of It All

Many parents sit in their offices, attend to their business, or work at their jobs with more or less satisfaction, depending upon various pressures that go along with the work. Yet they know that ahead of them lies freedom, relaxation, and good feeling. It is the hopeful anticipation of the upcoming night, weekend, or holiday, that keeps many of us going. Thus, while many adults overwork during the day, they are totally unwilling to do even minimal tasks at night. It is said that "the shoemaker's child goes barefoot" — because his shoes are to be made after work is done, and after work, no one wants to work. Even slaves were given at least promises of a time when work was done, a period of rest and relaxation.

Our children, however, are not that fortunate. When work is done there is always some homework, some study that could (or must) be done. "Yes, you can play," we tell our child, "after you do your homework." So the child sits and procrastinates, brooding and angry, and neither does the homework nor plays. Weekends and holidays are, at best, only partially enjoyed because hanging over the child is always some homework or studying for the next test. As a result, our children have lost the art of carefree play, the pleasure of going outdoors, the relaxed attitude and feelings of freedom.

So the father sits (deservedly, after a hard day's work), learning, studying, or reading — or, all too often, in front of the television — and must hound his child to do his homework, for so it is decreed. The child who finally does his homework needs help, and the father is annoyed. The father, remember, wants to rest; he does not want to help his child and thus himself go back to work. Needless to say, if it is a subject that presents difficulty for the parent, or if the father himself harbors negative feelings toward learning and homework (a definite possibility since he too suffered similarly as a child), the pot is primed with ever more anger that must lead to explosion. Moreover, the parent often sees the unfairness of all this and may side with the child, yet he must remain the enforcer for the school — another source of conflict.

This double bind generates frustration and anger that, too, is injected into the thickening clouds of emotional chaos. If, now, here comes the mother with her notions of what is to be done, or other children approach to compete for their share of Dad's time, the turmoil-to-be becomes a certainty.

As a result, parents and children who always have at least some hassles in everyday life are now blessed with additional fuel to keep the pot boiling. How much harm all of this generates can be only partially assessed by the multitude of problems that clinicians deal with when there are confrontations, battles, and wars between parents and children around the issue of homework. How many others keep the lid on tight but have the pressure cooker boiling away anyhow?

What Parents and Teachers Can Do

Fundamental changes in traditional education have come about primarily through riots. Unfortunately, the system could not be shaken until parents rebelled and no longer went along with tradition just because it existed. Parents demanded that the child must learn regardless of ability or motivation. Excuses were to be no longer tolerated. The proverbial horse should be led to the water and must be made to drink. As a result, progress came about. Additionally, there is now going on throughout the country experimentation and innovation and a demand for greater talent. The profession has been upgraded and teachers are no longer people who are just ahead of the child by a few pages. Teachers are now (we hope) innovators and scientists who search for newer methods and approaches to really reach each and every child.

Similarly, if we are to shake up the system and remove the tedious burden of homework and the havoc it creates, then a riot it must be. Teachers and parents should strike, and refuse to go along with this nonsense. They should band together and eradicate this creator of tension from the home. The home must be returned to its primary function, a place where one feels good, where relationships are the order of the day — not where enforcement and coercion take place. Teachers, in turn, freed from the hassles around homework, could then turn their attention to the real business of schooling — a joint venture into the world of learning where teachers and students are partners, not adversaries locked in a constant struggle of coercion and resistance.

To be sure, there is no argument with the need for review and the importance of independent study. There is, furthermore, much to be said for parents and children interacting in the process of learning. Indeed, how beautiful the sight of parent and child exploring the world of knowledge, studying, jointly learning and teaching one another. For that is truly the Torah way, the parent and the child learning, and learning to love learning. But homework as it is practiced in the traditional sense — where parents are enforcers — hardly ever does any one of these things, but rather separates, through strife and bitterness, whatever relationship does exist. Until newer and more imaginative ways will be found to do whatever homework was meant to do, it must not be tolerated in its present state. It must be surgically removed before the cancer of strife and friction engulfs our homes completely.

Chapter Nine

Achievement Motivation Reconsidered

A Second Look at Motivation

*P*arents are familiar with the ever popular children's games of "house" or "school." The little tots seem to delight in creating situations in which they which imitate their elders. In the process they are ready, indeed happy, to watch their "baby" in the doll carriage for prolonged periods, "clean" their house, "wash" the dishes, or "fold" the laundry. While playing school they listen to the "teacher," follow directions, and even take graciously whatever "punishments" are meted out.

Teachers relate with delight stories of first graders who are disappointed when there is no school or complain that they find that school is "more play than learning." Indeed, teachers have to promise that there will be homework and assignments at some future date, to the delight of the little scholars.

Whatever happens to this overabundance of enthusiasm, and

seemingly endless amount of motivation for learning and doing, as the child matures? Could we not capture this eagerness to learn, reinforce it and build upon this apparently natural and almost universal desire for knowledge and mastery? Instead, teachers and parents are forced to set up artificial situations to stimulate our children and to reward them in order to make them perform.

Can this process — the deterioration of an innate motivation for learning in children — be halted or at least slowed down? Or better still, can parents help develop, and then, together with the teacher, sustain and foster the child's innate need for achievement? A number of observable factors would dictate that the answer is yes. Achievement motivation can be fostered in children without extraneous rewards or reinforcement.

The Child's Need to Master His Environment

When children are able to do things, there seems to be a need for them to act and do them. Parents can see this readily when their child first sits up, walks, or talks. All that seems to be necessary is the child's physical or mental ability, an opportunity to perform, and an adequate model to copy. Once the task has been accomplished, the child, furthermore, tends to repeat his performance without any overt stimulation. This can frequently be observed when, for example, the child is first able to stand up. Without encouragement from others or any apparent need, he pulls himself up, stands bathed in a grin of satisfaction, and then plops down — only to repeat the process over and over again.

This rudimentary bit of behavior can serve as a model for more complicated learning tasks. It involves a principle which may be called "initiative, exertion, success, and repetition." *Initiative* to first stand up comes apparently from within the child — a drive to explore, to do what he is able to, to act and master his environment. *Exertion* as such does not impede the tendency to perform, because without exertion one cannot really speak of mastery. On the contrary, exertion in itself seems to be a motivating factor, because once the child can pull himself up without undue effort he ceases to do so, unless it is to serve another purpose. *Success* seems to be crucial. Without success, exertion is fatiguing. This success then becomes rewarding (intrinsic), with the parental smile of approval a further reward (extrinsic). The healthy infant does not exert himself unless such exertion is related to an attainable goal. *Repetition* is a corollary of success; success is a pleasurable state which demands repetition. What he can do, he wants to do. It can thus be said that success makes repetition both possible and likely to occur.

This type of behavior — involving initiative, success, and repetition — can be observed at all levels of maturity. It makes the homemaker decide to exert herself and bake a cake even though a similar one can be bought. It will limit her to attempt only those recipes where success is likely, yet, if successful, it will make for repeated efforts with the very same dish. This cluster of behavior patterns is responsible for children initiating various activities, delighting in strenuous games, and finding satisfaction in the same task even after innumerable repetitions. Knowing this should serve parents and teachers to foster achievement motivation in the child without artificial and extraneous methods or devices.

Fostering Motivation in the Home

All learning is dependent upon some initiative, a readiness to act on one's own. Individuals will act when it is their belief that there is a need to act, and that through an individual's own actions he can attain his goals. This calls for training in independence at a relatively early age in life and allowing the child to make more and more decisions on his own as he matures. For example, within reason he is to be allowed, and indeed encouraged, to make his own friends, choose his own clothing, and try difficult things without asking for help.

This demands a kind of attitude in the home where individuals are encouraged to be active and manipulate the environment, rather than be passive and pessimistic, with a kind of "what's the use" attitude. It calls for a philosophy of life that believes in personal responsibility for one's actions rather than a fatalistic and passive attitude toward life.

The need to exert oneself and to expend effort makes some frustration in early childhood necessary and beneficial. Obviously, ready gratification of every whim would stifle achievement. It would impede initiative and make effort unnecessary. Because success is so important to learning and fostering achievement motivation, tasks which are presented to the child must be within reach, albeit with some effort. Parents frequently make the mistake of encouraging the child to walk or be toilet-trained before he is ready, usually because the neighbor's child has already reached this milestone. As a result, the child develops a negative attitude toward such tasks and subsequent training becomes more difficult. Often parents give a child a bicycle or toy before it is within his reach to master them. To prove this point, parents need only check up on which toys are almost never used by the child; they are usually those which were given to him before he was able to master their use.

Gratification, Now or Later

Because the value of school tasks is not apparent or immediate, children need to develop an ability to postpone gratification, to do things now because of a reward later on. This is quite a difficult task for young children because of the intensity of their instinctual drives and because their concept of the past and the future is not fully developed. Nonetheless, postponement of immediate gratification can be developed. Children who basically trust their parents will have trust in the future because their parents say so, even if the concept "future" is quite hazy. Trust in one's parents comes about when there is a warm parent-child relationship, when promises are scrupulously kept, and when parents offer rewards with their demands. Such rewards need not, of course, be material ones. A sense of well-being, warmth, physical and emotional contact, a smile or a look, more than suffice. The ability to postpone gratification is crucial in many areas of life later on. It deserves much effort on the part of parents. Needless to say, such training should be gradual, with ever increasing periods of time between need and gratification. Of course, a warm parent-child relationship is in itself gratifying and can "take over" when the real gratification is in the distant future.

The Parent as Model

When the child acts like his parent, he more than imitates; he identifies with him and in a sense becomes the parent himself. This can be observed when the child takes over many of the parent's mannerisms, modes of speech, or posture. It inevitably involves the parent's code of behavior, his goals and aspirations, and sense of values. Not only does "the apple not fall far from the tree," but the apple contains the seed which grows into the very same kind of tree.

This kind of mechanism accounts for the known fact that children do not grow up as their parents want them to be. They rather resemble or become what the parents themselves *are*. It is thus superfluous to mention that parents should be adequate models for their children. It is, however, a sad fact that invariably parents demand more of their children than of themselves as far as achievement is concerned. As a member of a business organization, the parent may be satisfied with not being in the highest echelon — but the child must have A's and outrank his fellows. Adults know of their inefficiency and frequent mediocrity of performance, but as for the child — he must do his best.

In addition, there are many inconsistencies — such as parents professing love for learning yet hardly opening a book themselves. It is no wonder, then, that children are bewildered. They feel that parents are unjust in demanding more of the child than of themselves. In addition, they lose respect because of the transparent hypocrisy. As a result, the identification process becomes filled with anxiety and doubt. The young child who was so very anxious to be like Daddy is no longer so very sure. There will thus be less imitative play and less acceptance of the parent as a model.

Of course, no one is or needs to be "perfect." Indeed, woe to the "perfectionist" who drives himself to the point of mental or physical illness. Parents, like every one of us, need to recognize this. There are, additionally, variables in our makeup which make for success, where individual differences are important. None of us are equally endowed with mental ability, mental and physical stamina, patience, persistence, drive, and a healthy balance between safety and risk-taking. All of this is fine when individuals recognize all of this, yet try to "improve." For example, the mentally weaker individual could compensate by studying more.

Yet, when it comes to our children, we want our children to "be the best," to be whatever we — the parents — are not. That is both unfair and self-defeating. Parents should be more consistent themselves, show the way and model behavior rather than constantly demand or preach.

The School and Achievement Motivation

Much of what has been said about the home can be applied in school. Teachers know very well that "success breeds success." They should, however, make it possible for *all* children to be successful. This may call for many and repeated adjustments in curriculum-planning for a class as a whole and for the individual child.

Why do the very same children who clamored for homework in first grade and loved those little assignments come to loathe it later on? Obviously, if homework tasks would be introduced ever so gradually, with the likelihood of the child's being able to do the work at home, the child would not develop such an aversion to it so soon. So it is with most school tasks. Lack of motivation, and aversion to school tasks come about when tasks are too difficult, when success is unlikely, and when learning is then heaped upon earlier learning which never did take place adequately. Thus the child who lost out earlier in his school career rarely catches up.

More effort is needed to locate the child's level of achievement at the time when instruction is to take place and then introduce the slightly more difficult task — one that can be mastered with just a little more effort. It is said that frogs, who love warm water, have been boiled alive when the temperature of the water they were in was raised ever so slowly. Can our children, then, not be put into a comfortable environment and, when the "heat must be put on," can this not be done in a slow and painless fashion (and without boiling them alive)? Obviously, large classes, overburdened teachers, and a rigid, authoritarian administration are not conducive to improving the learning process. The teacher whose initiative is stifled cannot help but repress that of his students.

What is needed is greater flexibility from the top down to allow for experimentation and, if necessary, deviation from a too rigid curriculum. Teachers need smaller classes in order to better know their pupils and their abilities, and time in order to experiment and tailor instruction to individual needs.

Teachers know that before a difficult task is introduced, children should be given an opportunity to go over material they have already mastered. This helps the mechanism of "success breeding success." Frequently, however, insufficient time is given for such repetitive work which breeds good feeling and lays the groundwork for further learning.

A Delicate Transition

More important yet is the transition to more difficult tasks. These must always be ever so gradual if the child's early achievement motivation is to be sustained throughout his school career. To water down instruction indiscriminately will not do the job, for lack of a need to exert oneself will stifle motivation. Instruction should selectively be made easier and more difficult in order to assure success with some effort.

Children who come to school with strong achievement motivation and thus a good deal of independence will thrive when teachers call upon their students to take initiative and to actively participate in the planning and execution of what goes on in the classroom.

Thus, as in the home situation, a regimen of initiative, exertion, success, and repetition should assure each child the successful school career that is his due. This may sound like a tall order. It is, however, quite cheap and certainly worthwhile when one compares it to the heartaches, the failures, the wasted man-hours and lives, which come about when one's scholastic career was an unwelcome burden, where little learning actually took place.

Chapter Ten

On the Need for Self-Esteem

Self-Esteem: An Unfulfilled Need

very child has needs. There is the need to be fed and sheltered, to receive love and understanding, to have an opportunity to express oneself and learn, to live within a group, to be a member of human society. These are but a few of the many needs of the child. Some of these needs are more pressing than others; some are universal, while others are culturally determined. Certain needs are necessary to sustain life, while others serve to make life "worthwhile," to attain that elusive concept usually described as happiness.

Parents generally recognize the basic needs of the child that must be met to sustain life. Most parents, furthermore, understand that a child needs more than these basic necessities, and do their utmost to provide love, understanding, opportunities for learning, and so forth. This is so because the parent, too, experiences these needs, and as he goes about meeting them he learns, more or less correctly, how to do the same for his child. Yet there is one need, the need for self-esteem, which stands somehow separate and apart in that at the very time its foundation needs to be laid, it is rarely given the necessary attention. Childhood is the time when self-esteem is needed the most, yet provided for the least.

The Need and Its Development

Every human being must know that he is of value as a person, that he is a somebody. This must be so regardless of one's failures or shortcomings. Deep down within himself, in his most inner thoughts, every individual must recognize his worth, regardless of what he produces or contributes to society. There must be a reason for his existence.

Fortunately, total lack of self-esteem is rare in our society, but inadequate self-esteem is common, particularly in the school-age child. It manifests itself in depression, dejection, and an all-pervasive feeling of hopelessness which, if uncorrected, may cripple one's personality for life.

A person learns of his own worth primarily through the reaction his personality elicits from others. There are no real measurements or standards to guide one, but by repeated interaction with others an individual learns to introject what others think of him and then feel about himself the way others do.

Is the redhead fiery or the fat man jolly? There is no genetic reason for this to be so. But being told again and again that "you are acting just like a redhead" will make the person with red hair think of himself as others stereotype him. The same is likely true of the obese individual's jolliness.

It has been experimentally shown that certain minority groups have relatively low self-esteem because, it is argued, those minority groups introject the opinion of the majority. Another experiment which proved a similar point had a group of people contriving to raise the self-esteem of a shy and introverted individual through praise and attention. Amazingly enough, the subject of this scheme became a virtually changed person —

happy, well adjusted, outgoing, and friendly. More amazing yet, the change seemed to be permanent.

It is thus clear that having an adequate measure of self-esteem is vital; and this feeling comes into being through interaction with others. Man sees himself as others see him.

The Child: Captive of Society

There appear to be cultural provisions which, under normal circumstances, serve the individual to acquire and maintain an adequate measure of self-esteem during infancy and during adulthood. Yet the very same culture creates a setting during childhood which impedes, at least for some children, the development of an adequate measure of self-esteem.

The infant is born to a mother and father and, in the majority of cases, to a family group. The infant is accepted, loved, and provided for, regardless of his behavior or productivity. He learns of his value through the expressions he sees in others, which say, "Good baby, nice baby, we love you."

The adult lives within a family and within a larger group composed of friends, neighbors, business associates, and other acquaintances. This group, for various reasons, is likely to share similar interests and attributes such as levels of intelligence and socio-economic status. Being accepted by the group, and contributing to it, assure the individual of his worth: He is accepted, wanted, and needed. Should the individual fail to receive such reassurance, he is likely to break with the group and seek one which will provide the self-esteem he needs.

To be sure, one's self-esteem is not stable; man or infant constantly revises his estimate of his own worth according to the feedback he receives from others. But such fluctuations are not necessarily harmful. They may well be productive in that they cause the individual to make appropriate adjustments in order to enhance his self-esteem. Nor is the accuracy of his estimation, within reasonable limits, crucial. It is the existence of some self-esteem, some success, some worthwhile contributions to society which are essential.

Vulnerability of the School-Age Child

The child, specifically the school-age child, is not that fortunate. Such a girl, for example, upon entering the school, finds herself within a group that is new and very different from the family environment.

Within the family, the child has, under normal conditions, acquired the necessary measure of self-esteem due to the praise and love she has received from her parents and others. She may have had to contend with sibling rivalry or other problems, but she was an individual within a group that is more or less homogeneous in many ways — in intellect, socio-economic status, and physical endowment, for example. This is so because, generally, heredity and environment interact to make family members more alike than individually different. Needless to say, because of the nature of a family, individuals within it tend to support one another in spite of the many little frictions that do exist.

All this changes dramatically when the child enters school. Here, the child is thrust into a group which is heterogeneous in almost every respect — intelligence, motivation, socio-economic background, physical maturity, physical endowment. If the child is lucky enough to feel adequate in one or more of these attributes, she may well build her self-esteem upon that which she has, while relegating the attributes she lacks to a position of lesser importance. She rationalizes. Her estimation of her self-esteem may be inaccurate according to the standards of her peers, but its existence remains assured.

Suppose, however, there is a situation where a child cannot rationalize. Consider a young boy of average scholastic ability in a class of intellectually superior children within a society that holds intellectual achievement supreme. The child soon realizes that no matter how hard he tries, he cannot achieve as well as the others do. What road is open to him? He may try to excel in physical or social activities, and, despite the low value of this endeavor in the eyes of his subculture, he may succeed in building his self-esteem. However, should he be equally deficient in these respects, then his alternatives are drastically circumscribed. The child may redouble his efforts for a while, but when he fails, because of his innate limitations, he will tend to give up trying and withdraw from the battle. What is he to do now? He may daydream of grandiose achievement; he may become the class clown in order to get laughs rather than be laughed at; or he may react with overt hostility toward his teacher and classmates, only to receive less and less support from his environment — resulting in a total loss of self-esteem.

Let the average adult imagine being placed within a group that is affluent in every respect. Let him further consider that his outward physical appearance does not betray his "shortcomings." How hard will he try to keep up a front? He will lie, beg, borrow, or steal to match the economic status of his group. He will cram and study long evenings in order to meet the intellectual challenge of his group. He may assume a devil-may-care attitude and live the life of an outcast. But for how long will he "succeed"? He may compound deception upon deception, only to be found out in the end. But there is one important difference between this adult and the school-age child: An adult can escape this fate by removing himself from the situation, by finding a group level closer to his own. The child does not have this opportunity.

Concept of Individual Differences

We all pay lip service to the idea of individual differences, but what has realistically been done about this concept? All the schemes that have been tried — such as homogeneous grouping, or multiple track systems — do not fool the child. He knows all too well where he stands.

Not so very long ago, the child who did not achieve was considered lazy and stupid, which meant one and the same — he was not trying. Methods of motivation — the strap, the dunce cap, the knuckle-rapper — had little effect. Yet the efficacy of the method was not questioned; the solution was simply to design more effective torture instruments.

We tend to feel more sophisticated than our predecessors, but we may have finally perfected the best torture instrument of all — the psychological method. Let the child be ashamed, let him know how stupid he is. We may even attempt to sugar-coat the instrument by not telling him outright that he is stupid. We group the children, we assign grades, we examine — but we fool no one, least of all the child himself.

Finally he accepts his fate, realizes that he is no good, and loses his last ounce of self-esteem: He is a nobody. And what have we accomplished? Unless by some miracle he escapes his fate, the child will carry this burden for many years to come, if not for a lifetime.

There is a similar situation which, if perhaps not as serious, seems to be more prevalent within our more immediate subculture. Specifically, there are a great many children who are intellectually endowed and work more or less up to their ability — but parents and teachers often overestimate the extent of an individual's true ability. Thus there is pressure to achieve even more, which the child cannot do. Again his self-esteem suffers, though there is no basis in reality for the child to feel inadequate. One should quickly add that at times even specialists are misled in estimating ability. The gregarious child from a culturally enriched home is likely to fool the examiner until the hard facts of objective procedures face the clinician, who must then admit that during his first impression he had overestimated the child's true ability. The sad part in this scenario is that it is the intelligent, ostensibly objective parent who is implicated here (probably including psychologists), because a parent cannot be objective where his child is concerned.

Thus, for one reason or another, there are far too many children who feel inadequate and become part of a vicious cycle: They cannot achieve and their self-esteem suffers. Their anxiety is then aroused, or they give up, and they achieve less and less as time goes on — and the cycle repeats itself. Alternatively, they drive themselves endlessly to the point of mental illness.

What Parents and Teachers Can Do

One cannot endow the child with an ability that heredity has failed to give him. One cannot simply change societal values and aspirations. The parent of the child, furthermore, is more likely to be socially immobile — he is a captive of a subculture that greatly values scholastic achievement. Thus, solutions will be hard to come by, and even more difficult to implement. Nonetheless, an attempt must be made.

The family and school can be considered as a miniature society within a subculture, the Jewish Orthodox middle class, which in turn resides within a larger society, Western civilization. The family and school have values of their own. These values are generally influenced by the values of the subculture and those of the larger society. The intensity of such values, however, is amenable to change.

Parents and teachers can learn that there are values other than scholastic achievement. This may sound easy, but it is extremely difficult. But if the significant adults in the child's environment can find one area in which the child is proficient — unimportant as it may be — and then build his self-esteem around it through genuine praise and encouragement, they will have salvaged a human being and helped him to lead a life of productivity rather than to live a life of shame and unhappiness.

Basic, of course, is the need for objectivity in an endeavor which is by nature subjective. Parents, and to some extent, teachers, are not onlookers. They are participants. It is their child, their pupil. Therefore, the child's native ability should be objectively evaluated by an outsider, a specialist. Though the evaluation should not be taken as absolute and final, it must guide the parent and teacher in knowing what can be expected of the child at present. That information should be sealed, and available only to teachers to guide them in their expectations.

Even more important is the need for understanding. The child who is engaged in a day-to-day struggle needs, above all else, understanding. He needs an ally. To some, "understanding" may sound ridiculously simple and self-evident. This is not so. We are, after all, human ourselves, with needs — including the need to have our children succeed. There is a limit to our patience. Too often the parent or teacher cannot see why the child does not even try to help himself — why he alienates teachers and friends, why he fails to exert an effort. What we are really saying is that we cannot understand him. This is not an answer, but a question, a finger pointing at us accusingly: Why do we fail to understand him?

Understanding does not necessarily mean a study in depth, a total understanding of the child's personality. All that is needed is to understand his difficulties, to feel for him, to know of his struggle, to realize why he acts in a self-defeating manner. One who can thus understand the child becomes his ally, his protector, his idol.

Even if all else fails, the child who knows that someone really understands him knows that someone really cares. And even if only one person cares, the child feels that he is important to that individual — he is worthwhile, he is a somebody. The almost magic transformation of a child which at times comes about after brief contact with a teacher, a camp counselor, or a clinician is often nothing more than this: "Here is a person who understands me. He cares. I am a somebody."

In short, the parent or teacher who indicates to the child: "I know of your difficulties, I realize how you feel, I understand you, yet I accept and value your being" — this parent or teacher is performing a miracle. He creates a sense of adequacy in an individual who otherwise would be condemned to a life of unhappiness and oblivion.

What Should Be Self-Evident

On a much deeper level, one perhaps almost unattainable to the average human being, there should be another attitude altogether: Namely, that the innate value of man, his basic self-esteem, should be independent of what he does or fails to do.

It has been said that things are to be used, while people are to be loved. When things no longer work and are no longer useful, we throw them out. We do not do this with human beings. Although euthanasia has been practiced in the past and, to our dismay, not only continues today but has been dressed up as "medically assisted suicide," it is generally condemned. The Torah Jew is fortified in this belief that the value of all individuals is equal. *Halachos* (religious laws) dealing with murder do not factor in the age of the victim, the health of the victim, his imminency of death, or his contribution — or lack thereof — to society.[1] A

---

1. See *Rambam, Sefer Nezikin, Hilchos Rotzei'ach.*

human being is a human being; his value is infinite, and infinity divided by any number remains infinity. The value of man thus is intrinsic and not given to numbers or amounts. The human being is furthermore a *tzelem Elokim,* an image of G-d, again of infinite value or greatness. Thus when Jews are counted through the giving of a *machtzis hashekel* (the half *shekel* which eventually becomes an equal contribution for offerings meant to be equally shared), the "price" per head remains the same — the half *shekel* — for the scholar and the ignoramus, the wealthy and the pauper.[2] In the eyes of G-d, we are equal.

This brings us back to our original question: How do we handle our children on a day-to-day basis when one's value or worth comes into question?

It may be almost easy when, G-d forbid, a child is mentally or emotionally disabled, yet can be loved and can contribute, at times mightily, to the loving climate that resides in that house. But what about two children, one of whom has superior intelligence and functions accordingly, while the other functions intellectually at an average level, and cannot possibly compete — not with his sibling, nor with the majority of his classmates? What message do we send him? Do we say, "Work harder and you can do it" — and thus condemn him to chronic frustration and the pain of failure? Or do we tell him, "Well, you're doing your best and it's fine" — thus telling him that he is inferior after all?

Is there another alternative? Has the acquisition of knowledge, of skills, even of Torah learning, become in our psyche a material gain much like money, fame, or honors — something one gloats about to himself and to others: "I am better, I have more." The *mishnah* says differently: "If you have more Torah do not pride yourself, for that is the reason for your having been created."[3]

Obviously, it must be possible to attain a higher level in life, one where everyone is equal, where competition does not produce anger and frustration, where everyone should want to win, but where one benefits equally when his fellow or his brother wins. There must be a way for everyone to excel, for everyone to be a

---

2. See *Rambam, Sefer Zemanim, Hilchos Shekalim.*
3. *Avos* 2:9.

winner. Yes, this is possible — in the race to be a *mensch*, a loving human being, a contributor to the social-emotional well-being of all one comes in contact with. Those who participate in this race not only benefit themselves but, in a psuedo-contagious manner, pass on this attitude to society at large.

When this comes about, when being a *mensch* (in our case, a *Torah mensch*) is the ultimate, then all else should pale by comparison. This internalized feeling — "Yes, I am a *mensch!*" — would then add to and enhance the innate, axiomatic, unconditional feeling that "*I am*, because I am a *tzelem Elokim*, a human created in the image of G-d." Yes, man as a *tzelem Elokim* has value in that he is loving and lovable. The size of his brain, the strength of his body, do not make him better or worse. To use whatever ability a person has is good for the person and for society. But that does not make the man.

Be it in the family setting, or the school, or society at large, when being a *mensch* (or a *Torah mensch*) is the ultimate, then we start the race equipped equally, for regardless of brains or beauty, we can all be *Torah menschen*. Knowing this is the great equalizer that enables one to tell oneself, "Yes, I am a *mensch*, I am intrinsically worthwhile. I am loving and lovable. I have self-esteem, not because of what I can do or achieve, but because I am the ultimate of G-d's creations, a *tzelem Elokim*." Thus, the message from parents and teachers to our young should not be, "You are great because of what you achieve," but, "You are great because you are a human, and by your pleasant demeanor and your loving attitude are a true *Torah mensch*."

Chapter Eleven

To Be a Parent: The Whole and the Sum of Its Parts

hat does it mean to be a "parent"? What is the primary task the father is to perform, or the major role the mother is to play, in bringing up his or her child to be a person, a *mensch*, a happy and productive member of society? To stand guard over a child's health and safety, to have her brush her teeth and wash behind her ears — why not employ a professional nurse who could do all that more effectively and with fewer hassles? To feed a son — can we not engage a trained nutritionist to offer him the very best? To teach a daughter — why not hire a tutor or child psychologist? Why the parent, who is ill equipped to do all this, having had no formal training in child rearing, and whose emotional involvement beclouds rational thinking concerning how to bring up a child "scientifically" and "correctly"?

Yet the "untrained" parent it must be, in spite of knowing the vital all-importance of early parent-child interaction in shaping one's personality. Experiments in communes, even in well-intentioned and "scientifically" designed settings such as the kibbutz or orphanages, have failed to produce the ideal *mensch*. Indeed, in spite of the "professional" handling of their young by nurses, nutritionists, and tutors, there is scientific evidence that the "perfect" setting, the clean and well-run home for children, with good nutrition and attention to health, is no match for the "real mother" — even one who provides less than adequate nutrition, health care, or other comforts of life. For the long term, the real live mother, the constancy of the parent-child interaction, is more important than physical needs.

Certainly, then, the whole must be greater than the sum of its parts. The role of the parent as parent must be far greater than his or her role as nurse, nutritionist, or tutor. Indeed, this task of being a parent (whatever it may be) is so vital that to fulfill it we make do with less than perfect nutrition, health, and training for our children. What, then, is this role of being a parent as parent and nothing more than a parent?

Beautiful People and Happy People

Even superficial inspection of the world around us reveals to us the fact that people today are more "beautiful" than ever before. There they go with that fit and healthy look, laughingly baring their gleaming white teeth, off to enjoy life at the games, the theater, the beautiful places, facilitated by the pleasure machines and contraptions man is constantly inventing to provide amusement and fun.

Yet a trip to the psychotherapist's office, or even a closer look at these "beautiful" people, soon shatters this glowing picture. Within the deep recesses of her mind, the beautiful woman considers herself to be quite ugly — in spite of the endless adulation she receives. Inside, the brilliant and acknowledged scholar kicks himself for his many perceived stupidities, and the businessman worth millions labels himself as quite worthless. All the arguments in the world will not convince them otherwise, in spite of logical minds and factual evidence.

The staggering statistics of various addictions, broken homes, suicides, and conflict within homes and between people should convince us that the unhappy, no matter how beautiful they look, are the majority among us, not the rarity. In fact, there is strong evidence that the more beautiful they try to look — the bigger the (artificial) smile, the greater the involvement with clothing and good looks, and the more intense the chase after fun — the more unhappiness is being covered up. A similarly negative correlation seems to exist also between achievement and happiness. Overly high achievers tend to pay a price for their feats: a restlessness, an unhappiness, an inability to enjoy life without attaining in a superhuman fashion, be it money, position, or prestige.

Yet here and there one comes across that rare individual who has none of the beauty visible to the eye — no particular attainments, no outstanding intelligence or good looks, and no wealth to speak of. He does have, however, an inner happiness, a satisfaction and a contentment that is neither shaken unduly by adversity nor in need of constant reinforcement by way of praise from others or tangible achievements.

This seemingly illogical phenomenon, the unhappiness of the many who "have" and the contentment of those who are not that fortunately endowed, defies rational explanation. Obviously, then, there must be unconscious factors tucked away in the recesses of our minds that exude feelings of discontent in some and satisfaction in others. It seems as if the satisfied have an inexhaustible reservoir of good feeling that is only moderately affected by outer forces. The unhappy, on the other hand, have no such thing, but must seek constant happiness by way of outer sources — money, fame, fun. Like any addiction, such happiness lasts only as long as the source operates, i.e., as long as the fun or achievement is taking place. As tolerance sets in, the "addiction" then demands ever-increasing dosages or newer stimulants, and in the end really leaves one as empty as before he started.

Such unconscious factors — that reservoir of good feeling, or, conversely, the restless search for happiness — are assumed to be built in at a pre-verbal level, since the source remains unconscious and unavailable to rational discourse. Thus we should look for it in the child's early years, specifically in the uncountable messages the child receives from the significant people around her, her parents. *Transmitting the sum total of these messages may be regarded as the primary task of the parent as parent.* We will acknowledge the parent's role as nurse, nutritionist, and tutor, but only as secondary, and of significantly lesser, importance.

Acquisition of Self-Esteem

The knowledge of facts and skills comes about through relatively simple intellectual processes that require a source of information, a brain to understand, and an ability to remember. To know that two plus two equal four, we need a teacher or a book (source of information), an intellectual maturity to understand the abstract concept of numbers, and an ability to memorize the fact that two plus two equal four. The acquisition of beliefs and attitudes, on the other hand, is far more complex.

Beliefs and attitudes are acquired through signals and messages, verbal and nonverbal, with the latter having primacy over the former. The nonverbal message represents an unconscious pipeline that transmits such signals in spite of opposing signals that may be generated on a conscious level. Thus it is primarily not what we say, but what we really feel within — about a person, or concerning a particular situation — that tells others how things really are. These messages are then introjected and become part of the receiver's system of beliefs and attitudes. To the extent that such messages (a) are generated by significant others (such as parents), (b) are sufficient in frequency and, (c) have emotional impact, they become fixated and set. Their coming about at an early stage in life has particular significance because they prejudge and color all messages and signals that are to follow.

How does a child learn about herself? How does she acquire a self-concept, a notion that she is worthwhile and valuable as a human being? How does she learn which attributes, which factors make her a "being," and which make her into a "nonbeing"? Obviously, it is the myriad of signals and messages she receives early in life from her parents and other significant people, signals that are primarily unconscious but that tell her loudly and clearly exactly what she is and/or how she can become what she should be. What should these signals be, and how can parents know to generate and transmit them to the child?

Fortunately, nature does not leave so vital an issue to chance, just as it does not allow man to voluntarily control other vital body functions such as heartbeat or breathing. Nature sets up matters in a fashion that things turn out right — unless foolish man tries too hard to improve upon the already perfect design of man and his environment.

A human being is born not in a litter, but as a distinct individual — by him/herself, occasionally with a twin, and only rarely with more than that. The infant is totally helpless and dependent upon others for all her needs. She is a total receiver and a nonproducer. In addition, she is a "nuisance," upsetting the routine of the home, restricting the parents' freedom of movement, and keeping them awake at night. Yet this messy bundle of trouble is wanted — for herself, as an individual, as a being. There are no demands made of her, and her disturbing, messy condition does not prevent us from constantly signaling her that it's just great to have her around. The concept of "love" is not what we are talking about here. Love is for poets, and is a complex feeling that in excess can do as much harm as it can do good. It is also a cliché used to make parents feel guilty when we tell them that their child has problems because she is loved insufficiently. Except for rare cases, parents *do* love their offspring — and "more love" is not the panacea for all our emotional ills.

The vital series of messages essential for a healthy self-concept state simply but clearly the following notion: "You are okay just as you are; you're nice to have around." Period. This notion, together with the fact that the relationship is exclusive (because, right now, "You are the one and only one"), and the fact that the child's helpless condition extends for an appreciable amount of time, causes the child to learn that she has value — regardless of what she does or what she produces.

This idyllic situation soon is shaken as the infant matures and the educative process begins. Now there are demands, and restrictions are imposed. She is taught to improve her eating and toilet habits and her general behavior. The notion that she must become "better" then implies that presently she is imperfect, i.e., "bad." Self-concept then drastically drops and the endless search to become "better" begins — to be more beautiful or more intelligent, to have greater prestige or more money. All too frequently there is also rage, when the unconditional love becomes conditional and a neurotic compromise ensues: "I must please my parents to win their love — but I can't, because I am never good enough. So I keep on trying harder" — with frustration and with rage.

One hastens to add that children must be taught and limits must be set. We simply cannot go on and have a child remain infantile while we accept all her behavior unconditionally. The challenge requiring parental ingenuity is figuring out how to have the child become "better" while telling her at the very same time that she is "good" already as she is. This feeling of "being okay as she is" will form the inexhaustible reservoir of good feeling if she is to be one of the "happy people." To lack such self-esteem, on the other hand, will condemn her to become one of those who endlessly search — for beauty, prestige, money, or fame. Because there is no "best" and no perfection in this world, she is then condemned to the endless treadmill in order to be "better," in search of the elusive and unattainable "best."

This apparent contradiction — to signal the child "You are okay as you are" *and* "You can do better" — is not insurmountable. It calls for a qualitative approach and a quantitative one.

Qualitatively, there is a relatively simple but vital operation in distinguishing between the child and her actions. Basically, we must say, "You can *do* better," not, *"be* better"; or, "You are *doing* badly," not, "You *are* bad." For then we confirm the original message that "You are good as you are" — but what you *do* can be bad. This is far more than a simple semantic game. It is really a belief we are sounding: The value of a person (and, of course, the child) is not given to judgment. She has value — unconditionally. It is her activities that may need improvement.

Quantitatively, we must not allow our role as tutor or nurse to supplant our role as parent. As the educative process begins, and we make demands upon our child and place restrictions upon her, we must retain at all times our original role as the parent who enjoys his child regardless of her behavior — be it good or bad. In practical terms, this means to spend at least as much time interacting with our child in a non-demanding, non-teaching fashion as we spend telling, teaching, or correcting. This essentially is a good part of the psychotherapeutic process that every parent can utilize himself.

Parents are amazed when the therapist can get the child to do relatively quickly what they have been telling the child to do all along without results. The trick is really simple. The therapist divides the session into two parts. The longest segment of time is devoted to relating — call it nonsense talk, play, or just being with one another. This tells the child she has value, she is great, because "that person (the therapist) finds it worthwhile to spend his time with me." In the course of this interaction the therapist shapes the conversation so that the child *learns* by herself a little lesson, a thought, an insight. The lesson does not tell her she is imperfect or bad (which she would then resist), because it is learned rather than taught, and because it has just been proven to her that she is great.

The greatest compliment we can pay an individual is to want to be with her, for it tells her she has value, she is great. This operates only when this interaction is pure — without an ulterior motive such as teaching, fixing, correcting, or gaining an advantage. This — the psychotherapeutic message — is what nature provides for the infant automatically as she is thrust in an exclusive fashion into an all-accepting family situation. Parents interact with their young in the purest possible form — holding her, making nonsense talk, and playing with her. This essential series of messages must not be given up, and certainly not supplanted by the educative process that all too frequently tells the child she is imperfect and in need of improvement.

Chapter Twelve

The Quest for Happiness

*I*f there is one universal wish every parent has for his child, it certainly is the desire to have him attain a state we call "happiness." We are fairly safe in assuming that regardless of one's philosophy concerning exactly what happiness is or how it can be attained, its desirability is self-evident as a major goal in life. Nonetheless, parents rarely make a conscious effort to have their children become contented men and women, nor do they tend to weigh activities and experiences in the light of their contributing to, or detracting from, attaining this goal.

We know, of course, that happiness does not come about by merely striving for it. Happiness is a by-product of man's activities and experiences, and the ensuing state of mind. Thus we say: "Happiness is … a thought, a feeling, an experience." Yet, in reaching for this state of bliss, we seem to construct a relatively narrow road which we think leads us there, place the tot at its gateway, and prod him along — never stopping along the way to reflect whether this is the right path for the child or for anyone. It is not surprising, then, that in spite of parents' good intentions and sincere dedication toward gaining this precious state of mind we call "happiness," the goal remains all too often unrealized.

Happiness and the Value System

One develops a "road to happiness," a system of values, from several sources. First and foremost are one's early childhood experiences with peers and others, and learned attitudes from many sources — primary among them the religious and moral codes handed down through parents, teachers, texts, and society at large. These are then learned and become the individual's value system.

All of this may or may not take place through systematic efforts by parents and teachers. Thus, certain values are either learned through direct teaching, or are absorbed through processes of identification. In the latter case, the child, realizing what is important to his parents, teachers, and society, learns with perhaps less precision or consistency, but the effect of such learning can be just as potent.

This acquired value system then becomes the child's lifestyle, and the road along which his happiness is supposedly to be found. The exact nature of such a value system cannot, of course, be dictated by any one individual. Each person must turn to the sources at his disposal to fashion a lifestyle all his own. Our concern here is with certain aspects of the value systems that are prevalent today in our society and seem to have a direct bearing on happiness and personality development.

Values of "Investment" and "Intellect"

One such system prized in our society is the set of values which has an intellectual orientation, represses emotionality, and is generally future oriented, whereby one "pays" now and postpones gratification or joy for the promise of future benefits. Certainly, intellect has value as the major form of managing one's affairs within oneself, one's family, and society; reason should go before emotion. Also, emotions of extreme sexual or aggressive nature must be controlled at all costs. Thus we are taught to inhibit ourselves, to refrain from gratifying our impulses — to "suffer" now, for the benefit of a "good life" later on. All too frequently, however, intellect is used to exclude the emotional side of one's being so that one becomes ashamed of feeling or "losing control of oneself." We tend to be embarrassed, for instance, by unbridled laughter or uncontrollable tears.

Intellect is also prized for its own sake. Its use, in the form of hard work and self-discipline, we are told, will insure just reward. To get ahead, we must invest now. We must be frugal with money or joy in order to succeed.

For civilization as a whole, the overall value of such intellectual control, as subscribed to by the upwardly mobile middle class and culture — and even more so by our own Orthodox Jewish society — is not in question. What we are concerned with, however, is when intellect, future investment, planning ahead, and intellectual control become the sole determinants in life — and emotional joy and immediate happiness and gratification are severely downgraded. In that case, several possibilities may occur.

For one thing, children may be unable to follow this kind of regime, or they may simply be unwilling to do so. The adolescent frequently voices this very complaint and uses it as his reason for dropping out. He sees his parents investing in hard work, material things, and vague promises of future happiness. He sees little emotional freedom or true happiness in the here and now, and so he wants no part of it.

The younger child, of course, cannot rebel to such an extent. What happens, then, to his emotional life? Basically, emotions are dealt with either physically or mentally, or in a combination of the two. Mentally, when emotions are driven out of consciousness and repressed, they do not cease to exist, but linger on and affect us in many ways. They may become symptoms, the crazy little mannerisms most of us have, or they may simply weigh us down, affecting our entire character with vague anxieties or unexplained depressions. Physically, vital functions accommodate themselves to the demands of our emotions, and insidiously change their mode. Emotions are said to be implicated in a host of diseases, most prominent of which are hypertension, digestive disorders, and similar psychosomatic ills. The child's strong emotions, then, demanding attention, may also affect his glandular system, upset hormonal balances, and alter many of his vital life functions, such as respiration, heart rate, and digestion. Frequently, however, the child manages to develop "defenses," adapts to the demands made upon him, and develops a lifestyle that does, indeed, reflect the value of intellectual control.

The Price of Success ...

So the child submits. He forgoes the joy of emotions, of good feeling, of some fun, and of emotional relatedness to his fellow. Instead, he subscribes to the value of success and the supremacy of the brain. He becomes competitive — striving not only to achieve, but to achieve more than his neighbor.

We meet such specimens in many walks of life. These people, more often than not, are quite successful as concerns material goods, position in life, and the esteem in which they are held as orderly and upright citizens — yet their lives are, nevertheless, relatively empty. They drive themselves and others; they overplan for the future so that they cannot enjoy the present, they overbuy "insurance," literally and figuratively. Their contacts with people are orderly and controlled, but shallow; they have many acquaintances, but few if any intimate friends. When they have achieved their goals they cannot enjoy them, because enjoyment means to "give in" to their emotionality, loss of control, and general "looseness." Instead, they mobilize their intellect to get even further ahead. They never stop or slow down.

Because life's decisions are to be intellectually determined, and impulses, intuition, and "gut feelings" are downgraded, daily living can become somehow sterile. To get on with daily living, there may be endless ruminations, inability to make decisions, crippling doubts, meaningless habits or compulsions. There may be an excessive need to control oneself and others, to be right at all times, to save money or joy for future investments. If this is success — and society may rate it as such — the price is indeed a steep one.

... And the Price of Failure

When "success" in the material station in life is overvalued, and so are intellect and scholastic achievement, fear of the future and the need to assure one's place in the sun can become a nightmare. Indeed, schools and parents weigh and measure children incessantly through grades, tests, standards, and report cards. If there is no room at the bottom, children must scramble for the top.

In this respect, the adult is far luckier. We buy a home in a neighborhood of contemporaries, do business with people who are not very different from us, and mingle socially with those more or less our equals. If our neighbor has a second car, then we may have a nicer home — or we rationalize in a similar fashion. Our boys and girls do not have such luck. Their measure of success and self-esteem is based upon very narrow criteria which are very clearly spelled out. Their intellectual/academic standing is their — and frequently our — status symbol. Every child knows where he stands.

What, then, of the child who is not well enough endowed to give him a more or less equal chance with others? With emotionality and current joy in life downgraded, and intellect valued above all, what indeed does happen to his self-esteem? He is a failure! He cannot make it — and soon gives up trying. We may attempt to alleviate the pain by professing our love and by esteeming his value as a person. But the truth shines through: If we value intellect above all, and it is there wherein he is deficient, then his total value must sink with it.

What, Then, for Happiness?

The value of intellect, the postponement of gratification, and emotional control are not challenged as such. However, value systems must serve all children, regardless of their ability, and must not provide success at the price of a shallow and empty life.

The joy of living and being in the here-and-now must not be downgraded. Children must be scheduled for fun as well as for work. "What have you done for fun today?" is as valid a question as "Have you done your homework?" This joy of living implies a measure of emotional freedom and spontaneity. When parents ask,

"Why did you do it?" the reply (when uttered politely), "Because I felt like it" may well be valid. Everything need not have a reason. The saying, "All work and no play makes Jack a dull boy," does have some validity. The joy of living, concurrent with intellectual endeavor, will sweeten the workload and insure success — both in academic and professional achievement, and in the joy of living. Additionally, others will not be seen solely as competitors, but as friends and facilitators of a good social, interpersonal life.

The mad pressures for academic success and subsequent status in life must be challenged. On philosophical grounds, it is quite clear that it does not by any means insure happiness. Furthermore, it unjustly discriminates against the less able. For practical reasons, the stress thus generated may bring about dire consequences. At best, it will reduce efficiency or cause children to give up entirely; and at worst, it may cause emotional distress and possible maladjustment.

Whatever happened to the carefree, idle hours that boys and girls spent just being and living? Were these really wasted hours — or were they essential experiences in establishing habits in the joy of living? Happiness is a habit that must be fostered early if it is to be sustained, and even when it becomes necessary to postpone gratification, there must be some gratifying elements right now.

Like not putting all our eggs into one basket, children must have many areas from which they can draw a measure of happiness and success. Achievement should only be one of them. A rich and varied social life is another, and so is the ability to laugh and enjoy life. Personality must be many-faceted if it is to be rich and colorful and whole; intellect and emotion and feeling must all be a part of it. Then, when stress does occur, these various facets combine to support the ego, distribute the pressure, and thus ease the pain. All that is good in intellectual control, planning, and investment for becoming an upright and contributing citizen should indeed be valued — but not at the expense of happiness.

Chapter Thirteen

Winners and Losers: Man and His Competitive Existence

uman living and experiencing always takes place in an interpersonal context. An individual can be social, asocial, or antisocial; he can be gregarious or totally withdrawn — yet positively or negatively, a relationship with others always exists. Self-evaluation, regarding either personal or materialistic matters, is based solely on comparison to others. A person is not rich or poor, happy or sad — for there are no discrete measures describing human feelings or states. Rather, he is richer, poorer, happier *than* his brother, friend, neighbor, or other member of the human race. Thus, man always competes with his fellow, and either wins or loses as he experiences life and as he measures himself concerning personal worth, standing, or position. Moreover, as such "wins" or "losses" aggregate, he then actually views himself as a winner who is destined to win always, or a loser who is condemned to lose, no matter what.

Such competitive existence can become a burden upon life for several reasons. First, it makes of our daily lives a hassle in that there is a constant race to win against insurmountable odds — for there is always someone who is smarter or wealthier, has attained more, or does better. Furthermore, competition puts a distance between man and his fellow and contributes heavily towards his loneliness. More important yet, a chronicity, a habitual view of oneself that cannot be altered, may set in, leading to pathological states — the self-styled "winner" who has unrealistic expectations, and his counterpart, the "loser," who gives up entirely. Other people may develop neurotic lifestyles in which practically every experience becomes a matter of winning or losing, exacting tremendous emotional costs.

Whether the competitive spirit in any one single individual or in the human race as a whole is instinctual or learned, is academic. We know that certain societies do foster competitiveness far more than do others. Competitiveness, then, *can* be learned, unlearned, or modified. Parenthetically, we will concede that competition and the need to win, gain, and "do better" make for progress and growth. Yet its constructive quality must be measured against its destructiveness and inherent danger to man, for it is this correlation between competition and progress that should explain to us the significantly higher suicide rates in industrialized countries as compared to backward nations. Suicide is the extreme expression of total loneliness and alienation from mankind — an all too common malady in modern society.

The task of the parent and of all those charged with the education of the child is twofold: (a) to be aware of how competitiveness is taught and learned, and (b) to have the child acquire an optimal amount of the competitive spirit, sufficient to achieve personal progress without alienating him from those with whom he has to share his social existence, and without exacting an excessive emotional toll on himself.

Learning the "Business" of Living

Unlike skills and factual knowledge which are primarily learned through formal instruction, habits and traits are acquired informally and subtly as the child observes and takes in the world around him. More particularly, he notes the ways and dispositions of the significant people in his immediate environment — parents, teachers, siblings, and peers — and makes them his own. The child introjects certain traits of some or all of these people and identifies with them. The sum total of all of these partial identifications then add up to his becoming a distinct personality.

Because this type of learning is incidental through observation and depends on the way others deal with him, it cannot be taught directly. Additionally, when one is taught to do something which is practiced in the opposite manner, then all that is learned is hypocrisy and rage. To teach the child, for example, to share, to be giving and cooperative, while she observes us and sees our grabby and competitive behavior, is to lie to her in a gross fashion that cannot fool her. Such traits the child does not learn *from* her teacher, but introjects those *of* her teacher. There is, of course, nothing new in the fact that "Do as I say, not as I do" just does not work. What may, however, surprise us is the myriad of ways we manifest behavior, totally unaware that it is highly competitive and so (correctly) labeled by the child.

One of the most destructive (competitive) patterns in family life is the home that is run like a business, in which children "learn" of love, esteem, or privileges on the basis of performance as measured by parental demands. These demands are set by comparing the child's behavior to that of her siblings, cousins, or peers. At first glance it all makes sense. The parent cannot know what to expect of his child except by measuring her performance against some other standard, her sister or cousin. Furthermore, experience has taught the parent that business thrives when threatened by competition, so why not apply such sound business practice to the home — "for the good of the child," of course. Applying business principles further, demands and schedules of performance are then constantly upped, to increase "productivity."

Child's Reaction to Parents' Demands

To be sure, expectations of others, and of our children in particular, are essential for learning and for performance. But these expectations must be realistic, with a "stretch": "Yes, you can do better." However, they must not be used to further undue competition, nor to set up the home as a business in which one is rewarded, i.e., loved, when she produces. That would be conditional love.

The child, having no say in setting up these rules, reacts to the set conditions by either dropping out of the race entirely and/or constantly fighting her parents, or by racing ever more to keep up with the pack. In either case the result is rage, chronic anger against her parents and against the world. Such rage may be externalized, with the child becoming a hostile, chronically angry and negative person, or these feelings are internalized, leading to psychosomatic ills or manifested as depression or other neuroses. In any case, the rage is set up — to remain with the individual for life. The parents are hated for making her earn the love and esteem to which she should be entitled anyway, and then raising the ante so that she cannot possibly win. Others in the world — siblings, peers, people — are hated for being the instruments, the standards against which she is measured, against whom she must race. At stake is security, the ingrained feeling that she is a chronic winner of love, esteem, and privileges — that is, unconditional love — from those she is dependent upon, and who are significant to her. The outcome is insecurity, the nagging fear of becoming a loser, to which the child reacts by becoming ever more competitive, at tremendous emotional cost, or by completely giving up and dropping out, or by constantly making battle.

Practically, then, it is essential to be aware of the pitfalls of running a home like a business in terms of earnings, measurements, comparisons, and ever-increasing demands. This calls for strength in resisting "common sense" business approaches, no matter how tempting they appear to be, and not being trapped by the apparent short-term results they seem to produce in terms of heightened motivation. It also calls for ingenuity in lessening the impact of competitiveness that spontaneously comes about as siblings and peers become aware of each other's achievements or gains and then, to raise self-esteem, join the competitive race all by themselves. Children note readily how achievement is valued (or overvalued), then measure themselves and set up the win-or-lose race that can easily become pathological. In any family situation there is, of course, always the issue of winning and losing, as the child competes for standing in the family. This is the universal problem of sibling rivalry. Competitiveness, friction, and rivalry with siblings is inevitable, but it becomes aggravated when the total environment is highly achievement oriented and competitive, and is lessened when the social-cooperative mode of life predominates.

The issue of winning and losing is, moreover, at stake whenever parents and children engage in their many battles of wills during normal, everyday, parent-child interaction. Some of the child's demands must be denied, while certain behaviors must be exacted of him. Consequently, because (compared to his parent) the child is small and weak, he would naturally view himself as a "loser" — and then give up trying, or constantly make battle. The parent, on the other hand, cannot permit his child to always have his way, nor should he allow him to become a "loser." Parents must develop the art of *not* arguing things out to the point of winning or losing, but rather, of diluting issues or demands, and minimizing them so that there are neither losers nor winners.

Moreover, the child must "win" occasionally, and thereby learn two vital lessons: (a) that he *does* make an impact upon his environment; he is heard, and his needs and wishes are heeded, and (b) that it is all right to lose — as he in this instance sees his parent "losing" graciously, and surviving. More important yet, one must always be aware that winning against those we love is always a loss to the winner as well — for whatever one wins issue-wise, he loses in the all-important interpersonal relationship.

Sins of the Fathers

There are literally hundreds of situations in which we ourselves express our own competitive inclination — which our children then learn and copy. To be sure, the exaggerated need of the adult to compete and win is by itself likely the result of some residual complex around this issue, and thus not easily modifiable. Yet when we are aware of its effect upon our children, there should be greater motivation for change — lest our sins (i.e., "hangups") are visited upon our children, who then will continue to transmit these (neurotic) habits to their children, and so on.

People to whom achievement, gains, or losses are all-important and whose experiences are thus constantly measured in these terms express this exaggerated need to win. Symptom-wise it expresses itself in "wheeling and dealing," in excessive bargain hunting, or in getting "something for nothing." Similarly, people who *must* have the nicest home, the biggest car, or the smartest child, state clearly and loudly their chronic need to gain stature or self-esteem and be better than their neighbor or friend.

In such a home, the child is practically from the moment of birth poured into the mold of competitive existence, as expressed by parental behavior. These parents are concerned with quantifying details: How much did the baby weigh at birth? How much does he gain each week? These numbers only have meaning when compared to those of the child next door. Continuing, then: At what age is the child toilet trained? How soon does he walk or talk? How early does he gain admission into school? Did he get the best grade in his class, and if not, why did his friend manage to do better? If he did manage to get a 98 on the test, what happened to the other two points? Such a list is, of course, endless. What these behaviors have in common is the distinct expression of the need to win, to be better than the next one.

Even in social-recreational situations, the cocktail chatter is all too frequently spiced with a competitive spirit. A joke is made, and a repartee of witticisms follows in a "Can you top this?" fashion. A "philosophy" is expounded, and has to be argued. Similarly, we worry about how well we are dressed, how well we look, how "cool" we are, or how prosperous we look. Instead of letting go and being at ease, we wind up being under stress and on the alert to look good, to "win" and be best. Our children take all this in through observation, noting a word, a look, or a facial expression that clearly states the importance of the competitive mode of life.

How to Win Without Losing in the Process

Human experience always implies competitiveness with one's fellow. In moderation it makes for progress — but it also does have undesirable side effects. It always creates some stress and separates us from others. In excess, moreover, it becomes destructive and leads to psychopathology. The child learns the competitive spirit in numerous ways: (a) from the manner his own home is managed, as a "business" or as an all-accepting social-emotional haven; (b) by how competitive or socially cooperative his parents and other significant persons are; (c) by the extent that achievement is valued or overvalued; and (d) by how well parents manage to exact certain behaviors of the child and deny some of his demands in everyday life, without allowing them to become major battles in which there are losers and winners. Added to this is the all-pervasive, competitive climate that exists in a modern technological society, in the more immediate socio-economic group, and in the school systems. Complicating and confounding all this are sibling rivalries and excessive needs for security and standing in one's family.

Coping with all of this is no small task, and parents all too frequently throw up their hands in despair. How can one family change the system? Can one truly change society, the school system, and the competitive climate that leaks into our homes whether we like it or not? Parents forget, however, that it is they who create the basic miniature society our children first encounter. They are the ones who support schools and can (and must) have a say in their philosophical foundations. Finally, it is they, together with their neighbors, who make up the very society which creates the climate in which our children are raised — be it achievement-competitive, or socially-cooperative.

To be a "winner" is every child's right. The child can be taught how to win and how to lose if, and only if, winning and losing is not the major theme in our lives. To do this we must look carefully at our selves, and be willing to change ourselves, our methods of child rearing, our schools and other social institutions, and the very society of which we are part.

Individuals who learn and practice to lose (to a spouse, to a child, to a fellow businessman) — who learn that one does not need to be the very best, that one does not need to have the most — teach themselves that their positive self-esteem is solid and unconditional. On the other hand, individuals who must always be right, who must have it, and have it all, who must know the most and be the very best, teach themselves that their position is always precarious and one must always be at war with one's fellows.

Chapter Fourteen

The Overinvolved Parent: Anxiety and How It Is Learned

nderlying every neurosis or emotional disturbance there is anxiety — a gnawing sensation of
fear, of panic, or expectation of impending doom.
Childhood and adolescence are periods of stress and
anxiety, as the child gives up total dependency for independence, exchanging the "safety" of being nurtured by others for
self-determination and self-sufficiency. Residuals of these anxieties
remain with us through life. In moderation, they have distinct value
in that one learns to forestall danger and protect oneself from various situations that may endanger one, physically or psychologically.
Thus, for example, some anxiety in anticipation of a scholastic test
will energize the individual to study and prepare. Too much anxiety,
however, will make for panic, leading to a variety of reactions that
are in sum total regressive and/or counterproductive. Excessive anxiety may becloud thinking and cause confusion, thus impeding

optimal intellectual functioning. On the other hand, it may mobilize the individual, making him work hard and enhance functioning, but create excessive stress that will cost him dearly in total happiness and living. Finally, some individuals may attempt to escape the intolerable situation, invoking neurotic defenses that will lead to a chronic state of anxiety that is excessive and unrealistic. Such defenses will then be utilized whenever anxiety is encountered and thus make for the development of a neurotic personality.

Anxiety comes about in a myriad of ways that would require volumes to describe, and about which all is not really known at this time. Nor is it likely that the origin of human anxiety in general, or that of an individual in particular, will ever lend itself to be clearly traced. Yet there are some factors known to be responsible for this crippling condition that robs us of joy in everyday life. Children who are loved conditionally — if they behave or do as the parents demand — develop deep insecurities and anxiety. Competitive homes or overly striving ones, or those in which sibling relationships lend themselves to excessive rivalry, are similarly anxiety producing. Then there are homes where "the child comes first," where life revolves around the young, where every need is promptly met — and in these homes are frequently produced the most anxious children and neurotic characters of all.

Caring for one's child demands an involved parent who is physically present and free enough from personal conflict to be emotionally close. The two, however (physical presence and emotional proximity), do not always go hand in hand. Indeed, there are homes where the parent is verily omnipresent, involving himself totally with the child's physical needs — his eating, sleeping, learning, and so forth — yet remaining emotionally distant and psychologically nonsupportive. The damage that is generated in an overinvolved home stems from several sources.

The overinvolved parent finds meaning in life solely in the context of rearing his child. His life lacks purpose and he fails to find joy in anything but the child. He thus does not present a model for a satisfying existence the child could copy.

Overinvolved parents cannot be involved mates, so the marriage inevitably suffers, generating strife and constructing intolerable triangles where the child is pulled and pushed as his parents battle. The child then becomes a rival and a handy tool of parental warfare, seduced by one and rejected by the other.

Overinvolvement and Anxiety

The overinvolved home is an anxious home, because child rearing is all-consuming. The atmosphere bristles with a sense of urgency "to do for the child," to be involved with his every activity, thought, and feeling. The child breathes and introjects this anxiety, this sense of urgency and intensity. Moreover, the overinvolved parent inevitably clashes with the child as he makes neurotic demands of him to comply, to be molded into the "perfect being." The child is presented with intolerable choices and double-binding ambivalence: to comply because the ever-giving, sacrificial parent says so — and remain dependent, or resist in order to become independent — but risk losing parental love. In addition, child rearing becomes a chore — with ever more attention given to the child's structural (physical) needs, leaving little time for the vital emotional interaction that says, "All is well." Most important are the unconscious signals that emanate from the overinvolved parent, that create in the child feelings of incompetence and anxiety.

An important feature of general anxiety is dread, a kind of an ever-expectant feeling of "When is the other shoe going to drop? What do I have to attend to now? What needs to be done to avert hurt or pain, physical or psychological?" Where does this come from? Imagine the child in his room — reading, studying, playing, talking on the phone, or just relaxing. Now the front door opens; Mommy is home. The child has heard the door open; now he hears Mommy coming up the stairs. Now what? Does he continue doing whatever he is doing, and at most, Mommy will say, "Hi!"? Or does he go on alert and become expectant and hyper-alert? Will Mommy demand: "Why not study or go outdoors and play, or open the window or the light, or have some milk and cake, or ...?"

Yes! You Can Do It!

The infant attempting to feed himself, clumsily grasps the too large spoon, triumphantly calls out "M'self!" and inevitably misses the target — his mouth. There is more cereal on his cheeks, on the table, and on the floor than in his mouth, but there is triumph in his smile and victory in his shout — he has mastered. For this is his first successful attempt to master that which is imbedded in the matrix of the human organism: to do for oneself, to be competent and self-sufficient, to cope, and to master one's environment.

The involved and talented parent looks on, approving of this "heroic" feat, paying no heed to the mess, to the unconsumed nourishment, and reinforces this behavior. She says to the child, unconsciously but clearly: "Yes, you can do it!" This scene is repeated thousands of times, as the parent permits the child to do what he can for himself in various settings. And the message is reinforced and imprinted: "You are competent, you can cope."

The overinvolved parent, on the other hand, must save every precious morsel to nourish our tot. "No, you cannot feed yourself. I will do it for you. I will attend to your needs, and I will feed, clothe, teach, and nurture you." Repeated again and again, the signal is clear: "You are incompetent. You are dependent on me. You cannot cope." Additionally, the parent who has little joy in life now may derive "meaning" by being needed to raise and nurture the child.

Our tot matures and must venture forth into the "cold and dangerous world." The parent must carefully weigh and measure, and trade physical safety for adventure and growth. The choice is indeed a difficult one. Parental protective instinct is on the side of safety: "Let us be sure. Why take unnecessary risks?"

The optimally involved parent uses prudence, balancing the physical risks against the emotional stunting that overconcern will surely cause. She prods and reassures the child to risk the unknown, to enlarge his life space and to grow without fear. This parent risks, and prays and hopes. And she is rewarded by building into the child the ability to face the challenges of life without undue anxiety and with a feeling of power — that he can cope.

The overinvolved parent has no easy task. To begin with, her child is already timid, fearful, anxious, and afraid to go forth into the world, because he has never attempted to do so. The parent herself is overinvolved because of her own fears, apprehensions, and anxiety. And now she must let go — but how? There is misgiving and trepidation as she halfheartedly allows the child to go out, never really cutting the cord, never signaling to the child that he is on his own, that he can do it. At best there are admonitions to be careful, to watch out, and to report in. The parent says to the child, the adolescent, and yes, even the adult offspring, as he embarks: "Call me when you get there." What do these innocuous words say? They have but one meaning: "The world is dangerous. I am not assured that you can make it. I am afraid, and I do not trust you and your environment." Repeated thousands of times in various situations, using a multitude of phrases and facial expressions of trepidation, the message is clear: "The world is to be feared. To venture forth is dangerous. Anxiety is a way of life."

The Good Parent Is an Obsolete Parent

For the child to grow into a man (or woman) — confident, self-sufficient, able to face the challenges of life without undue anxiety and with the feeling that he or she can cope — the task of the parent is to slowly but surely cease being a parent. To do that is to give up control, to let go and signal the child: "You can do it on your own. You can conquer the world and need not fear." To love the child, to be concerned with his welfare at all times, is crucial — but not at the expense of emotional growth essential for life.

This does not come about by philosophical statements or words of encouragement. Self-sufficiency and freedom from anxiety grows in caring, but not overinvolved, homes. It is reinforced and imprinted onto the child's mind by hundreds of thousands of signals and messages, consciously and unconsciously, verbally and nonverbally. And it becomes imbedded into his psyche by parental attitudes, traits, and behaviors that say: "You can do it on your own. Yet you can always count on me."

Chapter Fifteen

Balancing Security and Satisfaction

ow do parents decide how their children are to be raised? How do parents select codes for their children's behavior and values with which to imbue them? Contrary to popular belief, books and articles by "experts" have only a minor effect in shaping parental behavior relative to their young. The bulk of child-rearing practices comes from the parents' own childhood, the parents' own personality patterns, and, most important, from the parents' own assignment of the relative import of life's experiences, which are then equally operational in relating to the child. The apportionment of significance to the various phases of the child's day-to-day activities develops traits, attitudes, and beliefs which then become his distinct personality.

Security and Satisfaction

Broadly speaking, man's existence in life can be divided between operations that insure him security, and experiences that give him satisfaction. To the former belong such basic needs as food, shelter, and physical health — and derivatives such as love, money, education, social acceptance and other cultural demands that secure and facilitate the procurement of our basic needs. "Satisfactions" are not that easily defined since they vary among individuals, and are easily confused with, and confounded by, our basic needs. Thus, for example, sitting by a glowing fireplace is pleasant, and having a nice home with a full larder is certainly gratifying. Yet such satisfactions are obviously related to our needs for food and shelter. More subtle are satisfactions that are related to love and social acceptance. Thus, one's enjoyment of his or her clean, well-run, and well-stocked home is always linked to subtle residuals of approval — external (from society), or internal (from one's own conscience) — that say: "You are a good girl (or boy)." Thus, a clear-cut distinction between security and satisfaction is not always possible, nor does it really matter if they overlap. If things satisfy and give us, additionally, a sense of security, that is fine.

Nonetheless, there are clearly pure satisfactions that have little to do with security, needs, or their derivatives. These are not a "waste," but deserve a place in our lives. Such satisfactions please our senses externally or internally, or are mentally satisfying in other ways. Foremost among them are sensations that please our palate (good food), our ears (good music), our eyes (art, nature), our muscles (play and sports), and other sensory apparatus. Then there are psychological satisfactions such as peace and homeostasis on the one hand, and, conversely, pleasure in being active, producing, doing, affecting our environment, and being stimulated by it. There is, furthermore, excitement, such as riding a roller coaster; mastery, such as solving a puzzle or climbing a mountain peak; and social interaction, such as relating with another human, a stranger, which may do nothing for our security nor hold promise for anything to be. Yet man is entitled to pure joy, which, in the religious individual, may add to his appreciation of G-d's gifts to man. It is said of *HaRav* Shamshon Raphael Hirsch, *zt"l*, that when asked about his vacations in Switzerland being somehow self-indulgent, he would reply that in the future world the *Ribbono Shel Olam* will surely ask him, "Shamshon, did you see my beautiful Switzerland?" Thus, enjoying G-d's bounties, within limits, may be a positive factor in our appreciation of the *Ribbono Shel Olam*, as well as being beneficial to our physical and mental health.

Finally, in a class by itself, there are the all-important satisfactions on a spiritual-civic level, having to do with "meaning of life" along the dimensions of ethical-moral-religious experiences. These may be highly personal or part of a social-religious system; truly and honestly experienced or only superficially subscribed to. For the common man such satisfactions may be hard to come by and are usually a lifetime undertaking. Yet striving to attain the unattainable, the meaning in life, is in itself psychologically satisfying.

Security, Satisfaction, and their Corollaries

Because security operations are vital to our very existence, experiences that threaten man in attaining them are always anxiety-provoking. For that matter, every act or function directed toward securing these needs is accompanied by tension, at least to some degree, since the task is vital and success by no means assured. Be it in the case of the infant crying for his bottle or the adult going forth to earn his livelihood, tension and anxiety exist. In optimal amounts, such tensions are useful in that they energize the individual to cry out, to do, to secure his needs, and to survive — and are thus satisfying. Thus, again, "securing" our securities is also satisfying. However, these securities should not be the sum total of our existence. The man who says, "I am a workaholic and I enjoy it," may indeed feel "happy," but he obviously has not tasted some of the more simple joys of life. Now one may ask, why look for "pure" joys and satisfactions when one can produce and satisfy security and satisfaction simultaneously? To answer this one should consider that since security needs always are accompanied by anxiety — because of their importance — the resultant satisfaction is also tinged with anxiety. Not so the experiences which are purely joyous and satisfying. Their pursuit is ordinarily free of anxiety, since the business of satisfaction is neither vital to man's existence, nor, at least in its pure form, is its absence felt as a loss. To the contrary, the pursuit of satisfactions is pleasurable in and by itself. Thus we speak of pursuit of happiness, since the search for pleasure is pleasure. Additionally, pure joy also gives man a much needed rest from anxiety — something that is sorely needed for mental health. Coupled with satisfactions of a spiritual-civic nature, it gives man the serenity he longs for and "meaning" that makes life worthwhile.

Thus we arrive at the following principle: Preoccupation with security operations and basic needs, while necessary, is fraught with anxiety — while the pursuit of "satisfactions" is experienced as pleasure. Experiencing the former without undue anxiety is, of course, also satisfying, yet should not be the sum total of life. Pure joy, relaxation, and recreation should also be part of our menu. Similarly, our spiritual lives also give us the satisfaction of serenity, security, and hope.

Putting all of this another way, one can say that man has four basic needs: (1) to produce, in order to be physically and financially secure; (2) to have a social-emotional life, in order to enjoy life and have the security of being connected to a group; (3) to have a relaxational-recreational life, in order to enjoy life and enjoy freedom from anxiety; and (4) to have a spiritual life, to give meaning to our existence and a connection with, and protection by, the *Ribbono Shel Olam*. This all comprises a kind of "*Shulchan Aruch*" (a set table, also the well-known Code of Jewish Law) with four legs.

Consider now the learner of Torah who *produces*: He learns and masters; he does so in a social-emotional setting, with the *chavrusa* (his partner in learning). This learning is, of course, spiritual, and can be recreational-relaxational, because of the joy all this generates. Thus one notices in certain *teshuvos* (responsa to halachic questions) a brief practical answer of right or wrong, permissible or not, and then a continuation of *pilpul* (Talmudic discourse) for "mental stimulation," Torah entertainment, recreation, and relaxation. "*Loolei Torascha shaashu'ai, oz avadeti ...* — Were it not for the joy of Torah, I would have been lost."[1]

---

1. *Tehillim* 119:92.

The Hierarchy of Needs

Because basic needs are essential for survival, they readily rise to the very top of the hierarchy of needs and preoccupations that concern man, child, and those charged with the care of our young. As the infant arrives home from the hospital, the mother is first and foremost concerned with the child's need to eat and to eliminate, with shelter and his general state of health. Only after all of this has been secured can the parent afford to turn to the "luxury" of seeking the less vital satisfactions. When all is well in terms of security, one can play, stimulate the infant, and socially interact with him.

The instinct for self-preservation creates the hierarchy of needs, and assigns top billing to food, shelter, and security. For example, it is reasonable to expect that any person arriving at a new place — whether a station in life, a camping ground, a new home, or anything else — would attend first to security needs before proceeding further. When these needs are met, and then maintained, there would be ample time for satisfactions and other useful experiences in life.

For the overinvolved parent, however, this is not to be. Meeting the child's security needs becomes an all-consuming and total task in life, leaving little room, if any, for satisfaction, pleasure, and emotional well-being. This legacy that the overinvolved parent bestows upon the child sets the stage for personality development, making the child similarly overinvolved with safety and security, avoiding pleasures and satisfactions which are seen as a waste, superfluous, and hazardous. The child grows up, becomes a parent (similarly overinvolved) and the sad tale continues ad infinitum. Life then is marked with anxiety and tension, with little freedom to experience joy and satisfaction. As my patients point out: "How much joy did I miss because of worry!"

The Overinvolved Parent and Neurotic Anxiety

The following analogy may help illustrate the nature of neurotic anxiety:

A city-state concerns itself with the needs of its citizens in a myriad of ways. These functions may be roughly divided between those that relate to general welfare during peacetime and those which are of prime import during wartime. Under normal circumstances, the services geared for peacetime produce consumer goods, provide for cultural needs, and offer entertainment. Only a minor part of the state's budget and business concerns itself with security. To be sure, there is an army and weaponry, but these are only of garrison strength, with its full complement in the reserves.

One day there is news of an approaching enemy. Peacetime activities are reduced to a minimum or shut down, the reserves are called up and the barricades are manned. The population waits with anxiety for the battle to begin — but the enemy does not arrive. Time passes and still the populace waits, for the anticipated war generates constant anxiety that does not permit the people to relax their alert. Their ears are strained to the point that even the sound of leaves rustling in the wind strikes terror in their hearts. Fear and terror are the fuels that feed the tension and maintain the anxiety. On constant guard, the people continue to wait.

That generation passes on, and the children take over. They have observed, they have felt, they have learned all about anxiety, tension, being on guard, anticipating the worst. There is no room for joy, for lightheartedness, for relaxation. There is only danger. The children carry on, until their children grow up and continue this sorry state of affairs, for the town has become fixated on fear and anxiety.

Emotionally and physiologically there are also wartime and peacetime activities with man. Foremost among them are anxiety and tension (wartime); and relaxation and satisfaction (peacetime). Physiologically, there is accelerated heart rate and blood pressure (wartime), and food consumption, digestion, and elimination (peacetime). To be sure, the emotional tension and elevated blood pressure have their usefulness during temporary periods of wartime. They provide the extra power needed emotionally and physically during these short periods, and generally return to normal when the emergency is over. When, however, the emergency is chronic and all is geared for wartime, with ever-heightening anticipation-anxiety that cannot be discharged, there is havoc within our emotional systems and their physiological counterparts. The nervous stomach, constant restlessness, and chronic anxiety of unknown origin are examples of this state of affairs.

Excessive concern with the child's safety fixates life around danger, fear, and anxiety. Controls are tightly clamped upon the child's activities. (No — don't go out! Don't sit around doing nothing! Don't seek unnecessary adventures [and joy]!) Did he eat enough, sleep enough, learn sufficiently, and wash behind his ears? Corollary to all this there is a sense of immediacy, of urgency. (Do it now, later on may be too late! Do it well! Be perfect! Protect yourself and you'll live "forever!") Happiness is traded for security. And perhaps the individual is somewhat physically healthier, lives a little longer, and produces a little more — if this can be called "living" at all.

Normal inclinations within the child to go out and enjoy life are thwarted, controls are arbitrary (at least to the child) and excessive. Why can she not laugh and play, why is she constantly being told, manipulated, and controlled, why does she breathe anxiety and tension? As a consequence, there are parent-child issues, there are battles, and there is rage. The child cannot hate the parent who is, after all, "doing all this for her," yet she cannot survive the smothering. As one young lady put it succinctly: "My mother loves: my teeth — to brush; my brain — to study; my body — to feed it and keep it safe; my hair — to wash it; but not *me* — for all of this is driving me insane!" Such a child either rebels and becomes an angry adult, totally complies and becomes timid and fearful, or internalizes all this and chokes on her rage as she develops an obsessional neurosis. All the while, anxiety is plentiful and satisfactions are kept to a minimum.

The overinvolved parent does what he does because of his own anxiety, likely learned from his parents, and now passed on to the child. Anxiety is a harsh master, constantly devising new security measures, which cause further anxiety as concern with security grows. The cycle must be broken. Helpful would be for parents to reduce their own anxieties. This may be a tall order, at times necessitating professional guidance. Short of that, it may be helpful to bear in mind the poor tradeoff that comes about when security needs are all-consuming. The parent who masters his anxiety as the child goes out, trading some security for satisfaction, learns how to deal with anxiety for himself and teaches the child how to enjoy life to the fullest.

Anxiety in appropriate measures is useful and is here to stay, yet it is clear that all of our defensive measures cannot prevent some of the accidents and sufferings that are part of life. Prudence modified with courage should guide us in striking a balance between total constriction and absolute recklessness.

Chapter Sixteen

Helping Your Child to Cope With Frustration and Anxiety

Developing an Immune System for Emotional Stress

arents who virtually give their child everything must also provide him with the wherewithal to tolerate frustration and manage emotional stress. We attend to the child's bodily needs, practice sound nutrition and health habits and know what to do for his minor physical ills. Similarly, by relating to the child in a particular manner, we fashion his early and most crucial psychological environment, thereby creating attitudes and traits that become his personality. Additionally, we maintain an emotional climate in our homes that is based upon our own feelings, attitudes, and behavior. Together, the way we relate to the child and shape his personality, the way we handle our own problems, and the general emotional climate in the home teach the child that minor conflicts and frustrations are readily overcome. A reservoir of ego strength is built up to help the child survive even major emotional traumas.

In addition, parents must develop the ability to administer "first aid" for mental stresses that will surely arise from time to time. The administration of psychological first aid will not only serve to relieve the child at that time; it will also teach the child mechanisms for coping with conflicts and frustrations which he can then use himself.

No individual escapes childhood without having suffered some frustrations and anxieties. The infant faces "problems" of getting the bottle and other bodily comforts. On a higher plane there are issues of being accepted and loved, and the vital matters of security, dependence, and independence to deal with. Later on there are battles of wills with parents, teachers, and the child's own conscience. There are rivalries with siblings and peers, and problems concerning aggression and competitiveness. Sexual behavior, both in its narrow sense and in its broader connotation of loving and relating, is a lifelong issue that has its germ in infancy, and so are hosts of other conflicts, issues, and problems that are part and parcel of the business of living.

The fact that these problems confront the "weak and innocent" child while still in his infancy is not unfortunate but a blessing, for only throughout the relatively long period of infancy and childhood can our child depend on his parents and learn how to manage his problems. Only then can he afford to make mistakes and be protected by his elders, and only during childhood do problems come along one at a time and in relatively minor fashion. Thus the child who is totally protected from all stress grows up to be truly handicapped as the frustrations and problems of living are later encountered. This is analogous to the individual who has not built up physical immunity to certain germs and then succumbs to even minor infections that are benign to others.

The parents' task, then, is not to shield the child from problems, but to create an atmosphere wherein emotional stresses are successfully dealt with, and to show how this is done. Needless to say, this atmosphere, or emotional climate, together with the development of coping mechanisms, will then become part and parcel of the child's personality and armor to withstand the stresses of life.

Problems accompany man throughout his life. Numerically they are beyond count, and because they are so highly individualized, it is simply impossible to teach our young how to manage each and every situation. Even were one to create a computer program which, when provided with data on all conceivable problems, would provide all possible solutions, the result would be disastrous. For then we would have individuals behaving reflexively, devoid of human emotion, feeling, and individuation. These are the robots so well described in science-fiction stories that conceive the perfect man as computerized, thought-controlled, and having all the answers laid out for him.

Yet time and again one encounters parents whose notion of bringing up their child is that they are to watch all he does, correct all his mistakes, protect him from all anxieties. One imagines these parents as sitting in front of a closed-circuit television camera which enables them to see all that their child thinks or does, with transmitters that send out electronic impulses to maneuver and correct the child's thoughts and actions. In its extreme, such an exacting and demanding attitude produces a particular type of neurosis, the obsessive personality. At best, it fails to do its intended job. Parents simply cannot be with their child at all times nor can they foresee the variety of problems that will confront him on a particular day. Parents do not know all the answers because some problems are just insoluble — they must be suffered. Problems also have nuances that demand one reaction at one time, and a very different one on another occasion. And most important, the child must learn to do for himself at some time in his life; independent thought and action are essential for coping as a human.

What parents can do, then, is not to rush in and help with each and every issue that creates emotional stress, but to imbue the child with a broader-based set of attitudes that are to be the child's armament in dealing with frustrations and anxieties. These traits and attitudes the child will acquire by breathing an atmosphere of mental health, by observing how his parents themselves handle emotional stress, and most important, how they react to the child's anxieties and frustrations.

The Emotional Climate in the Home

Phrases such as "a calm atmosphere" or "air charged with tension" are not merely figures of speech. These conditions exist. The trained observer or intuitive individual can walk in on a situation and actually feel the atmosphere. Nothing need be happening at that particular moment, nor are there any issues waiting to be resolved, but the air is already permeated with calmness or with tension. One may call this awareness extrasensory perception or empathy, or it may be the result of analyzing the sum total of minute but meaningful variables — facial expressions, body language, and all the other expressive modes available to man — that together tell us the climate. Yet at times there is a psychological climate, calm or tense, and this is what the child breathes.

The feeling in the air, be it one of calm or of tension, connotes also a "set" or disposition. Will the next moment bring calm or anxiety? It tells us now how the next question or problem will be dealt with. Thus the child learns to react to issues with calmness or with anxiety, or, worse yet, to be in a state of ever expecting calamity.

The emotional climate is created, of course, by parents and significant others who themselves are prisoners of their own traits and are beset by numerous pressures from within their being and from the environment. Their impatience and chronic anxiety and tension may thus be quite involuntary, yet this matter is vital enough to have parents make a concerted effort to discover which habitual behaviors create anxiety and which make for calm. These may be quite personal and specific, or more general patterns that are involved with the calm-tense dimension. Some examples follow.

People interacting with one another cannot help but get into each other's way. Parents have the right and obligation to teach their young, yet some parents are gifted in doing all this without creating confrontations. Conversely, the making of issues, an exacting and demanding attitude, and being critical call for confrontations and charge the air with tension. Children's needs and wishes can be respected, even when good sense dictates that they not be granted at that time. Children must be taught to postpone gratification, to modify their needs or to exchange them for others. They need hardly ever be told no. One can say, "Yes — but later," "Yes — but not quite what you wanted." Automatic nos create anger against the parent, followed by guilt and anxiety.

When problems are encountered which cannot be resolved with calm and reason, the parent's reaction will be carefully watched by the child. The ability to "let things be," and do nothing, is a worthy object lesson.

Parents who allow their child to "be herself," to make her own decisions without involving themselves, yet are ready to be involved when the child asks to be helped, give her security and support without robbing her of her independent being. Overinvolvement with children, even with the best intentions, cannot help but generate friction. People simply cannot think alike, and children can never be exactly as parents want them to be.

Parents who relate to their child in ways other than telling what to do or not to do, create a bond, a therapeutic partnership that gives the child the strength of an alliance, and security without the friction and anger that must come about when one is told what to do or not to do. Parent-child relations that exist solely in the "do-don't do" dimension make for strife without the balm of warmth and good feeling inherent in "just relating." One can relate with a child through play, sharing a thought, asking the child's opinion, an occasional "date" — your child and you sharing a pizza — and so forth.

One should weigh the gain of having the child do what is right, against the deterioration of the emotional climate that such an effort will bring about. For example, is hounding the child to brush her teeth or wash her neck worth the anger and hostility, and subsequent guilt and anxiety, this will generate?

Doing things with a light hand, accepting minor adversity and struggle with optimism, make for calm. Traveling the road of life as an adventure rather than an obstacle course to be overcome or plowed through makes for an ability to traverse life with calm and handle most emotional stresses.

The child must be taught by example how to express feelings and emotions, be they anger or love. Repressing feelings does not dissolve them. They continue to exist, and will surely surface in a more intensified fashion. These may be displaced anger, neurotic symptoms, or psychosomatic equivalents. Certain social groups, unfortunately, teach to suppress emotions: It is not nice to be overtly angry (misconstrued as being aggressive) or loving (interpreted as being "sexy"). Yet these emotions are the stuff life is made of. Thus one must learn to express them in a socially acceptable fashion, such as verbal expression of being displeased or feeling love. Parents can show how this is done and encourage the child to do likewise. "It is okay to tell Mommy that you are angry at her [and Mommy is not shaken by this, nor will she give in because of your anger]."

These are but few examples of the variables that color the emotional climate in the home. The "healthy" atmosphere is not easily come by nor need one strive for the optimal. Yet the healthy emotional climate is vital for emotional well-being and will help the child tolerate frustration and stress.

First Aid for Emotional Stress

Anxiety, like any strong emotion, colors the facts and interferes with rational thought. One cannot reason when one is disturbed. Thus the child who is flooded with anxiety needs symptomatic relief — an infusion of calm *before* the problem or the issue is discussed and before solutions are considered. Unfortunately, because parents are upset when their child suffers, the child's anxiety usually generates an anxiety reaction in the parent. Instead of relief, then, there comes about a reverberating system of anxiety in the child creating anxiety in the parent, which then aggravates the original emotional stress.

Realizing the importance of calm, parents should not attempt to probe or rush in with "solutions." By doing nothing and remaining calm, we transmit our tranquility to the child and give her relief. Speaking softly, we reassure her, "It will be okay, no matter what the problem is."

Because she is suffering, the child has a need to talk and communicate. Telling us her troubles has a cathartic effect in that it drains off anxiety, anger, and other emotions that are upsetting. To do this she needs a patient ear. We can slow down the torrent of emotional speech and tell her, "Yes we are listening. Slowly, take your time." And then, "Okay, tell me again. Explain further."

The art of listening is not easily come by. It calls for genuine concern and animated, live listening, without our talking or interfering with the child's thoughts. We interject a "hm" to show that we are truly there, listening, feeling, and having genuine empathy.

After the initial anxiety has been drained off, we join forces and show understanding for her agitation. Phrases such as, "I can imagine how angry (or frustrated or insulted) you must feel," give the child the notion that here is an ally, a co-sufferer who takes some of the burden off her shoulders.

We slowly attempt to minimize the issue, expressing the idea that it is perhaps not *that* important, or that one can *let it be.* We are extremely careful at this point not to give her a lesson ("You should have done thus.") Nor do we tell her how she should be feeling. For such a lesson would only frustrate the child more — why did she act so foolishly? If necessary, we file the information and correct her much later when the current upset is practically forgotten.

All of this, of course, may make parents feel threatened by the demands of having to be always calm, patient, giving, and kind. It should be remembered, however, that the "perfect" parent is as nonhuman as the "perfect" child. Still, it is helpful for a parent to sharpen his or her awareness of what needs to be done and what variables operate in order to help the child cope with emotional stress. In the process, of course, the maintenance of a calm home and proper emotional climate is a blessing to all.

Modifying Habits

Clearly, creating an atmosphere of calm, peace, and general optimism for our children and for ourselves is easier said than done. So, how does one go about it? Except for individuals who suffer from mental illness which calls for professional intervention, parents can do quite a bit for themselves and consequently for their children who "breathe that air," that is, they absorb and learn to feel and act in congruence with that emotional climate.

To begin with, for people to change, to modify their behavior, to act in an emotionally healthy fashion, one has to "pay," that is, to suffer the pain of doing that which one is not programmed to do or wishes to do. Conversely, to stop doing that which is emotionally or physically unhealthy, one also has to "pay." In a simplistic fashion, one who wishes to stop smoking or overeating must be ready to suffer the pain of depriving oneself of the "fix" the cigarette or the cake is offering. The good news is that when an individual truly wants to give up that which is unhealthy, and is ready to pay for it with the frustration this engenders, something else is also happening. That is, he is training himself to give up the addiction. He also learns to find healthy ways to give him that which he needs — pleasure, relief from anxiety or from boredom, getting his way, or getting things done.

Consider, for example, the mother who habitually screams, or the father who similarly hits, ostensibly to get the child to listen, but also — perhaps more so — to relieve her or his personal frustration or anger. This parent can learn to get things done with softness and with the assist of the natural need within the child to please the parents and win their approval. This gives the child the opportunity to do as the parent wishes, but without losing his or her individuality. "I do for my parent because I love her, and it pleases me to please her." Similarly, individuals who are impatient or intolerant, who, for example, cannot possibly drive within the prescribed speed limit, can learn, albeit with difficulty, not just to give up the temporary gain of getting things done instantaneously, but to really gain the ability to "sit," to wait, to enjoy the leisure of the drive and not just the moment of getting there earlier or out-racing the fellow in the next lane.

The major problem is that the pathologic way seems to pay off immediately, while the healthy way brings returns only in the long term. Thus, there is the uneven struggle between indulging (in the cigarette or cake, and savoring immediate gratification) and abstaining, or between yelling or hitting (which seem to bring instantaneous results), and speaking calmly and restraining one's hand (which is trained to hit). In both cases, choosing the second alternative leads to a happier, healthier, and more relational life — in the future.

Similarly so, when one fully understands its importance, one can learn to deal with excessive anxiety or overbearing seriousness bordering on mild depression. Anxiety per se can be seen as G-d's gift to man in order to prevent harm in the future or to make him feel more secure. In this day and age, one could say that locking one's door is prudent in order to avoid inviting a burglar. One could even make a case for two locks, and even for jiggling the handle to be sure it is locked. However, using more than two locks, or driving a few miles and then beginning to worry whether the doors were really locked, is catering to one's unrealistic anxiety. Saying, "It is better to turn back to check the doors, the gas, and the lights, rather than going on to my vacation destination and continuously worrying," is not really true. In the short run it may be, but one is training oneself to live a life of checking, of worrying, and of overconcern with security, with very little time for joy.

Similarly, the overly serious, the individual "burdened" chronically with one's duties and problems, is opting for a life where responsibilities are not simply things one needs to do for survival and to give meaning to life. They become the sum total of life and crowd out any thought and time for a life of joy and a life of mutual relationship and a sense of well-being with oneself, with a loved one, with one's fellow man — and with the *Ribbono Shel Olam*.

To be sure, achieving all of that is not easy. Yet when one truly makes the effort, it can be done. It may take a lifetime, but that is man's task — to make oneself into a patient, tolerant, loving, and optimistic individual. Needed is determination, the necessary investment of giving up old habits, and changing or modifying one's outlook on life. We do it with the readily available tools of a religious philosophy of *bitachon*, faith, and optimism, and the behavioral correlates to do, and not necessarily rush about. Confusion frequently exists concerning the concept of *zerizus*. The word means attentiveness, alertness, prioritizing, and doing what needs to be done. It does not mean the needless rushing about, harassing oneself and others. In the former mode it is in the service of the *yeitzer tov*, the drive for good; in the latter sense it serves the *yeitzer hara*, the evil drive, as evidenced by the harassment and strife it brings about with oneself, with others, and yes, *chas veshalom*, with the commands of the *Ribbono Shel Olam*, which are words of sweetness, of the good life, not one of harassment.

Chapter Seventeen

Some Thoughts on Discipline

The Problem With "Expert" Advice

O ne of the more difficult tasks in rearing our children is the establishment of effective methods of discipline. There seem to be more or less accepted norms in almost every area of child rearing except when we are called upon to restrain our children, to guide their behavior, and to transmit to them the dos and the don'ts of our culture.

We know approximately the proper amount and the kinds of food they ought to partake of for optimal health, how they should be clothed, the kind of medical attention they need, and what schooling is best for them. All of these necessary conditions can, furthermore, be clearly stated, and the well-intentioned parent can, if he wishes, follow the expert's advice to the letter.

Concerning permissiveness and restraint, what is optimal and what is detrimental in disciplining our children, the story is entirely different. What our "experts" tell us is quite vague, and when parents wish to follow their advice, they cannot be sure that under the specific conditions of their case a very different directive might not be indicated. As a result, parents can only be guided by their own inclinations and attitudes. Thus, discipline is effected with much doubt, in a haphazard and inconsistent fashion, which leaves the parent unsure, angry, and feeling all too often frustrated, if not guilty. These feelings of doubt, frustration, and guilt in turn make for more inconsistency, doubt, etc., and the cycle repeats itself.

The problem with formulas, rules, and "expert advice" is the infinite variability of human behavior and situations. No two conditions of human interaction are ever exactly alike, and what is good in one situation may well be disastrous in another. Thus, except for broad principles, no specific rules can successfully be laid down, and we must rely on sound judgment and good sense.

A more fruitful line of inquiry might lie in another direction. Parents need to be aware of what method they are using and how they have developed a particular set of attitudes in dealing with their children. In addition, parents should know why they frequently discipline their children in a fashion that is in discordance with their own good sense, which then makes them feel guilty after the act. What causes emotion to displace rational behavior?

Contrary to our beliefs, parents usually discipline their children in a manner dictated by a set of attitudes ingrained in their own personality rather than by the dictates of their judgment. These attitudes spring from three major sources:

1. All parents were children themselves at one time and learned through their own experience how children are to be dealt with. This, of course, would be all right if all their experiences were wholesome and generally well balanced. Supposing, however, the parent himself suffered at the hands of a tyrannical father or was overly indulged by a permissive one. Unbeknown to himself, this parent would tend to treat his child in a very similar manner or, by

reaction formation, in the very opposite way — either method lacking good judgment and balance.

2. We also learn how to discipline our children from a vague set of beliefs which are part folklore, part "philosophy," and part pseudoscientific knowledge. These beliefs vary and usually have subjective interpretations, but by and large several of them can be identified. There is, for example, the belief that one must "drive the devil" out of the child, which implies that children are innately bad and antisocial. Or, one speaks of the "innocence of childhood," which seems to say that all children are good and become corrupted only when they come in contact with society. Others speak of children as miniature adults, which would have one expect of the child behavior no different from what one expects of the adult. Perhaps this could explain the accepted practice during medieval times of punishing children no differently from adults, including their being subject to the death penalty. Still others would view the child as having no drives or inclinations except what society impresses upon him.

All of these beliefs may contain some truth. But each one by itself is sheer nonsense as a philosophy, and potentially dangerous. It is important to realize, however, that individuals rarely think through all the implications inherent in these beliefs. They are accepted as truths and practiced without conscious realization.

3. Parents have needs no less than anyone else. When they are angry they may lose control and tend to lash out no differently from the angry child who has a temper tantrum. Because adults control society, however, they may strike out when angry, but instead of explaining such behavior as a temper tantrum, we excuse it — indeed condone it — as "disciplining our children." What is really meant by the parent who says to the child he has beaten, "This hurt me more than it hurt you," is, "This has done me (the parent) more good as a physical outlet for my feeling of anger than it has done you (the child) as a disciplinary or teaching method." The "hurt" to the parent may be his feeling of guilt in abusing his child or the shame for having lost his temper. This, of course, is not to say that parents are not "entitled" to human weaknesses as well as anyone else. The point is that here again the child is disciplined not by sound judgment or even common sense, but by uncontrollable parental drives and needs.

In short, parents have, so to speak, built-in attitudes when they are about to discipline their child. Those have come about through their own childhood experiences, by having certain pseudoscientific beliefs which are common in our culture, and by their own emotional states. These have little connection with well-thought-out and rational approaches. Conversely, the totally rational approach — a cold-blooded method of control, rewards, and punishments — is equally harmful, for it lacks human warmth that shows the child that the parent does care and is personally affected by the child's behavior.

All of this is not meant to chide parents and reproach them for their weaknesses. Knowing all this, however, may help them take measures to minimize the influence these nonrational factors have when they are engaged in disciplining their child. There is no substitute for good sense and sound judgment when parents interact with their children. It is they, the parents, who endow them genetically, and it is they who must be entrusted with making judgments and transmitting the rules of society. What is important, however, is for parents to understand themselves and to allow their judgments to remain relatively free from the emotional pressures which are within every one of us, and the vague half-truths which, by their longevity, come to be regarded as truths.

"I Want My Child to Have Everything ..."

Parents frequently proclaim their intention to give their child everything they themselves have lacked and to "make something of him." Such thoughts undoubtedly are based upon altruistic motives and a sense of duty. Partially, however, they are motivated by the parents' own needs. There is nothing inherently wrong with this, but when these needs are exceedingly great, behavior will be expected that is more in line with the needs of the parents than can or should be expected of the child. When the child's behavior is poor, then the ensuing parental reaction may be caused by the parents' frustrated needs rather than the need to guide the child. Disciplinary measures then will be exaggerated, emotionally charged, and not optimal for the child's welfare.

Parents who have failed to realize their own ambitions, scholastically or economically, tend to use excessive pressure to have their child recoup this "loss." At best, such pressure would bring about friction, harassment, and much unhappiness. Furthermore, the strong possibility exists that the child will rebel, and the very opposite result to that desired by the parents will be achieved.

Individuals need to find meaning in life in order to suffer its hardships. When religion or philosophy fail to do this, parents may try to find meaning in life through their children. When this happens, the lives of the parents revolve entirely around their offspring, and their hopes and dreams become tied up with their children's lives. This may result in a child's inability to follow his own inclinations to lead a life for himself. Expectations as well as disappointments are then exaggerated, resulting in much friction and unhappiness. When the child finally must make the break, he may be unable to do this, or his parents may not allow it. Even if the child does succeed, the parent is then left to face a life without meaning and suffer the void of an "empty nest."

Children's behavior at times parallels that of their parents. This is so because both are human and because children tend to imitate their parents. When such behavior is not to the parents' liking, the ensuing disappointment in the child is compounded because it glaringly mirrors to the parents their own shortcomings. As a result, the parents' anger is similarly extended and the attendant disciplinary measures are way out of line.

All of this takes place without the parents' awareness. In fact, most of us would deny any such "selfish" considerations in dealing with our children. Nonetheless, they are present and do not allow us to deal with our children on a basis of sound judgment alone. These emotions make us distinctly human and should be accepted for both their positive and negative value. It is important, however, to realize that they do play a leading role in parent-child interactions, and thus to learn how to minimize or allow for their effect.

Parents and Children

Parents must discipline their children, control their behavior, teach them the mores of our society, and educate them to become useful citizens. In spite of the great import of all this, parents receive no formal training in how to go about it. Expert advice has its limitations, and should be considered with some skepticism. Our own need for being taught should not make us swallow the wheat and the chaff that is put before us. Some broad principles are useful, but the variability of life precludes precise prescriptions. Guidance must come from the parents' own good sense and judgment, which can and must be trusted. This would make for more self-assurance, fewer inconsistencies and doubts, less guilt — and thus less unhappiness and charged parent-child confrontations.

When doing for our children and guiding them, our needs should not be allowed to blind us. While parents may be entitled to have some satisfaction from their offspring, they should not vicariously relive their lives through them. Children do provide parents with the satisfaction of being needed, wanted, and loved, but an individual's total spiritual existence should not depend on it. And when our child's poor behavior parallels ours, we should, if we wish, direct the ensuing anger at ourselves rather than at the child. In fact, when this happens, the child's innocence is more clearly demonstrated than his guilt.

Rules and ways of dealing with children, and expectations and duties of the child, should be laid down *before* they need to be enforced. Consistent, well-thought-out ideas with cold logic will better withstand interference from our emotions. Being less harsh on ourselves will make for more realistic expectations of our children, allow for occasional transgressions, and make us react less violently when our children's shortcomings only mirror ours.

Two important factors should be kept in mind at all times.

To begin with, children simply do not understand why certain behaviors are expected of them, nor are they always able to comply. For example, the child obviously does not understand why one should eat with a fork rather than with his hands. To the contrary, it is pleasurable for the child to *"patshke,"* to handle his food with his hands as well as with his mouth. Additionally, standard forks are made for adults and may be quite difficult for the child to maneuver. It is similarly hard for the child to comprehend the need to sit "properly" at the table, especially when he does not possess the ability to sit for an extended period of time.

Then we should consider that the normal child wants to please and wants to be loved and rewarded. At the very same time, the child needs to have a say about his life, to have a will and *not* to be controlled and programmed. Let us think of the child who only knows how to comply and not express a will of his own. In the extreme, this makes for an authoritarian personality which believes that "orders are orders," even orders to kill and violate one's own human instinct of caring and kindness.

Obviously, then, a careful balance is in order, a type of weaning. To tell the child what to do, and explain why, and then to have the child modify these demands with his own will until his will and that of society converge and make him into a cooperative, yet unique member of the human race — this would be the ideal form and result of good discipline and teaching. Needless to say, the parents' own healthy, normal childhood, balanced perspective, and general calm will make for a discipline that is not rash and buffeted by the winds of emotions. Sound judgment, good common sense and firmness, together with warmth and acceptance, should prevail.

Chapter Eighteen

Effective Communication

*W*hen people fail to get along with one another, they frequently ascribe this problem to an inability to "communicate." Thus one notes of late an ever-increasing effort to effect a dialogue between races and nations, between parents and children, between and within religions, and so forth. There are untold numbers of conventions and meetings, conferences and assemblies, dialogues and encounters — all to resolve our many differences and frictions and general social ills. Offhand, it would seem that this is for the good. To understand, one must communicate. The results, however, are discouraging. All too frequently, meeting grounds turn into battle arenas, and encounters open up Pandora's boxes with devastating consequences.

Yet we continue to talk and seek the panacea for our social ills in the communication process. This is typical, for whenever a particular mode of behavior is found to be ineffective, we usually intensify that behavior, thinking that what is needed is more of the same. Rarely do we stop and think that what is really needed is a different approach altogether. We somehow "fall in love" with our behavior patterns. True, we are willing at times to modify or intensify them — but rarely are we ready to discard them entirely.

Inadequacy of Language

To the human being, language is, of course, the most effective and efficient mode of communicating ideas, feelings, or attitudes. Nonetheless, there is a particular inadequacy in the spoken word which is present whenever people with divergent experiences and interests attempt to communicate.

A perfect example of this would be the many verbal encounters that take place in the United Nations. Words are used, ironically, in an identical fashion by both protagonists, with apparently some vain hope that communication will come about. Thus, a representative of a free nation may hold forth on the concepts of democracy, liberty, and freedom, only to be followed by a spokesman for a totalitarian regime using the identical words, yet obviously wishing to convey very different meanings and connotations. A great deal of talking takes place, but communication is not achieved.

In a particular investigation, this writer found that certain simple everyday words such as *more* and *less*, *late* and *early*, have little definitive meaning to children. Yet these very same words do have a fairly precise meaning to one group of adults, and another meaning to another group — depending upon the group's culture and experiences. For example, "the meaning of life," or socially defined concepts such as democracy and freedom, certainly have different meanings to different social groups. This is so because words are more than symbols — they are concepts. Each word embodies a myriad of thoughts and attitudes arrived at by experiences and particular needs.

Parents, children, teachers, and schools are different communities, by virtue of different experiences, needs, and interests. For example, to be a "good" boy may mean to the parent that her son is primarily thoughtful and helpful. To the teacher, it may mean that his student is obedient (and not to be heard from too frequently), while to the school it may mean he obtains good grades and brings fame to that institution. To the child himself it may mean he is strong, assertive, and independent, and admired by his peers for his courage to stand up to his teachers and parents. Yet we use this word — and many others — as if their concepts are self-evident and universally shared.

Needed: Another's Viewpoint

What is needed, first and foremost, is the realization that while we may talk a lot, we may not really be communicating at all. We must, then, seek alternate methods, or at least ascribe the failure of communication to the inadequacy of the "word" rather than to the unwillingness of the other to listen.

One can begin by asking, "What does this mean to the other?" not, "What does this mean to me?" The parent informs the child that it is "late" and "past his bedtime." Obviously, to the parent these words are far more than a simple statement of time. They are concepts, and may indicate a concern for the child's health, as well as for his ability to arise on time and function well in the class-room. They may also connote the idea of a need for routine and order (and last but not least, some peace and quiet for the harassed parents).

The child, because of his fewer experiences and different interests, sees all this quite differently. "Bedtime" means pleasure denied, an arbitrary whim of his parents, or even banishment into the dark bedroom. He does not — and cannot — see, as his parents do, the connection between bedtime and its need and value to health and happiness. This is not to suggest, of course, that parents should shirk their duty of sending children to bed. But by understanding the child, and how he sees all this, we may change our methods and reason with him from his vantage point rather than ours.

There are, furthermore, words and concepts that admittedly confuse even the adult — yet are expected to make sense to the child. For example, the notion of assertiveness versus desirable social behavior plays havoc with almost all of us — and we never really know when to fight or retreat. Particularly in our society, controlling our assertiveness, anger, and aggression is a lifelong task.

Yet when the child comes home with a black eye, we may chide him for not standing up for his rights. At another time, when the tables have been turned and he "took care" of the other fellow — he is considered an aggressive bully. We rarely ascertain the real facts behind these encounters; yet even had we been there, the fine distinction of whether to fight or to run would have caused us some thought — with little assurance that our final move would have been the really correct one. Nonetheless, we attempt to teach the child to stand up for his rights but not to be a bully, expecting that the real knowledge of exactly how to do this will come from words alone. This is not the case.

Experiences Count More Than Words

What words cannot accomplish, experiences can. Allowing the child to make occasional excursions into the adult world — perhaps to stay up late on a special occasion — will give her the experience and the understanding of the connection between bedtime and fatigue and health far better than all the verbal arguments a mother could muster. Experiencing with her parents situations where critical distinctions between fight and flight have to be made will be far more potent lessons than dealing with them on the symbolic, verbal level. Thus, the more experiences a child has — and the more adult-like these are — the more she will see her world and her needs in an adult-like fashion.

The reverse is also true. Parents may be preoccupied with the needs of earning a living and providing for their loved ones. They may thus have little patience or understanding for the child's "unimportant" and "fleeting" little needs. An occasional excursion into the child's world will change all this. Parents may be amazed to learn, for example, that to the child a comfortable home and plentiful material needs are far less important than his stature as seen by his peers, or his prowess in the ball park. And this stature and the ensuing self-esteem are usually attained in ways that differ greatly from those that parents imagine. Being assertive (and at times rebellious) and physically strong, being admired and accepted by one's peers, having fanciful fantasies of omnipotence and similar "silly" notions, are the stuff children's dreams are made of. Most important, they give a child the feeling that he is a being with his own rights, yet is able to depend on strong and giving parents.

Parents need not be psychotherapists to interpret children's dreams and fantasies. In children, fantasy is close to the surface and frequently alternates and merges with reality. Thus, by listening and simply allowing the child to talk, we can learn to see his world as he does.

Differences in meanings will also be lessened when parents and children are united simply by sharing experiences, any experiences. Parents and children who have shared a delightful vacation, or the mother and daughter who have jointly completed a difficult chore, can then discuss differences of opinions which at other times would have been too hot to handle. Simply being together and sharing an experience tends to unite and create a bond that holds fast, even when disagreement will attempt to intervene.

It's the Salesman, not the Product

Communication can also be viewed as selling an idea, or buying what another person says. Thus the crackerjack salesman teaches us how to sell, for it is the salesman who makes the sale, not the product.

A vacuum-cleaner salesman calls for an appointment to show you the latest model machine. You tell him that the vacuum cleaner he sold you years ago is still working. He assures you that all he wants is to demonstrate the new product. You have no intention of buying his product, but figure you have nothing to lose by seeing what's available. So you agree. He arrives at the appointed time, and begins his spiel. To demonstrate, he first vacuums your rug. Then he presents some gifts for the kiddies and enjoys a cup of coffee with you, spending an hour or so of his own time. And more often than not, you wind up buying the very product you were convinced you didn't need or want — and you wonder why.

Similarly, you are invited to a gathering at an acquaintance's home to see a demonstration of the latest plastic kitchen gadgets and containers. First you socialize with your friends over coffee and cake and play a few parlor games, then you are treated to a product demonstration by a trained representative of the company. The very same mechanisms operate here to effect a "sale" as in the earlier example.

The vacuum-cleaner salesman, and the organizer of the Tupperware party, have used the most potent, if subtle, persuader known to man. They have set up an emotional climate that worked on you — largely unconscious, but powerful indeed. By vacuuming your rug and giving the child gifts, the salesman has done something for you that generated a need in you to reciprocate. The refreshments at the Tupperware party, and the little gifts distributed by the representative, create the same effect. The salesperson's spending an hour with you that he or she could have spent elsewhere — and perhaps made a sale — causes you to feel guilty for taking the person's time. And by exhibiting himself as being a nice fellow, or herself as being a fun-loving party organizer, he or she makes you unconsciously assume that the products for sale are equally nice. In short, the person, rather than the product, has been "sold." Hidden persuaders were called into play by creating an emotional climate that countermanded the intellectual barrier. You did not buy (rationally); you were sold to (emotionally).

All of us, at one time or another, use these emotional devices, and at time pressures, to get our way. Unfortunately, these methods, if misused, can be quite cruel — but they invariably work. The mother who constantly reminds her child that his poor behavior or lack of achievement causes her to feel sick or have headaches implants in him feelings of guilt — regardless of whether he then acquiesces or not. Suppose, furthermore, that the mother — or anyone else known to the child — then becomes ill, and perhaps dies. The child, who has difficulty understanding cause-and-effect relationships, can (and frequently does) consider himself responsible for this tragedy. This example is, of course, an extreme and relatively rare one, but there are numerous milder cases of "guilty" people who have been conditioned, i.e., trained, by parents who have used excessive emotional pressures to raise their children.

However, these emotional persuaders can also be used for the good. Parents are in a unique position in that they both give the child all his material needs, and "control" him in order to educate him. It must thus be expected that because of the giving, parents are loved; and because of the "controlling," they are resented. As a result, children have ambivalent feelings about their parents. Yet parents can lead with their giving side and underplay the controlling factor, and thereby use the love and warm feeling that is created to have the child comply. It is then not the guilt which is primary, but the need for love and approval.

With the parent creating a positive emotional climate, a need to reciprocate is engendered in the child to please that parent. Thus, while the child may not understand the importance of good behavior, or see the relevance of learning, he will, at least partially, comply to please his parents.

While verbal communication is essential in order to understand others, we frequently fail to truly comprehend because of the inherent shortcomings of the verbal process. This is particularly true of children who, because they have different and fewer experiences than adults, cannot see the world as their elders do.

It is important to realize, then, that much of children's misbehavior can, to a large extent, be ascribed to faulty communication. Understanding is enhanced when experiences, rather than words, are shared, and when parents honestly attempt to see situations from the child's point of view, rather than the adult's. Listening is still the most useful single process to accomplish just this.

Communication implies, of course, persuasion and receptiveness. Both are furthered when an emotional climate is set up that exudes good feeling and camaraderie. Parents who sell themselves have little difficulty in selling their edicts and directives.

Confounding Communication

More destructive than communication that is inadequate is communication that is vague, inconsistent, and confusing. While total accuracy and explicitness are not possible nor really desirable, persistent confusion can have serious consequences.

In a well-known experiment, dogs were trained (conditioned) to expect food whenever a circle was projected onto a screen. They quickly learned to anticipate their "reward" and salivated copiously upon sighting this circle. Subsequently, they were also taught (conditioned) to expect an electric shock whenever an ellipse was projected. Now they learned to anticipate "punishment" by withdrawing and showing fright at the sight of this ellipse. Thus they mastered both of these approach and withdrawal responses well, and as the experimenter alternated the circle with the ellipse, the dogs approached or withdrew without error.

Then, however, the (nasty) experimenter ever so slowly elongated the circle and rounded the ellipse at each subsequent exposure to make both forms more and more alike. The original approach and withdrawal responses continued for a while, until a point was reached when both forms were practically identical. Thereafter, all "normal" behavior broke down. Unable to discriminate, and "forced" to respond due to the previous conditioning, the dogs haphazardly and inappropriately approached and withdrew, froze in their places or ran around aimlessly. They defecated and whimpered and manifested "neurotic" behavior, due to communication that confused and confounded them.

It is similarly believed that certain schizophrenic reactions have their origin in "mixed messages" and "double-binds" — conditions where *to do* or *not to do* are equally threatening and emotionally dangerous, a kind of situation where the parent says to the child, "I dare you to do as I expect you to do." Thus the schizophrenic withdraws from the threatening world, alters his perception, literally freezes or acts wildly and inappropriately, and loses the ability to react "correctly" to other humans.

The "neurotic" dogs or the schizophrenic who reacts to a confounding and frightening world are, of course, extreme examples, and are cited solely to illustrate the point. Yet, to a lesser degree, all of us frequently engage in communication that is unclear, ambiguous, and confusing to our children.

The parent buys his child a box of crayons and large sheets of paper. The child draws, and is rewarded by his parents for his artistic skills with smiles and hugs. Then it's bedtime. The following morning the child awakes early, eager to continue drawing with his crayons. And here is this wall in the kitchen which beckons him to practice his artistry ... Before long there is quite a mural on this wall. The parents awaken, and the child anticipates more praise, smiles, and hugs. Instead, there is a calamity — a ruined wall and a scolded and punished child. Confusing, isn't it? How is the child to know the difference between a wall and paper? Is he old enough to understand? Or, at least, can we ourselves be understanding and now attempt to teach the child the difference?

A storm rages outside, with thunder and lightning. The parent holds on to the child. "It's nothing to worry about," reassures the parent. But the parent's body language, the grip and moist hands, send the opposite message. Yes, parents are human, and are given to unreasonable fears. Yet instead of sending confusing messages, let us attempt to explain to the child our foibles and exaggerated fears, and together learn to react to "threatening" situations in a more appropriate manner.

The Child's Need for Clarity

It is well known, of course, that children tend to see things in absolutes and extremes and find ambiguity distressing. Thus, to the child, yesterday was a million years ago, and a promised tomorrow seems to be in the very distant future. The past is long forgotten, and for a promise to be real, the child wants what he wants *now*. This writer, in a recent experiment, has similarly shown that young children have no real concept of indefinite numerical adjectives. For example, to the child the word *some* would seem to jump from its intermediate position between *all* **and** *nothing*, and be understood as *almost all* — or *nothing at all*. Telling the child to spend *some* of the time playing and *some* of the time doing homework will most likely result in far more time for play than for work. Is this due entirely to the child's selfishness or disobedience? Not necessarily so. Partly it is because the word *some* has no real meaning to the child. Partly it may be that time passes faster in play than in work. And partly it may be that the child may actually perceive the concept *some* differently at different times.

The younger child manifests this need for clarity by endlessly questioning his parent and wanting to know everything. The adolescent, too, sees things in black or white, all good or all bad, and then demands the optimal in life. He is thus drawn to the "isms" and extremes in politics because only they promise utopia. Only the adult, because he has had to compromise with reality, is able to tolerate vague and frequently conflicting values in life rather than absolute truths. Yet in communicating with their children, parents all too frequently forget that the young still live in the world of unambiguity and need clear directives and well-defined goals. Doubt confuses and frightens them. Children are particularly hurt by sarcasm and similar forms of admonition. They would take straightforward criticism far better than insinuations and remarks which confuse them and indict them as being worthless, without clearly spelling out why. We are invariably better off telling children exactly what to do or not to do and clearly defining limits, than vaguely telling them to be "good" or "well-behaved."

Being vague may be easier for the parent (and slightly cowardly), but it puts the burden of defining the term *good* on the child, which is of course an unreasonable demand. In addition, the child is then punished because "he should have known better." This is a "heads I win, tails you lose" proposition.

The Uncertain Parent

Parents are vague largely because of an inner doubt that makes them question their ability as parents. This may well be due to a general state of uncertainty in our society today. It is also fostered by the voluminous "expert" advice which attempts to spell out for parents exactly how to handle their children, and thus automatically builds in them a feeling that they really know nothing. This is nonsense. Common sense and sound judgment are still the parents' best guides.

Parents need not, and indeed should not, expect to know the "perfect" way to handle their child. What is needed is confidence and a sure stance in relating to children, regardless of the possibility that many of their child-rearing practices may be partially in error. Indeed, one wants to teach children to behave in a reasonably self-assured manner, using sound reflection, yet accepting the possibility of being incorrect. We want children to be neither impulsive, rash, and driven by momentary flights of ideas, nor compulsive, endlessly ruminating, doubting, and unable to make decisions. Parents who attempt to overly control behavior — their own as well as that of their children — to be perfect, usually create robots and automatons rather than self-assured humans who can also tolerate a moderate amount of doubt.

A crucial balance is called for, a sure-footed approach vis-à-vis the child, yet with a built-in idea that this particular mode may not be the only or perfect way. Total ambiguity and the endless search for perfection, overtly diametrically opposite attitudes, both foster confusion and doubt, the former manifesting itself in total lack of order and social control, and the latter in rigidity and an emotionally constricted life.

The father sends his child to bed without supper because of the child's misbehavior. The child is understandably angry and hurt. Yet he can retain respect for his parent because the father seems to know what he is doing. The child accepts the situation and no real damage has been done; in fact, he may learn to improve his behavior. However, should the parent, because of pangs of doubt, then sneak up some dessert for the little boy and even apologize for his "harsh" punishment, then this "lesson" may turn into a catastrophe indeed. For then the child is justifiably hurt by the parent's temper outburst, since the parent himself now regrets it. He furthermore loses all respect for the father's judgment and is utterly confused: *is* misbehavior punished by being sent to bed, or is it rewarded by a sneaked dessert and a humiliated father?

Parents possessing self-confidence in dealing with their children, who, in the process, make mistakes, will harm their children less than the parent who has no standards, one who endlessly seeks the "perfect" way, or, even worse, one who vacillates between these two modes.

Reinforcing Behavior

Confusion also comes about because there may be inconsistency between overt verbal statements and nonverbal feelings and attitudes. These may be conscious conflicts born out of doubt, but they may also be more basic, unconscious feelings not easily brought under conscious control.

The parent complains bitterly of her child's misbehavior. Everything has been tried — rewards and punishment, pleading and reasoning — all to no avail. The parent is adamant, and clearly and unambiguously exhorts the child to behave. And then one notes that as the parent denounces the child's misbehavior, there is a twinkle in the eye, a kind of secret delight at the child's devilish antics and his "assertiveness." Verbally, his actions are condemned, but covertly, he is admired. The child picks up this powerful nonverbal signal and his (mis)behavior is reinforced.

The power of nonverbal communication is usually grossly underestimated. Communication takes place through many modalities. A smile, a handshake, a look — all communicate, succinctly and pointedly, far better than verbal statements. Words can be carefully chosen, and reveal only what we wish to say; words both communicate and hide our thoughts. Our other modalities are less well controlled. Our features, the forced smile, the satisfied or the disappointed look, the way we hold our head or manipulate our body — all speak clearly, albeit unconsciously, and communicate unequivocally.

Here, too, differences exist between children and adults. The adult, as he perfects the verbal mode of communication, learns to hide real feelings. In the process, of course, he also loses the ability to read others except through their words.

Children, on the other hand, because of their verbal inadequacy, rely on other more potent and real indicators. They can thus know almost uncannily the adult's real feelings, of which he himself is unaware. It is thus believed that the infant actually senses the mother's feelings, her satisfaction or anxiety, and thus perceives his mother as satisfying or anxiety provoking. These perceptions may come about through the firmness of the mother's grip on his little body, the slight tremor, the perspiration on her palms, or other physical indices — or simply empathy, that mystical but real human feeling. Regardless of what it is, communication does take place. The parent's real feelings "speak" more clearly than the parent's words.

It is thus to be expected that at times all of us say one thing verbally while communicating through our other modalities the very opposite — and the child is confused. He may react to the verbal part of the communication, to the nonverbal, or to a compromise of the two (and develop neurotic symptoms which are usually symbolic compromises). Or he may act in an inconsistent, irrational, maladjusted fashion, or develop an elaborate system of behavior where there is an inordinate amount of energy spent on determining what is explicit and what is implicit in communication — and thus develop an obsessive lifestyle.

Situational Factors

Because parents are only human and are themselves exposed to assaults on their feelings, they cannot help but react to the child in part based upon their own emotional state, rather than purely to the objective situation. This is, of course, the human part of behavior. Should, however, the parents' emotional state fluctuate wildly and unpredictably, then the child cannot help but react in the confused fashion that causes withdrawal and irrationality.

Thus the parent who habitually tolerates certain behavior at one time and reacts harshly on another occasion to the very same behavior teaches the child nothing but confusion. Daddy comes home and our child rushes at him and is rewarded with hugs and kisses. Another time, Daddy had a fight with his boss (or wife). His mood is grim. He comes home and our child rushes at him, expecting to be hugged. Instead, he is pushed away and scolded: "Leave Daddy alone!" Now what does the child think or feel? Can he possibly comprehend these "temporary" conditions? More likely, he learns to see life as confusing and his loved ones as not to be trusted. Similarly, when rules seem to change at times — when guests are visiting, or other special occasions arise when social values such as honesty or generosity are set aside to suit parental rationalizations (or their pocketbook) — the child is naturally confused and learns little that is of value to him.

Some of this is, of course, unavoidable. What is important is that one consistent mode of reaction be dominant, one clearly defined value system be expounded, and then occasional deviations can be tolerated. It is the habitual vacillation, the frequent fluctuations, that are harmful.

Blocking Communication

Communication, of course, is the basis of understanding and the foundation of a relationship. Thus all is not lost as long as communication has not completely broken down. At all costs, then, parents must attempt to keep the lines open and to further verbal exchanges with their children. Frequently, however, and inadvertently, we block communication instead of generating it.

People want to talk, and children want — and need — to be heard. The psychotherapeutic process capitalizes on this need, and helps the individual verbalize — and then has the patient himself discover alternate and better methods of coping. Parents as well should utilize this tool.

The child comes home from school and announces that she has failed the test. The parent opines that the child has not studied sufficiently. The child, in order to defend herself, claims that the teacher or the test was unfair. With both parent and child adamant, no further communication is possible. The result in this vignette is an angry parent, a hurt child, and communication that has broken down. Nothing has been gained, and no wonder then when the child complains that she cannot talk to her parents for they just don't understand. All too frequently, a slammed door or temper outburst adds a seal to this broken communication.

Let us attempt an alternative method. The child announces that she has failed the test (and the parent senses that the girl wants to talk about it). The parent neither condemns nor shows disinterest, but in fact encourages further talk by simply saying: "Oh, you have failed the test." The child senses an opportunity to talk and sees herself in a nonthreatening situation. She is thus free to try out thoughts of having "an unfair teacher," but she can also entertain the possibility that she may have studied insufficiently. By simply reflecting the child's words and showing an interest without condemnation, the stage is set for the child to be honest with herself, to verbalize her defenses but also discover her mistakes. There is thus the distinct possibility, and indeed likelihood, that she will truly see her own error and subsequently correct it. The child has not been told of her sins; she has herself learned of her error. Most important, she has discovered that she can talk to her parents, and personality development is furthered through healthy parent-child interaction.

The relationship between communication and personality adjustment should not be surprising. Adjustment or maladjustment is largely the result of experiences in childhood, the most important of which are parent-child relationships. Relationships, in turn, come about through communication, verbal and nonverbal. Improving our style of communication, then, should better our parent-child relationships and thus further healthy personality development.

Chapter Nineteen

In Defense of Parents

The Name of the Game: Who Is to Blame?

One of the favorite mental mechanisms man uses to protect himself from emotional pain is scapegoating. This ploy comes in handy whenever one is unable to cope and, to escape the psychological pressure, blames others — individuals, groups, nations, or races — for one's own shortcomings, mishaps, or sufferings. Scapegoating can take relatively innocuous forms, such as the habit of blaming others for causing accidents which are in reality due to forces of nature or one's own clumsiness. For example, one drops a glass of milk and "explains" the misfortune by saying it happened "because you are making me nervous." Scapegoating can also be most serious, as in cases of paranoia, where all of one's angry thoughts are projected onto others: "You hate me, you plot against me," and so forth. The use of scapegoating is not confined to individuals. Politicians have used it to gain power, nations to find a pretext for war, and governments and social institutions to escape blame for their blunders.

In a strictly psychological sense, for the neurotic sufferer scapegoating is a defense against mental anguish and useful in protecting the ego. However, its indiscriminate and prolonged use is as harmful to the accuser as it is to the accused, for now there is no need for the accuser (i.e., sufferer) to gain insight into what he himself is doing or fails to do that is primarily responsible for his misery. No, now he carries his real or imagined scars like medals proclaiming to everyone the "true" cause for his suffering. Similarly, social institutions, in their zeal to defend themselves, come to truly believe that the fault lies elsewhere and not with themselves, thus obviating the need to look inward, to re-evaluate and mend their ways.

Parents as a group have become the target of such attacks with ever-increasing intensity. To explain the breakdown of law and order, society points a finger at parents and blames them for being too permissive. Social scientists, on the other hand, usually perceive them as being too rigid and constrictive. "Progressive" criminologists see evil parents behind every criminal, and the school explains away its failures by denoting nonmotivated students as products of nonstimulating homes, and misbehaving youths as the creation of undisciplined households. Of course, adolescents themselves blame all misfortunes in life and all their personal difficulties on parents and their cohorts, i.e., authority figures and the entire adult world. Finally, there is the psychoanalytic couch, where parents are "exposed" as the true villains for our neurotic sufferings.

This most regrettably but universally accepted belief is a distorted oversimplification of highly complex truths. It is reinforced by popular fiction and the performing arts, which depict psychoanalysis as primarily the uncovering of parental crime perpetrated upon the innocent young. The popularity of this belief is undoubtedly due to our own need to shed responsibility, unload any residual of guilt or blame, and find a scapegoat. So why not identify with all this, play the game and blame the parent?

Children's Needs and Infantile Dreams

Children need and should be entitled to have parents who, besides providing for their physical needs, create a home with an emotional climate that makes for healthy emotional growth. Minimum requirements would be for parents themselves to be free of serious neurotic difficulties. Such parents are able to set up rules that are reasonable, maintain discipline without being punitive, have order without rigidity, and be flexible without being wishy-washy. They are strong so that the child can look up to them for support, yet have some childishness in them to see things the way children do. They can laugh at things that are laughable, take a joke, and laugh at themselves.

These parents have an inner warmth that says to the child: "It's nice to be with you." They find their children pleasurable in spite of the burden they frequently are. They do not allow themselves to be pushed around by their children and then resent them, nor do they use their children to vent inner anger due to other frustrations in life. Parents such as these do not allow their duty to provide for their children's safety, physical health, and education to become so intense that all joy in life is squashed. They do not bug their young sons and daughters endlessly to eat, to be careful, to study, and to brush their teeth. They take some chances with the "important" things in life for the sake of enjoying life.

Added to the need for an emotionally healthy home, the child has dreams and fantasies of his own. He would like his parents to have no concern in the world other than providing him with pleasure. Yet he wants his parents to work and to furnish him with goods and services that make him secure. Our child would like his parents to be around when comforting and security are needed, but to vanish when he wants to "do his own thing" without interference. Similarly, he wants to be a one and only, yet have siblings to keep him company. As an adolescent he wants the parent to be concerned, but not interfere. He wants to share his thoughts with his father, but is unwilling to accept his opinion. He longs for mother's milk of sympathy, yet wants to reserve the right to be totally independent. Parents, he says, should show the way and set limits, except when these interfere with his own ideas. He wants to be scolded for his misdeeds, for this shows that his parents care, but is enraged when so punished. When it suits him, he wants his parents to be his pals, yet act their age and be adult.

The lists of children's needs and fantasies could, of course, go on ad infinitum. This sampling merely points out the complexities involved in being a parent who attempts to meet the child's realistic needs as well as catering to at least some of his fantasies.

The Child Is the Father of the Man

It is true, of course, that personality as a whole, and psychopathology in particular, generally result from one's early experience in life, particularly as one interacts with parents and with other significant people. It is also a fact that an individual's dreams and fantasies are shaped in accordance with the extent his needs are met: The healthier one's reality life, the less intense and less pathologic his fantasies.

It is equally true that the infinite variety of personality, interests, and attitudes in man — the "human" in man — comes about because of the myriad of ways needs are met and fantasies are satisfied. It is thus clear that a standard and perfect formula for being a parent is neither possible nor desirable, unless we want to produce robots who are programmed to think and dream alike — and act accordingly.

Because parents have their own problems, they cannot meet all the child's needs nor can they possibly cater to all of his fantasies. Thus no child ever escapes childhood without some neurotic complications due to real or imagined lacks in his early life. The process of psychoanalytic psychotherapy, as a necessarily highly simplified model, is to first separate the real from the imagined. Then one works through these early relationships, perceiving one's parents and one's early life differently through understanding, insight, and alternate ways of seeing what has happened and why. Finally, one learns, through the context of patient-therapist relationship, to "cut the transference," i.e., to act now on the basis of what is desirable here and now, to behave as an adult to further one's interest, not as a child who re-enacts and replays outdated angers and ineffective ways of functioning.

In short, not all of children's problems are due to the inadequacy of parents. Nor are parents free of attempting to provide, as much as possible, an emotionally healthy climate. Yet, in spite of the best of intentions, psychopathology can come about because of other factors such as children's unrealistic expectations, harmful experiences outside the home, or social pressures or hypocritical philosophies which reside in modern society. Thus, when help is needed, one should avoid the pitfalls of blame, and concentrate on relief, healing, and help.

Chapter Twenty

Checking Up on Our Children's Mental Health

The most pressing health problem confronting us today is that of mental ill-health. Serious mental illness affects 10 million Americans. Over 19 million suffer from anxiety disorders; depression strikes 18 million, and suicide is the third-ranking cause of death among the young. While medication and psychotherapy help the more seriously afflicted, little is done to treat the less obvious manifestations of mental ill-health — general unhappiness, malaise, marital conflicts, parent-child conflicts, inability to get along with others, finding work and staying on the job, and so forth. Thus, vigilance at a most early age for early signs of emotional disturbance is in order.

How is one to check up on mental health? Who is to diagnose? What are the instruments available to us? Where does one begin? There are no mental thermometers or pulse rates to guide us; no sniffles or sore throats to attract our attention. There are by far too few clinicians to see every child individually; nor has it been demonstrated as wise to give every child a periodic mental-health checkup.

Thus the task must fall into the hands of those who deal as a matter of course with children on an individual basis — the parent and the teacher. The only method available is that of observation, specifically observation of behavior — eating, sleeping, fighting, learning — in short, all that which we observe in, and experience with, the child.

One cannot, of course, evaluate every bit of behavior, nor would this be advisable. One can, however, be on the alert for signs which should make one pause and investigate further.

The Concept of Normalcy

The adjective *normal* can be thought of as *ideal* when, for example, one describes body temperature or the form of a newborn child. It can also be used to mean *typical* or *average* when, for instance, one speaks of intellectual ability. Speaking of human behavior, however, the term *normal* is not useful when used as an adjective in this sense. The very same behavior which might be ideal in one situation might very well be far from perfect in another. Nor is *typical* exactly what we look for when we strive for normalcy in behavior. To be typical is to be ordinary, if not mediocre; that is not the goal of normalcy.

"Normal," when used as a description of behavior that is desirable, can be used only for the particular situation in which it takes place. There is no behavior which in itself may not be proper under certain circumstances. The how and when must determine whether it is desirable or not.

Much has been learned about human behavior from the study of the mentally ill. That is because the behavior of the mentally ill is generally not different in kind, it is different only in degree — it is exaggerated or inappropriate. This has unfortunately led to the situation that one cannot look at a mental-health column without reading of one or more symptoms of mental ill-health which he finds in himself. Certain terms have slipped into our vocabulary from the mental-health field which have no justification for being used with the mentally healthy, certainly not by the layman. One who is repeatedly upset by certain situations is said to have a complex; one who is easily aroused is called hysterical; one who resents being injured by others, a paranoid; and so forth.

The fact that the paranoid has feelings of being injured and persecuted by others is by itself not the determinant that labels him as sick, any more than his having a brain makes him mentally ill. Having a brain is part of a human's equipment, and feelings of injury or persecution are part and parcel of feelings that are human. It is the exaggeration of feelings, their inappropriateness, and a preoccupation with such feelings that makes the important difference.

Thus it cannot be said that a particular form of behavior is abnormal. What parents and teachers should be on the alert for are indicators of gross inappropriateness and gross exaggeration. When reactions are more than normally intensive, when a typical behavior takes place too frequently, when behavior is too rigid or too erratic, when behavior seems to be completely wrong for the time or place — then the alert should be sounded.

Appropriate or Inappropriate?

A single example will suffice to illustrate how one can judge whether behavior is appropriate or not. All of us are familiar with temper tantrums. It is that manifestation of rage which almost every child displays — a syndrome consisting of screaming, kicking, a red and purple face (and a parent who then either kicks back or begs the poor darling to calm down).

We think that with maturity, rage simply vanishes. What, then, gives rise to adult anger, stress and tension, the general grim faces we encounter, the strife, marital conflict, complaining, cursing, gossiping, and sarcasm — and essential hypertension or violence?

These, too, are obviously reactions to rage — temper tantrums which have been modified and appear in a more mature (and socially acceptable?) form.

One does not expect the school-age child to have a temper tantrum, but we expect him to react in some fashion when incensed. Thus we expect boys to hit, girls to pull each other's hair. Similarly, when adults are angry we expect women to gossip, executives to get high blood pressure, and certain personality types to resort to violence — all manifestations of rage. We thus expect any of these kinds of behavior of certain people at certain periods in their lives.

We neither expect a very stereotyped or predictable way in which one will always react, nor do we want to be shocked by a kind of behavior which is "way out." Behavior will most likely be modified by one's age, his station in life, and the time and place. Extremes in behavior will extend only to an allowable point; they will happen infrequently; they will be neither stereotyped nor rigid; they will be appropriate to some extent, even if undesirable.

At times, when life is not that good, adults fantasize. To the degree that such fantasies lead to constructive action, this is certainly laudable. Yet even when such fantasies are temporary escapes from harsh reality and lead nowhere, they are still useful no less than an "escape" to a ball game, an entertainment, or a brisk walk to "get away from it" — all, of course, within limits. Similarly, young children also have a rich fantasy life. They speak of imaginary friends, of becoming a powerful superhero, and so forth. All of this, when occurring occasionally in a mild form, is certainly not harmful. But if a child daydreams frequently or hallucinates even occasionally, it should cause us concern.

Thus it is not the isolated bit of behavior that should be reacted to, but the exaggerated behavior, the typical behavior which occurs too frequently, rigidity of behavior, or complete inappropriateness which should sound the alarm. For any behavior to be judged inappropriate one must consider the child's age, the situation at hand, how exaggerated the reaction in itself really is, and how frequently it occurs. One should note whether the reaction is automatic and stereotyped, erratic and "senseless," or spontaneous and somehow fitting the situation, at least as seen by the child.

Parents and teachers need not be experts in mental health. The child's every move or behavior need not be observed or evaluated. Parents and teachers, however, have invaluable experience with children and can easily determine when behavior is inappropriate. When such inappropriate behavior does occur, the extent of its inappropriateness must be judged. Parents and teachers have the responsibility to note when help is needed, and see to it that help is forthcoming.

Understanding, Empathy, and Emotional "Band-Aids"

Ideally, of course, we should be looking not only at controlling behavior, but more importantly, at understanding inner feelings. Do we not occasionally read newspaper reports of a brutal killing or series of killings by an individual who had heretofore been a quiet, exemplary citizen? This may be extreme, of course. However, since society does demand control of extreme behavior — even while inner feelings of anger, resentment, frustration, or psychic pain or hurt remain — what happens to these repressed feelings? Well, they can be displaced: upon oneself as depression, or upon those weaker, more vulnerable, and more accessible, such as one's spouse or children. These feelings can also be kept in perpetual check, held back fiercely from expression. On the outside this strategy may look good, but what does it do to the inside? Does it cause chronic stress — the feelings demanding expression, and/or social withdrawal, thus shutting the gate? Or does it become unbearable to the point of an inner implosion with dire consequences to one's physical or mental health?

Unfortunately, unlike physical ill-health, which one usually recognizes and attends to, when it comes to mental health or emotional well-being we are not that ready to recognize the problem nor willing to do something about it. A variety of mechanisms work against us. There is shame. There is denial. There are feelings, really rationalizations, such as "Well, isn't it normal to be angry or sad when ... ?" and so on. In the case of our children, there is also the avoidance of feeling that one has been a less than perfect parent. So life goes on, and one comes to accept one's own and one's children's emotional state as is. "That's life, no one's perfect, and no one is really happy."

To be sure, no one is always happy. Life has its ups and downs. Furthermore, the best of parenting and the most ideal social situations do not guarantee the most ideal emotional adjustment. Thus, freeing ourselves from unjustified guilt, parents and teachers must learn to recognize children's emotional problems, be they normal or potentially ominous, and to deal with them.

Frequently, all that is necessary is to help the child express his deep inner feelings. This can be a powerful first-aid tool for all of us — to verbalize in a socially acceptable manner our feelings of anger, pain, hurt, love, and longing.

Oh, what relief for the sufferer to be heard, possibly to be understood, and to receive some empathy from others instead of the usual admonitions ("Why are you always angry/ depressed/ worried/ fidgety/ late/ disorganized?") which never help but only add to the sufferer's feelings of helplessness, stupidity, and alienation. In addition, such comments label the individual: "You adults call me angry or nasty, so I might as well continue to be as I am." This is blaming the sufferer, which helps no one and guarantees that the maladjustment is maintained.

Parents and teachers need not be, nor should they be, psychotherapists, just as they are not medical doctors. Yet everyone must know how to recognize a problem and the rudiments of first aid. Honest, genuine, empathetic listening — to hear the inner child — is such a tool, available to all of us.

Let us also consider the following possibilities:

(a) This child who fails to conform and is disrespectful: Is he simply a "bad" kid who needs to be shown that the adult is boss — and to do so the child must be punished? Or is this a hurt child who incorrectly (and at times correctly) sees himself as singled out for persecution?

(b) Is the child who always moves about, unnecessarily handling papers, pencils, and other objects while the teacher is speaking, simply playing or showing disregard for the teacher? Or is this child restless, unable to concentrate or unable to sit still? Do we really know at what age and for what length of time a child can sit and concentrate in accordance with the program of a school, which has neither scientifically investigated this matter, nor ever experimented to determine for how long an individual can sit and concentrate? Such a study would have to consider general age, the particular child, the difficulty of the material, the interest level — and the ability of the lecturer to keep everyone awake. (Look around during a rabbi's Shabbos *derashah* and observe the listeners, the fidgeters, the sleepers, and the snorers ...)

(c) Does the disorganized child, the one who is always late to class and with his homework, simply wish things to be as they are, or is there something emotional operating here? Note, in the adult world, individuals who are invariably late, messy and disorganized, yet wish — and frequently, genuinely so — to "improve," yet are powerless to do so.

(d) What about the quiet, serious loner? Does he really choose to be as he is, or does he need to be provided with opportunities to interact socially, to loosen up, to be less serious?

(e) How to understand the overachiever, the grim competitive student, who must get the best grade? Is he simply ambitious, or is he compensating for some negative inner feeling: "I am socially retarded, but scholastically the best," or, "I have been scolded and I feel worthless. I'll show them!" No wonder, then, that one all too frequently finds "model" students depressed or even suicidal.

This discussion could go on and on, because the human being is unique, and so is his behavior. If man is to be perfect, then we would all be clones. Children, like adults, should be permitted and even encouraged to be themselves. Yet some gentle help to add and improve is always helpful, while criticizing, labeling, and jumping to conclusions as to what is wrong with them, never is.

Chapter Twenty-one

Children Under Pressure

adly enough, society has become inured and hardened to violence. We have become used to hearing about violence between nations (war), between spouses (domestic abuse), and toward minorities and similar "others" (hate crimes). The news is brimming with stories of individuals who commit violent acts during robberies or as acts of revenge, random killings carried out to "relieve" the murderer's inner frustrations, and suicides — violence toward oneself, the ultimate freedom from frustrating misery.

But when it comes to violence among or by children and youths, society is still shocked, particularly when such violence is at first glance inexplicable. So answers are sought. Medical scientists are looking for a gene responsible for aggression. Behavioral scientists are looking for explanations: Is violence on television to blame? The ready availability of guns? General permissiveness under the guise of liberalism? Loss of respect for social institutions — government, religion, law, marriage, authority, elders? — and so forth. Society quakes in the wake of Littleton, Jonesboro, and a host of many other, albeit less outrageous, reports of violence in the schools. What to do? Obviously, there are no simple answers, nor are the forces which generate violence necessarily uniform. Let us first consider the origin of aggression.

Not everyone who is aggressive to the point of being physically violent is a product of a society ruled by the fist, the knife, or the gun. There are children and youths raised in civilized homes with kindness and consideration who, nonetheless, because of unbearable frustrations, "relieve" themselves through violence.

Is there anyone around, no matter how gentle and civil, who did not at one time or another have a fleeting thought of smashing his fist into the wall or into someone's face, or even of killing? To be sure, most people will never take such violent action, but the thought, the feeling, is there — because of frustration and anger which are boiling over. Such feelings mostly "evaporate" as life goes on and other good feelings supplant them, or they may lie dormant for very long periods, and then — when other angry feelings are added, and all of it becomes unbearable — an explosion will take place toward others or toward oneself, verbally, physically — or violently.

Obviously then, we should look toward frustration that is unbearable in order to understand aggression and violence. We may then also learn that aggression and violence which reside in many of our youths is not that new or novel.

> *Four days before [he] ... killed his parents with an ax and then threw himself to his death from a water tower, he was reprimanded by his ... teacher ... He was worried about it. He told the boy [his friend] he had three options: "I can beat up the teacher, I can intercept the letter [of reprimand], or I can kill myself."*
>
> *... He was not seen by his classmates as an overly aggressive striver ... they saw him as a humorous boy who joked and teased good-naturedly and who enjoyed sports. And yet ... after the suicide-murders, another picture ... emerged, that of an adolescent tormented by unattained and secret aspirations ...*
> *(The New York Times, February 3, 1975)*

To make page one of *The New York Times*, the copy has to be unique, exceptional, and particularly "news." The typical, common, and representative do not make the headlines. Yet one knows that the extraordinary and the special are simply the extremes of the common we encounter in everyday life. Rare is the child who kills randomly or kills himself and butchers his parents — but far from rare are children who entertain such thoughts. Anyone who works with children on an intimate level, listens to their fantasies and analyzes their dreams, can vouch for that. Unbearable pressures, untenable double-binds, and chronic stress generate frustrations and rage that demand expression in violence to oneself and/or one's tormentors.

Humans are actors who mask inner feelings and strivings for various reasons, one of which is that society does not tolerate the expression of raw emotions. Thus, as the child develops, he tries out various roles, frequently antithetical to his real self, to defend himself against mental stress and frustration generated by unattainable needs. For example, the overly passive boy may be attempting to hide and counter inner feelings of rage, or the good-natured tease may well be covering up frustrations and anger. With time, however, such defenses tend to break down, particularly if and when additional stress is encountered and roles of passivity or playfulness are no longer adequate. The individual then shifts to a different role in order to cope, or his rage may break through in violence.

Thus we find in children and in adolescents stable behavior that is deemed more or less desirable or undesirable, periodically changing behavior, or radical changes that represent a breakdown of defenses and an emergence of inner needs and secret strivings. Fortunately, feelings of rage do not always lead to violence, for anger and aggression are deemed to be ego-alien and are quickly tucked away into our unconsciousness. Yet even when this is accomplished, there remain scars that manifest themselves as neurotic symptoms or styles of life that are marked by conflicts, pressures, and general unhappiness.

The Child as an Extension of His Parent

Generally speaking, one may classify children's stress as emanating from two major sources.

First come the personal frustrations, the anger, the poor habits and coping problems of parents and significant others that are visited upon the child as the two interact:

The father comes home after a spat with his boss. He is angry, frustrated over his inability to "tell off" his superior, and tense, afraid of losing his job. He snaps at his wife, who may understand, and at his child, who likely does not. The child's friendly greeting is countered with a frown, a dismissal, a rejection.

The teacher has difficulty maintaining discipline in his class or he had a fight with his wife, and is charged with anger. The pupil who asks a "stupid" question or does not pay attention is rewarded with sarcasm, with hurt and pain way out of proportion to his "transgression."

The mother burned a cake and feels stupid for having wasted time and effort. She encounters the child, and she projects her self-disgust upon him. Now *he* is stupid, noisy, a pain in the neck.

Needless to say, parents and teachers who are chronically dissatisfied or angry interact with the child with impatience and intolerance, or inject anger into every one of their verbalizations. The child then either learns and copies these poor behavior patterns, or creates his own maladaptive ways of coping with them as he fights back and defends himself. In any case, maladaptive behavior is basically learned. Its source can frequently be traced back to the child's mentors — parents, teachers, and other significant individuals.

The second set of pressures comes from value systems inherent in society that are projected onto our children as society, parents, or teachers use children to make up for their own failures and inadequacies. The notion, "I want my child to have everything I never had," goes far beyond acquiring toys and goodies. We want our child to be the best — the smartest and the healthiest, the best behaved, the cutest, the most popular, and the happiest — forgetting that striving for the best precludes happiness and satisfaction. Yet, "I want my child to have all that because I did [do] not have it" must prevail.

A destructive double-bind is thus created by making the child's self-esteem contingent upon the schedules of achievement we map out for him. He is only "good," i.e., accepted and loved, when he is "best." This becomes a compelling need which breaks his will to defy us and assert his "self," which in turn has a vital need of its own — to be oneself, to be independent, to be "me." His choice, then, is either compliance to maintain self-esteem as he destroys his ego, or defiance to assert his ego but lose self-esteem. Alternately, he may use role-playing and maintain a facade of one attitude or the other while the antithetical need boils away inside his inner self. Thus there is always ambivalence — to comply or defy? — and pent-up rage that will surely erupt one day or be discharged into neurotic symptoms which are basically compromises of compliance and defiance.

Parents and teachers justify their pressure tactics by proclaiming that it is in the very best interest of the child. "The child must be told." "He can do better." "She must learn responsibility." Yet when such pressures produce misery, anger, and irreparable adult-child animosities — in addition to being counterproductive — one must ask why adults persist in continuing along this track. One tells the child to do his work, to be sociable, to be productive — and the child refuses to comply. The request is repeated, the child counterattacks, and performance further deteriorates. Yet the adult continues along this road. We ask the parent or teacher why he does not give up these counterproductive admonitions. The answer one gets is the nonsensical, "Well, the child must be taught; he must be told what to do." Obviously, then, when rational people practice methods in child rearing that have no value to the child, there must be some value to the adult as he does what logic dictates not to do.

Such an individual expresses dissatisfaction with himself, a need for self-improvement, or simply frustration and anger at the expense of the helpless child — helping neither himself nor the child. To the contrary, the endless hounding and nagging, the fixing, correcting, criticizing, and pressuring for more and greater perfection set the stage for internal dissatisfaction leading to neurotic behavior or outright rage. Or at best, the child or adolescent complies — learns to lead an unsatisfactory life, and then himself becomes a nagging parent or teacher.

The Child as Society's Whipping Boy

Society is made up of individuals who have a more or less common value system. In turn, of course, society shapes a person by imposing upon him/her that value system — what is expected, what has value, what is frowned upon, what is legal and moral and what is not, and much more. By society we may mean one's immediate family and one's close-knit community, such as the one the Torah Jew interacts with in *shul* or socially. Alternately, one can look at society in a topographical fashion, noting the frenetic pressure which exists in the big city or the relatively calmer life of suburbia, or the even more peaceful existence inherent in rural living or in the ideal Torah kibbutz.

Whether we admit it or not, we are living in a materialistic, competitive world which accomplishes a great deal in technology, in enhancing human comfort, in entertainment devices, and yes, in great medical advances and other very worthwhile endeavors. Yet that materialism and competitiveness and the need to achieve ever more, and the pace at which we are tackling these challenges, adversely affect interpersonal relationships, intrapersonal feelings and our emotional-social lives. Like it or not, *"Asoi vie ess kristelt sich, asoi Yidelt sich"* — our surroundings do affect us, no matter how committed we are to Torah life. One may even wonder if, at times, to have our children learn and know more may be tinged with materialistic-achievement needs, rather than learning because that is what Torah demands of us. Let us be sure that *kinas sofrim*, the competitiveness of scholars, furthers only knowledge and not, G-d forbid, raw strife, competitiveness, and unhealthy needs.

Don't Teach Me — Fix My Child

There is a well-known story of the father who desperately wants his child to become a decent person and a productive citizen. So as the tot proceeds to enter school, his father wags his finger and says: *"Nu,* when will you be a *mensch?"* The child enters high school and again the father admonishes: "When will you become a *mensch?"* He is a Bar Mitzvah, he becomes engaged and he marries — and at each junction of life the father asks the perennial question.

This continues until the day a child is born to the son, who now himself becomes a father. The father — now grandfather — comes to see his son and grandchild to offer his good wishes and blessings. As he approaches, the son-turned-father hastily shouts: "Stop, Father, don't say a thing, don't ask me when I will become a *mensch*. For me it's too late — but the little one, let's begin to make him into a *mensch*."

The notion that one teaches best by modeling behavior rather than telling and teaching is clear to everyone. Less obvious, but perhaps more important, is to be aware that one should not teach the child the very things one is lacking himself. Such teaching, telling, and "fixing" is always tinged with anger which resides in the mentor. This anger is then visited upon the child, who now turns this anger into resentment and rage, in part because anger simply begets anger, in part because the child sees the hypocrisy, and because he must choke on his feelings and is forbidden to respond.

Parents must encourage children to express feelings — yes, even feelings of anger, albeit in a socially acceptable fashion. This is first aid for mental health. Feelings of anger when expressed early in the game will not turn into rage and into violence. Moreover, when parents are "big" enough to see that what they want of the child is really what they desire for themselves, they will learn to desist from this destructive path. And if they are "very big," they can even admit it to the child and thus teach him that one is never perfect and can admit to it without harm to one's inner pride. When this happens, then both parent and child can go on to learn, to improve, to do better — each one by himself, or even jointly, when the parent stops teaching (*to*) the child, but learns *with* the child.

Chapter Twenty-two

The Unhappy Child

nderlying most common emotional disorders is a feeling of helplessness and despair. In its most terrifying form, it is found in psychotic states or in a severe neurosis. To a lesser degree it is present in practically every negative emotional reaction, both "normal" and abnormal.

Adults have come to accept periodic feelings of unhappiness that cannot be explained. Thus we periodically "feel blue," or "have gotten up on the wrong side of our beds," or "just aren't ourselves today." Occasionally these conditions may last for somewhat longer periods and require professional help. Yet, by and large, we look at these moods as being "normal."

There are, furthermore, individuals who do not suffer periodic depressions, but whose mood is generally subdued. They seem to lack a zest for living and are prone to be melancholy. Yet these people can function well in society and are accepted as productive, if somewhat too serious, individuals.

Children's Moods

Concerning the child, our attitude seems to be quite different. Childhood is supposed to be the period of happiness, a time of carefree abandon and freedom from obligations — verily, a bed of roses. Indeed, parents usually become angry when the child speaks of feelings of unhappiness or depression. This is so, partly because the child's unhappiness tends to reflect upon our adequacy as parents, and questions our "goodness" in giving him sufficient love. Thus we repress and deny the fact that children, too, can be unhappy and suffer from anxieties and depression.

In truth, children are prone to periods of sadness no less than are adults. Their life is not one series of blissful experiences. Indeed, their suffering is more intense, and frequently more devastating. Children cannot understand or verbalize their feelings as well as adults can. Thus they cannot find relief by talking things out. Furthermore, their ego structure is relatively weaker and less stable, and their moods swing more frequently and more intensely. When they are unhappy, they are intensely so, just as their happiness is enjoyed more fully. It is this instability of mood that helps to mislead us. We deprecate their unhappiness, because we see them soon thereafter happily at play.

Unless the child's unhappiness is relieved, a habitual depressive disposition is established and he is likely to bring into adulthood this proneness for feelings of unhappiness and a vulnerability to depressive moods. The habit is learned. During adolescence children usually progress to more frequent and more intense mood swings, or they may develop a mild but all-pervasive depressive personality structure, being not really sick, but somehow never really enjoying life. Reactions differ, of course, among individuals, just as the reasons for these moods have diverse etiologies. Nonetheless, the mere fact that depressed personalities are shaped during childhood should make us more attentive to children's moods and feelings.

Only the foolhardy would attempt to formulate a global theory of anxiety or depression, one that would explain satisfactorily its nature in every given case. As it is with most emotional disorders, each individual presents a unique condition which calls for a research project all its own — to understand the reason for its development and to formulate a plan of action to resolve, or at least relieve, the problem.

To what extent hereditary endowment is involved is unclear, though it is suspected that some factors of temperament and disposition are inborn. Almost from birth some children do seem to be more or less alert, sensitive, or indifferent. Some infants do cry and fuss and seem to be unhappy, while others apparently have a relaxed disposition and seem to be content. Yet for practical purposes, little that is useful is known at this time about the genetic influence on mood.

Similarly, the child's intelligence, his body build and his nervous system — all hereditary factors — are obviously implicated. It is these factors which subtly but surely make us react to the child in certain ways and, in turn, make him act uniquely and expect a particular response from others.

Functionally, it is believed that the child's earliest environment, the first and perhaps second year of life, determine his basic outlook on life — trusting optimism or fearful pessimism. Involved are the qualitative relationships with his mother and other important people, the presence or absence of warmth, empathy, and feelings over and above meeting his physical needs. (Unless parents have such instinctual warmth and insights, books or articles will help little. Therapeutic intervention is the only known method to help parents "learn" and develop these necessary attitudes and feelings.) To be sure, when genetic factors operate, then even the warmest of parents, the most accepting and well meaning, will encounter great difficulties because the child himself will push away the warmth that is offered.

A fruitful avenue to explore is the period of childhood, when much learning takes place, and attitudes and moods are similarly learned. It is, after all, the aggregate of feelings, attitudes, and dispositions that form what is known as one's personality.

The Learned Depressions

The development in childhood of a depressive disposition may come about through simple imitative behavior or a failure in maintaining an "economy of happiness."

We know, of course, that children learn more by imitating their elders than by formal lessons. They become individuals who are kind or cruel, earnest or playful, primarily by observing their parents and adopting their ways. This is so obvious that repeating it should be pointless. Yet one continues to be amazed by the fact that in counseling parents, one hears fathers and mothers complain mostly of those shortcomings of their child of which they themselves are "guilty."

One is reminded of the father who was beating his daughter because her suitor found her wanting in that she was not a *bas talmid chacham,* a scholar's daughter. This is supposedly a joke — but on whom? Parents endow the child genetically, and also with habits, attitudes, dispositions, and models. Ignorant parents ask why their children fail to learn, unscrupulous men want to know why their children steal, and depressed women are angry when their children are unhappy.

The unhappy home produces unhappy children. Apathy, lack of involvement, and a lack of zest are learned. To treat the child, one must first treat the parents.

Probably the most basic psychological need is a feeling of worth — the possession of an adequate self-esteem. It is this feeling that seems to come closest to the vague concept we call "happiness." It is also a total lack of this self-esteem that can drive man to total despair.

Hopefully, one's basic self-esteem is laid down during the early years when there is an overabundance of love, when love is truly unconditional ("You are loved because you are"), when every little accomplishment is showered with praise, when frustrations are at a minimum and demands are few. This basic parental investment bears interest, and thus a satisfactory "economy of happiness" becomes possible. However, life being as it is, there are numerous assaults upon one's self-esteem. Parents become angry, friends may dislike the child, or his ability is questioned — and a deficit comes about in his economy of happiness. Fortunately, there are other experiences, happier ones, that "balance the budget" and restore, if not improve, the state of this economy.

Supposing, however, these assaults are excessive, or the

restorative income of satisfactions inadequate. The economy of happiness is now upset, a loss of self-esteem develops, and a depressive mood sets in.

Drugs and alcohol, food or entertainment, or all the things that supposedly make us happy, are at best temporary measures whose efficacy lasts only as long as they stimulate our nervous system, our palate, or our senses. Our basic and more permanent sense of happiness and well-being reaches us through that general feeling of trust and optimism laid down during infancy and enriched through the "income" from our environment.

As the child grows into adolescence and adulthood, there come about other factors that affect self-esteem for better and for worse. The adolescent must compete with others, and define his masculinity or her femininity. The adult must earn a living, maintain a household and function in a mature social manner. He or she must be "competent." On the negative side, the erstwhile unconditional self-esteem is challenged by the ever growing demands of "growing up." On the positive side, the adolescent or adult can choose his peer group and socialize with people whose socio-economic state is similar. Additionally, the adult is not chronically measured and weighed and compared to others.

The child is not that fortunate. His task is to acquire an education, and there are ready-made devices to measure his success or failure. His task is clearly defined; it is measured, and constantly compared with the accomplishment of others.

What, then, of the child who cannot succeed or ends up to be low man in his peer group? Must he be doomed to an irreparable loss of self-esteem, or must he act out in order to forcefully gain the satisfaction he does not find at school?

The key to a lifetime of adequate self-esteem must thus be the early-in-life learned unconditional love and worth, where competency only adds to one's well-being, but is not the determinant of one's success as a human being.

Implications for Home and School

During childhood, children learn from their parents' moods and dispositions, just as they learn behavior in general. The child's basic self-esteem regulates his moods of happiness or depression, and needs a periodic income of happiness to maintain itself.

What can the home and school do about all this? Parents must learn that skills and achievement are desirable in order to make life richer and more comfortable. However, achievement by itself cannot and must not substitute for happiness or self-esteem. The worth of the child must be governed by his *being*, not by what he is *doing*. Assaults upon his self-esteem should not be used to motivate him to learn. Self-esteem is too vital to place a price on it; the child's worth must be self-evident. Such an outlook might be viewed as being unrealistic and smacking of a vague philosophy. Yet parents can learn to enjoy their children simply by interacting with them as humans, without making specific demands of them.

The school must provide for every child, particularly for the slow and less well-endowed ones who need to bolster their self-esteem. Schools should not employ competitive methods to motivate children, an obviously unfair state of affairs and potentially dangerous to many children. Since the school professes to deal with the whole child, there must be opportunities for satisfying experiences for every child, over and above scholastic attainment. Parents should not accept a verdict that "the child refuses to learn." The proverbial horse *can* be led to the water and *can* be made to drink — when that drink is flavored appropriately and when it can be digested.

Chapter Twenty-three

Your Attention Please!

ow does one deal with that "nudgy," obnoxious, attention-seeking child? Here he sits in the classroom, forever demanding attention: acting the clown, calling out, rattling his belongings, or just being different in order to stand out. There he is at home, wanting what he wants when he wants it, instantly, outshouting his siblings and his parents, dominating the family's time and attention. At the table or in the car he must be heard first, and, if at all possible, exclusively. His needs predominate and have priority over those of all others. Yet when asked to contribute his services or attention to family matters, he is unwilling to do so.

Interestingly enough, when questioned clinically, this child sees himself as the victim rather than as the perpetrator, and blames others for his woes. Without therapeutic intervention, this "obnoxious" behavior pattern usually accelerates and worsens. Our child is unable to learn that his behavior, rather than improving his position, in actuality pushes him out of the family or social circle. He accomplishes nothing, but the behavior pattern persists.

We label all of this as "attention-getting behavior," as if such identification of a trait solves anything. We then either dismiss this matter by saying, "That's the way he is [and nothing can be done]," or take punitive countermeasures, believing that, "He must learn his lesson — he must keep quiet." Neither of these approaches work, and the situation not only remains, but worsens.

What does the child really need? A little food (far less than the baby-food jar prescribes), a little shelter (far less than our modern homes provide), and lots of attention. In this attention lie the psychological underpinnings of security, love, power, self-esteem, and much more. The need for attention is not solely a childhood phenomenon. Adults, as well, need attention. We dress up to catch the eye of others, drive prestigious cars, beautify our homes, act witty, attempt to appear prosperous, and so forth — all in order to draw the attention of others.

Conversely, we shout or act obnoxiously to intimidate others; we seek the sympathy of others; we walk and talk with mannerisms that supposedly convey meaning to others. To the extent that such maneuvers satisfy our needs, yet are socially accepted and valued, we speak of one's adjustment or maladjustment. Yet the fact that individuals persist in maintaining maladaptive behavior patterns teaches us that what is maladjustment in the eyes of society is an adjustment and adaptive behavior as (incorrectly) perceived by the protagonist. So, too, the child persists, and the (mal)adaptive behavior is maintained.

Attention and Security

An individual feels secure by virtue of the psychological assets he possesses. These assets may be one or more, or a combination of, several phenomena that "guarantee" one's physical, social, and emotional life. First, perhaps, comes a feeling of faith in oneself, one's loved ones, society as a whole, and a socio-religious system one believes in. Then there is money, the "guarantor" that supposedly buys all possible material goods, love, prestige, and power.

Equally important are the experiences of the past that help us predict the future. These experiences give us the sense of security, the belief that "I have managed before, I can do it again," a feeling that things somehow work out, and that the future will not necessarily be worse than the past. Needless to say, there are numerous other assets that are of universal value or are valued by an individual, correctly or incorrectly. The important thing is that every adult has something.

Our child is not that fortunate. He has no past to guarantee the future, no money to give him power, and self-esteem is only in the process of emerging. Concepts such as faith in others or in a social system have no meaning to him. All he has is the parent who, it is hoped, represents security to provide for his physical, social, and emotional needs. Yet this source of security is constantly in danger. First, it must be shared with his siblings. Then there are the outside obligations and personal needs of parents — jobs, social commitments, a need to read, rest, and so forth — that compete with the child for the parent's time and attention. And when parents are depressed, anxious, or emotionally preoccupied, then even when they do attend to the child, they remain emotionally distant, and the need for attention remains unsatisfied.

Thus one notes that children are most demanding when there are guests in the house or a sibling has a friend over. Our child pesters us just when we are busy on the phone or in a rush to go someplace. When the baby has to be fed or a sibling is ill, then sibling rivalry adds to his misery, and he becomes "just impossible." And when the parent has a headache or is depressed or anxious, this child shows no consideration whatsoever; he is totally "selfish."

The truth, of course, is otherwise. For it is at these times — when the parent is able to give the least attention — that the child's "security," i.e., attention, is threatened the most. Unfortunately, modern society demands a great deal of us socially and emotionally, and parents suffering from impatience, headaches, depression, anxiety, or lack of time are far from rare. To get him "off our back," we then attempt to pacify our child with toys and "things," which at best are poor substitutes for our attention. And when this finally fails to work, we say, "He is spoiled — he has it too good." Again we label, but accomplish nothing.

Thus we may understand why "good," productive, charismatic parents frequently have — all things being equal — the greatest difficulty with their children. These parents have more "competitors" for their child's need for attention. They are busier, admired by others (who are rivals to the child), and usually more impatient. This productive parent then says: "All my work is for my child; why is he so angry?" Indeed, this parent gives his child all the "things" that should make him happy. What he forgets is that it is this very productivity that robs the child of the parent's time. The "things" he gives the child are poor and unreliable substitutes. If the parent has fallen into the trap of buying off the child by giving him the "things" he demands, then he is doubly so in trouble. The child now wants the parent (i.e., attention) *and* the things. Neither one of these satisfy him. The attention is insufficiently and only grudgingly given, and the "things" are inadequate substitutes.

The Child and His Choices

The child must have "his" attention. He has several choices at his disposal. If he receives his due, then all is well. If he does not, he may use pseudo-adaptive methods that may receive social approval, but in their extreme form demand too high a price. Thus he may become overly striving, highly competitive, seductive, or a "goody-goody."

Alternately, he may be drawn to people, things, or systems which promise that highly coveted individual attention. He may join gangs where he is "special" in some way, take to the bottle or to drugs that seem to give him "love," or fall for psychopathic charlatans who peddle pseudo-love and attention. Thus, for example, do unscrupulous operators invent "religions" or "isms" that draw tens of thousands of unhappy youngsters with the promise of love and attention.

Finally, he may attempt the "obnoxious" route. "I dare you to ignore me," he says. For instance, he stomps his feet as he walks. As a child he annoys, in the classroom he clowns, and as an adolescent he acts out. When we punish him, saying, "He is asking for it," we are indeed telling the truth as it is, for when attention cannot be gotten in an adaptive fashion it will be wrenched from us in a maladaptive manner. Once this is "learned," it becomes the only way known to work, and the cycle is set up. The child demands and annoys, the parent withdraws, so now the child has to demand more. In another scenario the child is obnoxious, the parent reacts ("proving" that the obnoxious behavior "works", i.e., attention is bestowed), and this behavior is learned and reinforced.

To Give the Impossible

Our child arrives in this world and is given intense and undivided attention. For his sake and for the sake of those around him he must be weaned — but how? Attention means time, patience, and a status of uniqueness — all highly prized and not readily available commodities. Yet with some ingenuity it can be done.

First and foremost, parents and teachers and all those dealing with children must realize that "attention" is the child's lifeline, not an undeserved luxury. Secondly, our child will get it, if not graciously, then with rage and turmoil, even if he drives himself to insanity in the process as well as seriously disturbing those around him. To give him all the attention he wants, even if such were possible, would only make him into an addict craving for even more. So we must wean him; he must learn to do with less and manage with substitutes.

With some ingenuity, numerous possibilities can be explored. The talented teacher can talk to our child, yet attend to the entire class and interact with each child individually — all at the very same time. He uses his eyes — a look, a wink, a gesture. He scans the entire classroom, resting momentarily upon each face, and transmits unspoken messages: "I hear, I see, I am attending to you." Similarly, the parent can feed the child, yet interact visually or verbally with someone else. He can be on the phone with whoever is "important," yet put his arm around the child, implying, "It is really you who are important."

When in a hurry (implying lack of time for the child), one can "take time" in the form of only one minute, but with total attention. The parent thus says, "Attending to you comes first. Here is my first installment in the form of one minute. The rest will follow." At the dinner table or in the family car, the parent can orchestrate the children so that each and every one has his say yet is able to await his cue, knowing for sure that his turn will come. That parent does not throw up his hands in disgust or have his own temper tantrum. No, he wields his baton, holding one, yielding to the other, or he brings about a performance in concert: "Let's hear what Aaron has to say, so Sarah can respond and we all have a conversation."

Every child can be unique, as every human truly is. One person is helpful in special situations; one child is athletic; another is pleasant to talk to. As it is with food or rest, attention given before it is direly needed requires far lesser amounts than when it is wrested from us by the "starving" child. Similarly, gifts given when not expected or asked for are more potent than the present wrenched from us through emotional blackmail. The spontaneous gift, however small, makes the child think: "As busy as she is, my parent is thinking of me."

Giving the child independence, exposing him to various social situations, having him explore the world, and allowing him to find his own pleasures will equally so give him healthy substitutes for parental attention, and make the weaning process easier. Conversely, the dependent child says, "You have caused me to be socially backward, so now you attend to me."

When parents take total responsibility for their child's "fun" by demanding that he be always happy, and suggesting sources of fun, then the child may well turn to the parent and demand constant entertainment. When parents are depressed, anxious, or preoccupied, it would be best to remove themselves entirely from the scene, rather than be *near* the child but not be *with* him.

With patience, ingenuity, and a little time, a great deal of attention can be given. Then with tokenism and substitution the weaning process can take place. If the parent can truly enjoy the time he spends with his child — even at the "expense" of his job or household duties — then both parent and child will gain in pleasure, in meaning, in time well spent. Is this not what life is all about?

Chapter Twenty-four

The Stubborn Child

hy are some children stubborn and contrary? Why is every demand made of them resisted fiercely, and every request countered with "no"? Such children make life miserable for themselves, and for their parents and teachers. Their need to say no, to argue and to bicker, seems to transcend the child's own needs. It would seem as if the result of whatever is going on is of no importance other than to serve as a vehicle for these children to prevail with their no and contrariness.

As adolescents and adults they have difficulty in getting along with others, because they somehow must say no. When we suggest to meet at 6, they counter with, "Why not 7?" They ask us our opinion, then proceed to argue against it. Every utterance is dissected, every opinion questioned, and such hassles become a burden people are unwilling to tolerate. As a result, these no-sayers remain alone and alienated. Yet as long as their no prevails they are willing to lose all, and they frequently succeed in doing just that.

Stubbornness, like all human traits, is learned. Children are born neither compliant nor defiant. Obviously, then, it must be something we do, or appear to be doing, that becomes a model for the child to be obstinate, stubborn, and contrary.

Arbitrary and Reasonable Styles in Child Rearing

What does it mean to the child when we are arbitrary? How does he feel when we say, "Do it because I said so, and don't ask any questions"? Obviously, he feels no different than does anyone who is ordered about without rhyme or reason: He is enraged. The arbitrary approach suggests to the child coercion and total disregard for his own needs and wishes. This he must oppose at all costs. Indeed, he is willing to destroy himself in order to save his will, his being, his need to be himself. Thus there is set up a power struggle between parent and child. The arbitrariness of the parent is met with blind resistance in the child. The child now "learns" the arbitrary style. He, in turn, generates his own arbitrariness, only to be met by parental resistance — and the spiral of ever-increasing strife is fashioned. The parent, in his frustration, heightens his arbitrariness, for "the child must learn to listen," and the child resists with matching ferocity.

This battle of wills never really ends. Long after the child has grown up, even after the parent has departed, the phantom struggle against authority, i.e., arbitrariness, must go on. In its extreme, this tragic drama is finally acted out in mental hospitals where individuals sit with passive resistance, "enjoying" their gain in saying no to mankind.

On the other hand, the reasonable style generates in the child numerous thoughts and feelings that are positive. He learns that people do not live by power but by reason. Thus he can listen to reason, and himself employ reason as he interacts with others.

In addition, feelings of self-esteem and self-worth come about: "I am a somebody, I have ideas, I am worth listening to." Moreover, the reasonable approach sets up conditions that make child rearing easy, if not pleasurable. This is so because reasonableness suggests, as the dictionary defines it, being agreeable, being moderate and nonarbitrary, and using sound judgment. Who could refuse any demand that is moderate and agreeable, and dictated by sound judgment? Should the reasonable style prevail in our homes, our children would have little difficulty with such reasonableness, and in turn learn to become reasonable individuals.

The Difficulty With Being Reasonable

Why, then, do adults act unreasonably, or at least appear to our young to be arbitrary and capricious, particularly when reasonableness is easy on our children and ourselves, while inflexibility and arbitrariness make child rearing a chore? Yet, since parents frequently find the authoritarian-arbitrary route the one which seems to get immediate results, there are obviously certain difficulties with the reasonable approach. These seem to stem from several sources. To begin with, there are parents and teachers, themselves products of arbitrary child rearing, who find it only natural to act likewise in relation to their young. Then there are spurious beliefs that "parents *must* be listened to," as if such a decree is axiomatic and automatically known to all infants and children.

Similarly, some adults deem it insulting having to explain to their charges the whys of their directives, while others believe that children must learn to take no for an answer as an exercise in self-discipline in order not to be "spoiled." Still others fear that giving a reason for their demands might give the child an opening, an opportunity to question the parent's reason. Thus parents, for one reason or another, frequently subscribe to the authoritarian-arbitrary approach in child rearing, and unreasonableness prevails.

Learning to Say No

Besides the arbitrary approach that generates negativism in children, parents actually teach their children to say no. We know, of course, that behavior is learned through modeling — the child observes and copies. Thus our child copies what we do, rather than what we want him to do.

Faulty child-rearing practices, which rely on verbal admonitions rather than on modeling, are heavily loaded with literally hundreds and thousands of dos and don'ts, and equally as many nos. So our child learns not what we want him to do, but how to say no. Thus we observe our child, in tragicomic fashion, muttering no endlessly to himself, or as an automatic response to any question or request. Behavior remains unchanged, but a new repertoire of no and negativism has been learned.

The many nos we direct toward our children are not necessarily due to any evil or selfishness within us. Nor are all nos the result of our arbitrariness. Many nos originate from certain environmental conditions in our lifestyle, personal hangups, and social expectations that make us seem arbitrary to our children and make for the proliferation of nos and don'ts. We pride ourselves that ours is a child-oriented society. Indeed, nothing is too good for our children. Yet our environment is structured to restrict children's natural tendencies to explore, to do, to play, to experiment.

Here we have a beautiful, pastel-colored wall. What an ideal surface for our child to write on with the crayons we bought him! There is the highly polished cocktail table. What a perfect roadway over which his cars and trucks could travel! We must say no to these activities, but can the child really understand? Do we appear reasonable to him? Then there is the carpet and our richly upholstered dining room chairs. The child should eat but not dirty the chair, walk about but not leave footprints on the carpet.

There is the backyard and sidewalk where the child may play, but she must not wander into the roadway. There are knobs and buttons on stoves and appliances to which she is naturally attracted (note the popularity of the busy-box), but which she must not touch. Cupboards are filled with our best chinaware that seem identical to the toy dishes we buy for her. There are the attractive knickknacks that invite touching, or mommy's rings that look so pretty. Again we must say no, and again no.

What Can We Reasonably Expect?

Besides our physical environment that makes for constriction, there are social expectations that make us exact behaviors of our children that may be unreasonable for any given age. Can young children really sit still when we expect them to, or for the length of time we require of them? Can they walk when they are pro-grammed to run? Can they resist hopping on and off the curb in order to walk "properly" and safely? Can our child understand that it is reasonable to be denied a lollipop in order not to spoil his ap-petite or invite cavities? Or go to bed, just when he is having so much fun? Can he grasp that it is great to play but not to get dirty? Can he comprehend that it is fine to climb a tree, or run about, but that one must also watch out and be ever so careful? When children are older, how do they feel when we tell them to go be independent and have fun, but to report to us at an appointed hour? In all of these cases our restrictions or nos may or may not be reasonable, yet they surely appear to the child to be arbitrary, capricious, unreasonable, and constrictive.

What Parents Can and Must Do

For our child to become a reasonable, flexible, and accommo-dating adult, we ourselves must assume a reasonable posture. This does not by any means imply a wishy-washy approach.

To begin with, the child's wishes must be respected, though not necessarily complied with. This means that we must listen and truly attempt to understand his side of the story. Occasionally letting him "win" does not imply inconsistency, only that we are reason-able, human, and able to lose. This will enable him to do likewise.

Bickering, nitpicking, and endless argument have no place in the home. Such a style is self-perpetuating as a way of life, and ac-complishes nothing. Notions such as "Parents must be listened to," "Children must learn self-control and how to take no for an an-swer," or "Father knows best" make no sense to the child. Children should believe that, though parents know more, they are not infal-lible. For the short term, the idea that parents do have flaws may make the child feel a little less secure, yet it will save him the bitter disappointment later on. However, because parents are not ab-solutely sure of their position is no reason for the child not to comply. The parent may say, "I believe that this is not quite right," even though he has no real evidence that this is so. Feelings and hunches also have a place in life.

Similarly, parents need not fear explaining their wishes to the child. To do so is a sign of strength, not of weakness. Such a parent does not fear being challenged, yet can stick by his guns regardless. Saying: "I want you to do thus because of such a reason" softens the arbitrariness, but need not dilute the power of our conviction, nor the expectation of being listened to. Even if the child cannot comprehend the reason or agree with it, there is still the satisfaction that his wishes are not simply dismissed out of hand. There is a reason why or why not. Even the very young child at a pre-verbal level can distinguish between the arbitrary no and the reasonable "because ..." Our tone of voice, our posture, our facial expression tell it all.

Some Practical Suggestions

With a little ingenuity we can almost completely avoid the harsh and cold nos that sound so oppressive and arbitrary. We can usually present choices that are agreeable to us, yet make the child feel that she, too, has some say. For example, we can say to her: "You can have orange juice or grapefruit juice," "You can go to bed any time between 9:00 and 9:30," or, "You cannot have soda, but you may have punch." With a little thought we can say, "I don't think so," "Better not," "Perhaps later," "We'll see," or use other, similar phraseology that conveys the meaning of no, yet provides substitutes, possibilities, and notions of reasonableness. Phraseology such as "Because I don't want you to" should have no place in child rearing.

Of course, no one in his right mind would advocate disregard for order or for property. Yet, to avoid sounding arbitrary and harsh, and to save our child from pathological rage and frustration, our physical environment must be rearranged and child-proofed. Attractive items which are breakable, expensive, or dangerous must not be permitted to beckon our child so that we must stand guard with our nos and don'ts.

Perhaps, when children are very young, our furnishings should be more sturdy and more resistant to children's handling. Rooms can be rearranged, furnishings can be shifted around, and fragile knickknacks kept out of reach. And some chances must be taken with our child doing some damage if he is not to be bombarded with endless nos and don'ts. Most important, some space must be provided for him where there are practically no restrictions to his handling materials or exploring space.

Concerning the child's safety and his acquisition of "good manners," one must look at things from the child's point of view. Is it really possible for him? Does it seem reasonable to him? Honestly, we do not know, for we are adults and do not feel like a child or think like one. Only on the analyst's couch can we, for example, recover an experience where a 3-hour car ride was experienced by the child as his being literally chained and imprisoned.

If we are hung-up on dirt and orderliness, overly anxious about physical safety, and excessively concerned about what our neighbors will say, let us not bequeath this neurotic legacy to our children. Our society is in the grip of an epidemic of emotional maladjustments because of such concerns. These make us appear to our children as arbitrary tyrants who care little for their wishes and happiness.

When dispatching a child to bed to protect his health, or depriving him of candy to assure the health of his teeth, or disallowing freedom of movement to keep him safe, saying to the child, "It's for your own good," has little meaning. He simply cannot understand. To him, such actions or restrictions mean arbitrariness and unreasonableness. All we accomplish then is to have him become a stubborn and contrary individual, albeit physically healthy, blessed with beautiful teeth, and oh so safe!

The avoidance of strict rules bordering on tyranny does not mean anarchy and total disregard for health and safety. What is necessary are rules which are reasonable, possible trade-offs between joy and safety, and some ingenuity to do what is good for the child in a manner he can digest.

Chapter Twenty-five

The Hyperactive Child

arious behavior disorders ranging from mild to severe, with diverse etiologies or origins and expressing themselves very differently, are frequently identified by a major symptom: hyperactivity. The afflicted child is described as being unable to sit still, squirming incessantly, getting into things (both literally and figuratively), poking and pushing others around him, flitting from one thing to the next, and being unable to stick with any one activity for an extended period of time.

One result of this behavior is that the parent finds it exasperating to keep up with the child's demands for attention or to run interference for the many troubles he gets himself into. Admonitions or threats are to no avail. One gets the uncanny feeling that the child deliberately gets himself into trouble and actually invites the resulting punishment.

Since he cannot attend to the task at hand, nor sit still long enough for learning to take place, the child usually develops similar problems in his school environment. Unable to concentrate, he cannot learn, despite his possessing the ability to do so. This inability to concentrate is usually interpreted as an unwillingness to learn, and sets the stage for teacher-child conflict. However, because of his hyperactive disposition, he must do *something*. This takes the form of poking or pushing others, moving about incessantly, producing various noises or distractions — all to the annoyance of the teacher and his classmates. It is no wonder, then, that even kind and understanding teachers describe such children as obnoxious and exasperating, and as greatly disturbing to the normal conduct of the classroom.

Yet beneath this willful and destructive behavior, one can detect a good deal of unhappiness and, quite frequently, a real — albeit frustrated — effort to control motility and conform to the environmental demands.

Diagnostic and Descriptive Problems

What can parents and teachers do to help this child? A good deal of caution is in order when one attempts to fit any one child into a category on the basis of a symptom or behavior description. First and foremost is the problem of measurement and lack of objectivity. The child who may be designated hyperactive and troublesome by one adult, may seem to another to be quite normal. Furthermore, each adult has periods when he can tolerate this difficult behavior, more or less, depending upon his own state of emotions at that time and the particular situation which is frustrating the child. Thus, for example, the very same behavior will seem to be different when the parent is tense or trying to sleep than when he is relaxed or in the mood to do things. Similarly, the teacher who is presenting a new and difficult lesson to his class will react to annoyance which would go unnoticed in a "doing" situation, such as an arts-and-crafts period.

Secondly, it is far from resolved whether hyperactivity as such is an entity that can be treated or considered by itself. It may well be that a number of different disorders manifest themselves in hyperactivity, much as elevated body temperature is a symptom of a variety of physical ills. In addition, it is not at all clear whether or not every type of hyperactivity has a different meaning, and we may be lumping together under one heading very different behaviors, which may or may not require different ways of handling.

Nonetheless, the condition is prevalent enough, and sufficiently disturbing to parents and teachers, to make it worthwhile to consider the various possibilities. Specifically, one wants to know what has brought about the condition, what one can do to alleviate it, and to what extent we can "force" the child to inhibit motility, to sit still and pay attention, and to manage himself in a fashion which will not annoy the adults to the point of exasperation.

Inhibiting Motility

In observing "normal" motility, one notes at least three factors which seem to be implicated: age, neurological organization, and emotional state. Though these may be separated for the sake of clarity, an interrelationship among them obviously exists.

None of us, of course, is ever perfectly still. Imperceptible as they may be, some body movements always take place. Similarly, all of us have limits to what extent we can attend to, and persist in, a task, and to what extent we can be distracted. By comparison, the infant *always* squirms and moves about, attends to things only fleetingly, and is quickly and easily distracted. As he grows older, a distinct progression in all of this is noticeable. He squirms less, is able to attend to things for increasing periods of time, and is less easily distracted. Though not the only factor, physical maturation is thus clearly implicated as inhibiting random movements, enabling the child to attend to and to concentrate on one task for increasing periods of time.

Secondly, certain kinds of brain damage manifest themselves in disturbed motor function, such as tremors, paralysis, or spasms. Such disturbed motor function seems to be "driven" and not under the control of the individual. Movements come about without having been initiated by the individual, and are executed not in accordance with the individual's intent. To the observer, the person thus afflicted is constantly on the move, and his physical movements are distracting to others and even to himself. It is generally believed that certain hyperactive children suffer from this type of minimal neurological dysfunction and thus are not in complete control of their movements. Nor are they as able as others to attend to relevant matters, and to shut out distracting stimuli. As a result, their behavior is "driven" and their personality adversely affected. Their general intelligence may not necessarily deviate from the norm, and they may appear to be normal in every other way. Yet their ability to inhibit motility, to attend and concentrate, and to tolerate distractions may be impaired.

Finally, there is also a relationship between emotions and body movements. The very word "emotion" connotes "to move." The surge of strong emotions seems to produce an impelling force to move, to do something. Behavior manifestations of emotional origin are many. There are tremors, general agitation, random body movements and tics, and also purposeful behavior to work off the accumulated "psychic energy." Thus housewives throw themselves into housecleaning; men have spurts of work activity; others chop wood or go out just to do something. Similarly, the hyperactive child may be suffering from emotional problems of which hyperactivity is the result of emotions that seek expression in activity.

Unfortunately, because the hyperactive child's behavior invariably brings him into conflict with adult authority — his parents and teachers — and frequently with his peers as well, interpersonal relationships deteriorate, thus aggravating the original problem and compounding the difficulties. A vicious cycle is created, and the hyperactive child is, at least to some extent, frequently socially maladjusted. There is always, then, an emotional component that accounts, at least in part, for the child's hyperactivity, frequently secondary to the original problem, but equally disturbing.

Diagnosis and Treatment

By no means are all children who are brought for examination because of hyperactivity found to be so clinically. Frequently, the condition is rather superficial or transitory and symptomatic of some emotional disturbance related to the child's present interpersonal life and/or with school adjustment. When the underlying cause is discovered and parents and teachers take steps to improve the situation, the symptoms often disappear.

When, however, a chronic situation exists, careful study is in order to determine the possible causes and to find ways and means to ameliorate the condition. The first question we should ask ourselves is whether there is now also a disturbed parent-child or teacher-child relationship. Usually this exists, at least as a secondary condition, as evidenced by the mere fact that the child has been brought in for study. We can pinpoint the conflict area further by determining whether the child is more hyperactive with some people or under certain circumstances. For example, one frequently finds that when the child stays with a relative or when the family is on vacation, things dramatically change for the better. Obviously, then, certain conditions or particular relationships which are in need of change are implicated.

When this part of the "vicious cycle" is broken, all concerned usually find themselves dramatically relieved, and the air is cleared for a concerted effort to ferret out the problem and to solve it. Curiously, when the secondary problem is resolved, more often than not the primary problem no longer exists. This is so because the original cause for the child's hyperactivity and disturbed behavior may have been transitory or developmental and had improved spontaneously long ago. Another possibility is that the improved emotional climate that has been achieved serves both the current conflict and the more chronic problem, which was largely emotional to begin with.

In any case, regardless of the cause, present relationships must be improved before any real solution can be hoped for. This, of course, is more easily said than done, because involved here are not only the child's behavior, but the parent's or teacher's emotional state, the anxieties the child arouses, the adult's self-concept which is threatened by the child, and the unconscious conflicts that this disturbed relationship has aroused. Nonetheless, it is a task which *must* be accomplished.

Hyperactivity that has its origin in a developmental lag or in neurological dysfunction is usually associated with other symptoms which can be detected by psychological tests. In that case, the perceptual-motor area is disturbed and intellectual functioning is quite uneven. This may manifest itself in general clumsiness, disturbed gait, or ineptness with pencils or crayons. Developmentally, the child may have begun sitting, standing, or walking at a relatively late age, and did not master other motor tasks, such as bicycling or skating, as well as other children do. In the school situation, reading, writing, and spelling cause him particular problems, which are especially frustrating, because general intelligence is not impaired. The child himself is frustrated: "Why can't I master these skills as others do?" Here, too, there is generally an emotional component which aggravates the situation, at least in a secondary fashion, and thus needs resolution. Yet even here, where the problem is organic, there is a good deal that can be done. If the situation is due to a developmental lag, expectations relating to inhibiting motility, concentration, learning to read, etc., should be drastically modified, and formal learning may have to be postponed. Older children in whom neurological dysfunction is assumed to be responsible for learning and subsequent behavior problems may be helped by allowing for their deficiencies rather than by trying to overcome them through force.

Specific methods and procedures are available to teachers trained in special education. Expectations should be lower and a relaxed climate will be helpful. In general, hyperactivity and clumsiness must be overlooked, because *intentional* inhibition and control of motor function by the afflicted child usually result in the opposite, while a relaxed attitude brings better results. This is similar to the fact that when we carry something precious and are particularly careful *not* to drop it, or drive a car while being tense and are consciously intent on *not* having a mishap, chances are greater for an accident to occur than when a relaxed attitude is adopted.

In the school situation, the child must be given greater leeway in performance, and neatness should not be stressed. The child should be permitted to use special "crutches," such as stencils or rulers. Extraneous distractions should be kept to a minimum, and learning periods kept in line with the child's concentration span. In some cases, certain medications may help relax the child, and though these will not cure the condition, they may help the here-and-now secondary situation. Psychotherapy to provide a corrective emotional climate is almost always helpful. Specialists, including neurologists, psychologists, and educators skilled in special education, should be consulted. So-called resource rooms are useful, but care needs to be exercised not to allow the child to be stigmatized.

Prognosis

Prognosis is generally not particularly poor. If the hyperactivity has a largely emotional basis, or at least a secondary emotional problem exists, this can be dealt with, though time and effort will be needed. Hyperactivity or disinhibition which are due to a developmental lag are best left to maturation and nothing should be done. Of course, the emotional climate must, in any case, be kept at an optimum state.

Hyperactivity, concentration problems, and perceptual-motor dysfunction which have a neurological basis may improve spontaneously; children frequently outgrow it.

In other cases, individuals develop compensatory mechanisms that overcome more or less successfully such deficiencies through the cultivation of certain interests or the pursuit of certain tasks that do not endanger their self-esteem. This, of course, is far easier for adults than for children. Administration of drugs should be left in the hands of experienced experts, and should always be monitored.

Parents and teachers usually have stereotyped expectations and molds into which all children must fit. This must not obtain in dealing with the hyperactive child. Flexibility, a relaxed attitude, and modified expectations should be the rule. In addition, because this child is forcibly placed with other "normal" children who *can* do things, his self-esteem is constantly under attack, and therefore he needs much support from all those around him.

Unfortunately, the hyperactive child engenders in the adult a mirror response: the adult, too, becomes agitated, excitedly eager to "do something." This is not what this child needs. A calm attitude and low emotional intensity are called for to soothe the child and relax him. Regardless of the origin of his particular condition, this is an effective antidote for excitability or hyperactivity. The good news is that when properly dealt with, such children, when they reach adulthood, frequently become successful in many endeavors, though they may continue to be unable to sit and read for extended periods of time. So what?

Chapter Twenty-six

Children's Aggressiveness

Overt and Covert Aggression

he term "aggressive behavior" is usually reserved for situations when some physical act of violence takes place — temper tantrums, hitting, shouting, and so forth. Practically all parents are concerned when their children manifest such behavior, and usually concerted efforts are made to control aggressiveness. By and large children do learn to control such aggression, and parents then consider themselves successful in having taught their children how to suppress their hostility.

This, however, is not the entire story. Frequently, aggressiveness is not that simply dismissed. It goes underground and reappears in a disguised form as sarcasm, gossip, "practical joking," and other emotionally hurtful behavior, or it lies dormant for periods of time, only to explode in violence later on. Furthermore, with some people it can become converted into mental or physical illness. Thus, while overt aggressiveness has been controlled, its roots have not been destroyed. The child has learned to control his acts of aggression; he has not learned to manage his feelings of hostility and aggressiveness.

Thus one finds within a law-abiding society relatively little, if any, overt physical aggression. However, instances of interpersonal friction, gossip, sarcasm, hurtful witticism, chronic complaining, and similar types of behavior are commonplace. Additionally, there are many mental or physical ills that have their origin in, or are aggravated by, improper management of one's aggressiveness.

What is needed, then, is the management and alleviation of one's inner anger and hostility rather than the control of manifest aggressive behavior. Managing one's feelings is far more difficult than controlling behavior. It is relatively easy not to strike an adversary; it is practically impossible to "turn off" one's feelings and suspend anger, hostility, or other emotions. Emotions and their management are part of a person's character. They develop over a period of many years; any change, if at all possible, takes much effort, time, and determination. Character is formed during the very early years of an individual's life. It is shaped by numerous factors, including genetic endowment and environment, and principally by the way the child is dealt with by his parents and other important adults during these formative years.

In considering the control of aggression, then, it is important to turn to the early years and understand why aggression occurs in the first place, how anger is to be dealt with, and how it can be expressed in a socially acceptable manner.

Aggressive Behavior in Infancy

Feelings of anger and hostility are inevitable in the process of growing up. Every child must experience at one time or another frustration, the thwarting of a need or desire. Even the baby who is "born with a silver spoon in his mouth" cannot obtain instant gratification of all his wants. He, too, must wait for mother to come running, warm his bottle, or change his diaper. He is also faced with "powerful" forces which are frustrating him and with which he cannot cope at all, such as pain, boredom, or illness. Additionally, the child must frequently frustrate his own need to lash out at his frustrating "adversaries," i.e., parents, siblings, or peers, because he has learned that to lash out is to invite ostracism or counter-aggression. The reaction to frustration is anger; and the infant, who cannot state his feelings, shows the very same physiological reaction to anger as does the adult — flushing, accelerated heartbeat, thrashing about, and crying.

Parents may handle this type of situation in one of three ways. They may let the child cry it out in order to "teach him" frustration tolerance; they may be at his beck and call to answer his every need with dispatch, or they may find some method between these extremes. Common sense dictates that a middle road is best. It is important to know, however, where this middle road is *as the child sees it,* and the likely consequences of too much or too little frustration in infancy.

The infant lives in the present. He does not have the concept of time, nor does he relate the experiences of the past or the expectations of the future to his present needs. He cannot know that because his mother has fed him in the past, she will not abandon him in the future. Nor can he conceive that there is a refrigerator nearby with an adequate supply of milk, and that he is among adults who care. Thus, to need food and not have it immediately is obviously a frightening experience for him. His world is hopeless and harsh; nobody cares for his needs; he is angry. He cries, thrashes about, and may exhibit physiological correlates (such as holding his breath) because he is terrified.

He has not learned to tolerate frustration; he has learned to view his environment with anger and distrust. In extreme cases such children grow up lacking a basic trust of their environment and of people. They need everything — and they need it now. They cannot wait and postpone gratification, because if they don't get it now they're afraid they never will. They are perpetually angry. Later on they may handle their anger in various ways in order to exist in society — displacing it on the young and helpless, cloaking it in some fashion or even internalizing it. These mechanisms may make life in society possible, but they do not serve to lessen the perpetual anger within.

Conversely, children whose every whim is satisfied with dispatch learn to view their environment as a never-ending paradise where every wish is fulfilled. They develop a degree of optimism and expectation that society does not tolerate. To get their way, such children later on manipulate their parents by whining, begging, complaining of aches and pains, or employing threats of one kind or another. Even if parents are willing to tolerate such behavior, others are not. The result again will be aggression, because this child does not know what it means to be thwarted. When subsequently frustrated, he will be angry and strike out.

The middle road does not simply mean halfway between two extremes. What is needed is a slow buildup of frustration tolerance, together with the development of a basic trust commensurate with the individual's age and understanding of the world around him. The adult, for example, can go hungry for hours without undue feelings of frustration when he knows that food will be available at a more or less specific time and place. The hungry child can be placated by being told that supper will be ready in half an hour or so. He will not be satisfied when told that a much longer wait is necessary. The infant cannot be calmed at all. No explanation or assurance will help. Thus there is a gradient in the ability to tolerate frustration, which depends upon understanding, previous experiences, and a general trust of one's environment. The infant has relatively little understanding; his past experiences are not readily related to the present and future, and his basic trust is in the formative stage. At this point in the infant's life, an excessive demand to tolerate frustration can have the very opposite effect. He may learn not to trust, to seek always immediate gratification if he is to get any at all.

To be sure, there are situations when frustration is inevitable: the infant is in pain and we cannot relieve it; the grocery delivery is late and there is no formula for a bottle. There is still something parents can do. Remembering that the infant's anger is aggravated by his feelings of hopelessness about the future and a lack of trust, we can provide at least an environment that shows that there is hope, someone does care and can be trusted. Words have no meaning, but soft reassuring sounds, patting the baby's head, holding and cuddling him speak a powerful language of trust and concern. These gestures can substitute, at least for a while, and show the infant that his environment is not sterile, someone does care, and help is forthcoming. That is why kisses can heal wounds and holding the hungry infant will stop his crying until the bottle is ready. Infants do have a way of "knowing" through empathy of this concern, and will thus be helped to develop a basic trust and tolerate frustration temporarily for ever-increasing periods of time.

Aggressive Behavior in Childhood

Aggressive behavior during childhood does not appear suddenly out of nowhere. It is usually a more "mature" expression of earlier aggressiveness. The child who hits or throws temper tantrums has "graduated" from an infancy of excessive crying spells, holding his breath, or similar behavior. The task for the adult, then, is not just to control the child's aggressive behavior, but to change the feelings and attitudes which have developed during infancy and are responsible for the manifest aggression. This task is a most trying one for parents and teachers. On the one hand, the child must be shown love, concern and acceptance, while at the same time his behavior is not tolerated and openly disliked.

Unfortunately, aggressive behavior has a way of perpetuating itself. The aggressive child is unhappy and angry and lashes out. This behavior provokes retaliation from other children or adults which, in turn, makes for more unhappiness and anger — and the cycle repeats itself. This cycle can be broken when one intervenes, not at the "lashing out" stage, but at an earlier one where there is just unhappiness and anger. When an adult interests himself in the "why" of a child's anger and unhappiness, several avenues are opened by which overt aggression can be averted.

If the child basically distrusts people and manifests such distrust by anger and aggressiveness, an educative process becomes necessary to show the child that people can be trusted. The one adult who really cares can become the prototype for all of humanity and show the child that others do have regard for him. As is true with education in general, the process is a lengthy and arduous one, but not impossible. Most important, it is the only effective way to deal with such a situation. To be successful, the adult must have an honest interest in children in general, and in this child's problem in particular. It requires much time and patience and persistence even when the child, in order to test the genuineness of the adult, reacts with hostility and distrust.

Of particular importance is to teach the child to express feelings, even angry ones, provided this is done in a socially acceptable fashion. The child says: "Aunt Soshie is coming. I hate her." You, the parent, are shocked. Another time the child goes even further. When you, the parent, have to deny his wishes, he shocks you with, "I wish you weren't my mommy!" Teach him: "Yes, sweetheart, you are angry. So say it, but say it nicely: 'Mommy, I am angry because you do not do as I wish.' That's okay, and I, the parent, am sorry that you are angry — but such is life." One has negative feelings, and one should and needs to express them. But to be a social being, this needs to be done in a socially acceptable manner.

There are situations when the child's character is not truly set in being perpetually angry. There may be simply, for some reason, frequent occasions which rightfully arouse feelings of anger. Here one can implement the aforementioned lesson by giving the child an opportunity to express his anger verbally to a sympathetic adult without fear of ridicule or ostracism. When the adult recognizes and accepts such feelings of anger, a kind of catharsis takes place — some of the anger is spent in speaking of it and the need for an overt act is lessened. There is no particular magic in accepting or recognizing feelings of anger and hostility. The child, for example, feels that he has been cheated in a competitive game. He swears vengeance and readies himself to seek out his antagonists and punish them physically. All that is frequently necessary is for the adult to say, "Tell me all about it," and while the child does so, to interject with statements that reflect your recognition and validation of the feeling of anger. Thus, telling the child that you understand his anger and frustration serves to take the punch out of it and helps him express it at least in a minor key.

There are further occasions when there is anger without the child consciously knowing its cause. In such situations, anger and hostility can be channeled and acted out without harming anyone. Activities which involve competitiveness, ambitiousness, or achievement are, within limits, socially acceptable and even useful. They may at the same time serve to express unconscious feelings of aggressiveness and should be encouraged.

All these methods — re-education, catharsis, or displacement of aggression in a socially acceptable way — can be used successfully at one time or another before aggression becomes overt and turns into hostility. There are times, however, when one is confronted with the final act and must cope with children who are about to act aggressively toward adults or toward other children. How does one manage at such times?

The Management of Active Aggression

It has frequently been said that it is well to let children express their aggression. To suppress aggression, it has been argued, is psychologically harmful in that aggression not discharged builds up internally. Conversely, when it is permitted to be expressed, it drains off the hatred and maintains an equilibrium. Such arguments are unsound and just not true.

In the first place, even if one allows a child to act aggressively towards him, such behavior will not be tolerated by others. The child who has habitually been expressing his aggression will only be doubly angered when he comes in contact with his larger society which will not permit him to do so any longer.

Furthermore, repeated aggressive behavior without restrictions will simply teach the child that this is "normal," it is sanctioned and is a "successful" way to deal with others. His once tentative trials of aggressiveness become rewarded and the aggressive habit is formed. Research clearly shows that this is so. Expressing aggression does not reduce subsequent tendencies to act aggressively.

So the child must be stopped. But how? Forceful physical

restraint is obviously not the answer, for such restraint or counter-aggression points out to the child that aggression is an effective method with which to get one's way. He is simply too weak at this time and cannot be "aggressive enough" — he must bide his time or pick on those weaker than he is. Again, research supports this to be so. Children who are punished physically are more aggressive and tend to use violent action to get their way. Physical punishment becomes a "model" for the child, showing him how one copes with problems. Aggression begets aggression. On the other hand, gentle, loving restraint may be in order when things get out of hand. One then holds — with love — yet restrains the angry child.

Skillful teachers and parents have somehow a bag of tricks, an armament of methods with which they are able to prevent aggression from becoming overt. They maintain a climate of tolerance and emotional well-being where even the usually aggressive child tends to be less so.

When, however, aggression is about to take place, timing is essential in moving quickly before the act. Again, astute adults seem to have the ability to sense when trouble is about to erupt, and they quickly use diversionary tactics to avoid the clash — a change of activity, a rearrangement of groups, and so forth.

Children can be shown that social living is not merely restrictive, but has a positive value. Let us take an example. The child has a doll which she is asked to share with another. To share means to give up — an idea the child deems to be a loss. The young child cannot be expected to realize that our entire social system is based upon sharing. With but little ingenuity this can be shown. Instead of giving up her "mother-child" doll play, it can be extended to include the other child as "father" or "big sister" and heighten her own enjoyment. Children can understand social concepts if they are concrete and meaningful for them. They will not understand, nor willingly cooperate, when decisions are arbitrary, when the adult moralizes or simply disapproves without explanation. Very young tots, who simply grab, obviously cannot be reasoned with. Nonetheless, the adult should not himself grab the item back. Gentle removal may help, or distractions — or substitution of another toy.

In general, aggression thrives when there is habitually too much or too little discipline or direction from adults, when standards are excessive and arbitrarily enforced, and a generally tense atmosphere prevails. Adult interference can be effective when it is fair and consistent, when the adult believes in what he does, and when *together* with disapproval of the child's *act* there is basic understanding and acceptance of him as a person, including his feelings.

Chapter Twenty-seven

Violence and Your Child

Man's Search for Explanations

an's interest in knowing himself is probably as old as man himself. In times of social upheaval, or when individuals engage in particularly antisocial behavior, this interest becomes heightened. Invariably, people want to know why the assassin committed his crime, why a group has taken to violence, or why a social system has broken down.

Pat answers and explanations do not seem to be too difficult to come by. Each of us has his theory about why there is violence in the streets, why sexual morality has broken down, why youth rebels. Behavioral scientists, too, come under pressure to do their share of explaining, and some have indeed "found" *the* reason for these outbreaks of overt violence and immorality. They are not difficult to find. Read your newspaper — there they are.

We have been told that to blame are the impact of television, the breakdown of parent-child communications, youth's alienation, inadequate family cohesion, youth's reaction to sexual repression, to excessive permissiveness or, conversely, to too many restrictions, and so on. The explanations are duly catalogued and shelved, and life goes on.

The Danger of Oversimplification

Such explanations grossly oversimplify the complexity of human behavior. It is naive to single out one factor or one type of experience and blame our ills on it. Human behavior is the result of a great many factors. It is "overdetermined"; that is, multiple factors combine, cancel out, and interact in a fashion that makes it practically impossible to disentangle the threads.

We search for simple and quick explanations because behavioral eruptions frighten us. We must know why it happened! When the villain is identified, we sigh with relief. Yet, all that comes about is the (false) relief of our anxieties, the knowledge that the blame lies elsewhere, and that "something should be done about it."

A more profitable course might be to learn more about how behavior takes place, identify the factors that are likely to steer a child one way or the other, and then manipulate these factors — adding them to, or subtracting them from, the child's repertoire of experiences. Environmental experience and the child's genetic endowment act and interact to mold behavior pattern tendencies. Some of these factors are amenable to manipulation, others are less so. By identifying them, parents would have some guidelines in knowing what to provide and what to withhold. And those factors that cannot be manipulated could be compensated for, or at least understood.

To illustrate these variables, let us follow a hypothetical child from birth to maturity to see the factors operating to produce an antisocial, "acting out" individual. For the sake of illustration the portrayal will tend to go to extremes. We need not expect any one child to be afflicted with all of these conditions; nor are they the only ones that could bring about a more or less similar end-state.

They will help us, however, to generalize for other factors as well as almost any behavioral dimension.

Let us call this: *"The Story of Joe: The Making of an Antisocial Character."*

A Prototype of Violence

Almost from birth, Joe was a difficult child. He cried frequently and with great intensity. When Joe needed his bottle or a diaper change, he needed it *right away.* If hurt or hungry, he could not be distracted by being held or comforted until the bottle was warmed or the pain subsided.

When the pediatrician ordered scheduled feeding, Joe could not comply with a preset schedule, nor carve out for himself any regularity. With demand feeding, his parents fared no better. They could not predict when he would be hungry, when he would sleep, or when he would move his bowels.

The lack of regularity or any form of rhythm or cycle made restful nights impossible. With nerves on edge, fights erupted within the family and heightened the tension, including Joe's. Mother dreaded feeding and bathing times. Joe made his parents feel helpless and inadequate. He came between wife and husband, and he interfered with the smooth operation of the household. Nights out could not be planned. Daddy began to stay longer in the office. The other children were neglected and soon came to resent their brother. Joe's parents alternated between being angry at the child and feeling guilty for their perceived inadequacies as parents.

His parents' inability to provide for his needs beforehand, together with the intensity and the immediacy with which Joe demanded satisfaction, combined to make life unpredictable, tense, and fraught with anxieties. That was the result of Joe's temperament interacting with his environment.

The very young child does not comprehend language. But he does understand gestures, facial expressions, and the language of being held — warmth, strength, closeness and satisfaction, or distance, hesitance, and mutual dissatisfaction. Our Joe was no exception, of course. He instinctively sensed all this, and became even more unhappy. This unhappiness now combined with his temperament, and he came to react with even greater intensity and irregularity.

Maturity Compounds the Picture

As Joe got older, toilet training was a nightmare. Because of Joe's irregularity, his mother could not catch his bowel movements and habituate him to use the bathroom. Joe lost patience quickly and could not sit still on the toilet seat. Conversely, because his needs were so urgent and immediate, Joe could not wait long enough to go to the bathroom and go through the ritual of undressing and preparing to use the toilet. The resultant upsets again added to frustration and mutual dissatisfaction. The mother was angry with Joe's noncompliance, and Joe was furious about the demands made on him.

Again environmental elements were added. Because parents usually believe that toilet training is more amenable to direct teaching than sleeping or feeding, physical coercion was introduced. Joe was *made* to sit on the toilet seat and punished when he soiled himself. But Joe knew how to retaliate: by withholding his bowel movements while on the toilet and soiling himself while off. The accumulated tension and ill feelings of the past negatively colored this parent-child confrontation which, in turn, became the prototype for disciplining the child. Physical coercion, harshness, and a battle of wills became the mode.

Friends and Television

Joe began speaking relatively late, and verbal intelligence trailed behind his motor abilities. He used his hands to make his will known. He pointed and tugged at his mother, and later on pushed and shoved to get his way. When angry, Joe did not rely on verbal insults and subtle sarcasm. He hit. This, together with his relatively poor interpersonal experiences during infancy, made peer relationships difficult, a situation which added further to unhappiness. He thus drifted towards children who were more action-oriented than verbal, who were also "outcasts," unhappy, and prone to violent reactions. At this point, his parents may have tried to coerce him to select better friends. But his strained relationship with them only added to his determination, because by choosing undesirable friends, he also retaliated against his parents.

Because verbal pursuits were not satisfying, Joe never read or looked at books. He did things or watched things that were being done. Television became a natural outlet for his interests and fantasies. Of particular interest to him were shows which depicted much action rather than verbal exchanges. And when action was violent, Joe would vicariously become the powerful hero taking revenge on his frustrations *and* on those who frustrated him, thereby setting in motion fantasies of physical power and violence.

The Family

In general, Joe's family was not a harmonious one. Opinions were rarely exchanged and calm discussions infrequent. A difference of opinion usually resulted in a heated argument. Dinners were either silent or argumentative, or eaten in isolation. Family trips were infrequent, and there was lacking the hard-to-describe, but readily noted, qualities of warmth, love, and togetherness.

Joe's parents may have paid lip service to a value system which encompassed religion, ethics, and social responsibility. In practice, however, his father was an irascible, angry, and impatient man, due to longstanding as well as more recent personal frustration. Joe could not discuss his problems with him; most communications were a brusque yes or no, do or don't. Dad felt that he deserved to relax in front of the television set when he came home tired from work, and that he should not be bothered by the children. When Mother did manage to cajole him into interacting with the children or disciplining them, he considered it an imposition and he resented his wife's pressures. He would get angry and hit the youngsters, thereby teaching Joe that reaction to frustration is violence — even though this violence may be out of proportion and totally unrelated to the present stimulus.

At School

School, too, was not a satisfying experience for Joe. Hypermobility, basic lack of verbal ability and of important verbal experiences, and inadequate achievement motivation, singly or in combination made learning a chore to be avoided. In addition, Joe's "acting out" behavior brought him into frequent clashes with his teachers, who felt that he was willful and disobedient. The better teachers did try to reason with Joe and win his trust, but his previous experiences with authority figures — his parents — caused him to transfer his negativism, hostility, and distrust toward all authority and the entire adult world.

The Stage Is Set for Violence

Joe's war with his world was now in progress. In comparison with the establishment, Joe felt relatively weak and helpless, and his antisocial reactions at this time were relatively mild. He was biding his time. With growth would come strength, membership in a gang would provide power, and a fortuitous situation would provide the spark. The "mechanics" of violence he already knew: his minor conflicts with society, the trashy comics and television shows, and the exchanges of ideas within the gang had taken care of that.

All that was needed was the trigger. A particularly intense frustration, an exhorting leader, a pseudo-cause, or simply an accumulation of anger could perform that function. In the absence of the challenge, struggle, and reward of education, violence often becomes the logical alternative to achieve power, prestige, and excitement. Thus the stage was set, the actor well trained and rehearsed and ready to act — with violence.

The Basic Factors

In trying to extricate oneself from the myriad of combinations and possibilities this vignette is trying to present, one becomes aware of three clusters of factors which can, at least for the sake of clarity, be dealt with separately. They may be called (1) *potential*, (2) *predisposition*, and (3) *precipitation*.

1. We readily see that Joe's basic makeup provided him with a good *potential* for his subsequent violent character formation. His intensity of feeling, urgency, and his inability to conform to schedules are the equivalent of behavioral inability to tolerate frustration and postponement of gratification. Thus, these behavior traits were in a sense present at birth. Similarly, his pattern of intellectual and language function "made" him do poorly in school and facilitated physical violence while retarding verbal discussion. These are but some examples of the innate potential for subsequent behavior which differs from child to child.

2. *Predisposition* is the aggregate of potential plus experiences, plus the interaction of the two. In the case of Joe, it is the frustrated child, the angry parent, *and* the angry parent adding frustration to the already frustrated child.

3. *Precipitation* is the spark which finds more or less flammable material in what we have called predisposition.

Intervention Always Helpful

It should become apparent that our ability to manipulate these factors, to run interference with them, varies. We can do least with native factors; we can do most with experiential ones — with precipitation someplace in-between. Yet there is always something that can be done. For the sake of brevity, one or two examples will suffice:

Joe's parents might not have been able to lessen the child's need for immediacy or intensity of feeling, but they could have understood that his need neither reflected upon their adequacy as parents, nor was Joe's behavior totally voluntary and driven by an innate evil. Then, instead of anger there would have been understanding, warmth, and love. These would have soothed the infant and taught him feelings of security — that momentary lacks or discomforts can be tolerated because other people care and will provide.

Had Joe's parents been happier and calmer, the child would

have learned to react to frustrations with calm and reasoning. Interacting with Dad, Joe would have tried to imitate him, would have talked about his problems and thereby ameliorated his unhappiness. Mother could have read to him and helped him to become more verbal. And the family doing things as a unit would have lessened Joe's need for fantasy, retaliation, and trashy television programs that fed his warped ego.

Taking into account Joe's vulnerability, even as an outcome of previous mistakes, there are still things that could have been done. Joe could have been shielded from intense frustrations; undesirable comics and television programs could have been replaced by equally interesting but less harmful things to do. And the gang leader or cause can be dethroned by the parent or teacher becoming the hero and developing a cause.

Rarely does a single factor, no matter how traumatic, shape character by itself. A factor only adds to the already existing ones and merely helps steer matters in a certain direction. Because of this, intervention is always helpful.

The important question is: How much are we doing now to counteract what has gone before? The knowledge that every minute experience has an effect on shaping character may be frightening, but it is equally encouraging because the possibility of intervention through the provision of other experiences removes finality and gives us a second chance, no matter what has gone before.

Chapter Twenty-eight

Youth in Need of Direction

The Adolescent Protest

Wile adolescence has always been considered a difficult period in parent-child relations, the proliferation of individual youths who "drop out" of the traditional home and school setting — and also form groups to "support" one another — have escalated these individual battles into what one may call a major war between society and its adolescents. Whether we call it alienation, generation gap, youth dropping out of society, or simply rebellion, the symptoms are similar enough, and they seem to endanger our existing moral code.

Parents are concerned, and rightfully so, for no class or group is being spared. Newspaper headlines fan our fears by ever increasing reports of youthful runaways who are being sought in the streets or other unsavory hangouts. Violence surfaces among ever younger children, and, with guns readily available, it is becoming ever more deadly. Schools have become armories with guards and metal detectors, yet hardly a day passes in which the press does not report of violent crimes by or among young people.

Other youths drop out by forming groups of outcasts or losing themselves to the Internet, television, or other fantasies which modern technology provides. Virtual reality may replace reality, and the chat room provides a social outlet for the socially inhibited — or kindred spirits who allow and encourage a host of perversions or other antisocial attitudes. There are others who simply drop out by withdrawing into themselves, into a kind of semi-depressed state — dysfunctional in school, at home, within themselves, and with others. Life, to them, is a drag.

To "identify" themselves as a society within society, there is then a need to be outrageous — in dress, in jewelry attached to the most intimate body parts, and in language spiced with profanity. All of these are used to shock others, and to find support in this society of dropouts.

Additionally, one frequently finds mature adults grotesquely imitating such groups by adopting "hip" dress and language, and admiring performers who have made outrageousness into an art form. Thus, with the adult imitating the dysfunctional, rather than showing the way, there have crept in doubts regarding our "normal" value system and our institutions — marriage, law and order, government, polite social conduct, modesty, and all that civilized society stands for. As a result, there is conflict and there is doubt. These new doubts in our value system, and the seriousness with which we take our protesting youth, are eroding sound parent-child relationships, and may well bring about a perpetual state of confusion for society, which in turn encourages the dissenters.

What about the Torah world? Once again, we are touched and affected by the world around us. On the positive side, there are "drop-ins," the *baalei teshuvah* who have had enough of these doubts of the world around us, and have embraced the security and the assuredness of the Torah world. Yet, sadly enough, there has also been an erosion in the opposite direction.

Cause and Effect

Those who study human behavior and society have striven to find the causes for this state of affairs. Culprits were readily found: The technological revolution, overly busy parents, and a host of other villains have been named. All of these, individually and in combination, are thought to be responsible for these restive stirrings of our younger generation. This, of course, may be so. There is, however, one additional culprit, possibly the chief one, that must be mentioned: the doubt which we ourselves have in our value system. Not only has doubt been the result of the adolescents' protest, it is also the avenue which has paved the dissenters' way. And because doubt is both the cause and effect of the adolescent protest, we are indeed in danger of a self-perpetuating doubt system consisting of doubt, dissent, and further doubt.

Among the young adult's many psychological needs is a clear recognition of the meaning of life and an attendant value system. The adolescent needs to know who he is, what is expected of him, what the important values are in life, and what the business of living is all about.

In this need for meaning, the adolescent is not unique. All human beings must have a value system at all stages of life. The intensity of this need is, however, greater for the adolescent, and its fulfillment more difficult.

The very young child lives more or less in the here-and-now and considers himself the center of the universe. Parents, siblings, and society are merely appendages, there to satisfy his needs and wants. At that stage, he gives little thought to higher meanings of life. As he becomes socialized, he slowly adopts the value system of his parents and society without much question. He does so because his parents are to him all-wise and powerful and know what is best; he has relatively little choice about it; and he really has seen little else which could be an alternative. The child has no problem with "the meaning of life."

The adult, on the other hand, is well aware of some of our value system's shortcomings. He is, however, realistic. He is likely to discount utopian ideals, and generally does not indulge in philosophical speculation. Instead, he is practical; he takes operating ideals for granted in spite of the many inconsistencies and discrepancies between the ideal and the real. For example, he may believe that all politicians are crooked yet subscribe to our political system, he may preach scrupulous honesty yet deviate slightly on occasion, or he may proclaim a true belief in religious principles yet fall short when it comes to practice. To help him juggle pragmatism and idealism, he invents maxims which he accepts without either fully believing or questioning them. To reassure himself about his behavior, for example, rather than to make a statement of truth, he says that honesty is the best policy — and really sees himself as scrupulously honest. When necessary, he can always "rationalize" to explain his own lapses. The adult is too tired and too busy to change the world. He is satisfied to survive in it with a modicum of ego-integrity.

The adolescent views all of this quite differently. He is young and feels all-powerful; he is optimistic. The whole world is before him; he is going to conquer it and make it better. Youth learns about ideals not from practical experience, but from books and teachers, sources that are to a degree abstract and removed from the day-to-day business of living. He takes such ideals seriously, and can afford to want what is ideal. Because the best of social systems is far from perfect, because the adolescent had no hand in having contributed to our imperfect society, and because the ideal world has been described to him, youth feels impelled *to do something* to change the world for the better.

Quest for an Ideal Society

It has been said that all of mankind's contributions to this world have at one time been far-fetched and unrealistic dreams of individuals. Similarly, the man who succeeds in remaking himself must at one time have wanted to remake the world. We must indeed strive for perfection in order to climb at least partway up its ladder. Thus there is purpose in youth's romanticism and ideals, and it is in this purpose that the seed of progress for a better world can be found.

There are, however, by-products which can spell danger in youth's quest for the ideal. In its search for perfection, youth is readily attracted to those systems that claim to have a perfect formula for living: the extremist "isms" and their programs. Thus, adopting an extremist stance, youth tends to believe that if authority is important then dictatorship is perfect, if democracy is good then anarchy is great, if sharing is laudable then communism is ideal.

This pull toward an extremist position is not always complete. At times the pull merely breaks the adolescent loose from the moorings of society's value system and leaves him floating, rejecting the imperfect parental standards without accepting a substitute value system. This seems to be what is happening in modern society when youth has an ever-widening view of the greater world.

Belief in Values, and the Need for Direction

The rapid technological change which modern man is experiencing has shaken our belief in facts which have hitherto been taken for unshakable truths. Indeed, textbooks and college courses are continually being revised to supplant what was new only yesterday. Thus knowledge today is to a large extent tentative. As a result, there is doubt whether this "new" knowledge will endure — and this is as it should be of most, if not all, the physical sciences.

In addition, because of the vast amount of knowledge that is required for each of the sciences, there is more and more specialization so that no one person can know all there is to know in any one field. Needless to say, few, if any one of us, can claim real knowledge in more than one area. As a result, there is a proliferation of expertise, and reluctance on the part of the novice to venture into a field he knows little about. This self-professed ignorance is all too apparent.

It should be remembered that the great discoveries of our day have been in the physical sciences and technology, and that our abilities in human relations have not kept pace with these rapid technological advances. One can point to little progress concerning human behavior and the ability of man to live with his neighbor and with himself. Indeed, judging by the state of affairs of society, national and international, it would almost seem that we have regressed.

The popular press, women's magazines, and books by experts in child rearing have obviously contributed to these self-doubts. To be sure, there is always something that can be learned by parents and by teachers. Yet that must not engender self-doubt in the adult that sends the adolescent a message of, "Yes, our parents, our teachers, also don't know what life is all about." On the other hand, the arbitrary attitude — "Do it because I said so!" — is equally dangerous. For it allows the adolescent only two unpleasant choices: total rebellion, or developing a meek, passive, and easily influenced personality.

Indeed, one doubts whether we can ever bring about new discoveries to perfect our society or to develop magic pills for the ultimate in human behavior. This is so because man's basic needs and pressures, his nature and nurture, are age-old, yet unlikely to ever change.

If we are to learn how to manage all this more effectively, then our sights should be turned toward man's past, his history, with all its failures and its glories. Man has had ample experience with value systems and moral codes. The fact that none of them have ever proven to be perfect is probably due to the basic imperfections in man rather than to a system's shortcomings. Each society, every subculture, and every man must choose for himself the value system and code of behavior that has stood the test of time. Technology may facilitate communication or help us obliterate each other more efficiently, but is unlikely to provide us with a perfect code of behavior.

Youth Wants Direction

Every child needs to feel that he has a wise and all-powerful parent who knows all the answers. As he matures, he himself needs to acquire that wisdom and power in order to eventually function independently in society. In the process, he inevitably must come in conflict with his parent's directives and doubt his rules and moral code, partly because they are not perfect.

Because the child knows that he cannot win this battle, and because of his love for his parent and his trust that his parent does know what is best, an identification process takes place. In spite of the many parent-child battles and experimentation with extreme attitudes, the child or youth adopts more or less the very code he was fighting, but now calls it his own. As the very true adage states, "The apple does not fall far from the tree."

Supposing, however, the parent himself is uncertain of his value system and only hesitantly directs his child. The child loses respect for his parent and for society, whom the parent represents. The child does not fight in this case because he is not forced to do so; he becomes apathetic and indifferent, a drop-out from society. If an identification process does take place, it is with the parent's indecisiveness, dependency, and ever-shifting attitudes that remain ungrounded upon a solid value system. In addition, the child falls easy prey to anyone who does promise direction, regardless of its validity.

The child will forgive the parent who directs him forcefully to abide by society's code — if it is clear that the parent believes in what he is doing. The child can then respect the parent, disagree with him, and eventually adopt some, if not most, of his teachings. The child cannot forgive the father who teaches him nothing or, worse yet, directs him in a halfhearted way, for then the child is deprived of the security of a knowing father.

Humility is not always virtuous. To the child, the parent must deliver the moral code justly but with firmness. Forgiveness, love, flexibility, understanding, and making allowances for the child have nothing to do with, nor may they affect, the parent's own belief in his code and the assuredness with which it is imparted upon youth. Since the apple does not fall far from the tree, youth which drops out and falls will land by the tree whose roots are inadequate and whose branches failed to nurture and hold firmly the tender fruit.

Fortunately, the Torah Jew has direction which has sustained

Jewish society at all times. One may have questions, but, as the saying goes, *"Fun a kashya shtarbt men nit"* — one can survive and live with a question, without knowing or understanding. But there must be a firmness in our beliefs, which youth can adopt and live with. If we believe in our physicians and mechanics, we should certainly believe, *lehavdil*, in the Word of G-d.

Chapter Twenty-nine

Torah and Mitzvah: Learning, Doing, and Being

hat does it mean to be a Jew — in the fullest sense of the word? Obviously, a Jew is one who learns Torah and does *mitzvos* as prescribed in the Torah, one who behaves in very specific ways towards G-d and towards his fellow man. A Jew also has a certain set of beliefs, attitudes, and opinions congruent with *hashkafah*, Torah philosophy. Yet there is more. The total Jew feels and thinks in a uniquely Jewish way. Consequently, he acts in various unspecified and not formally legislated ways in a manner that befits a Jew. He thus *is* and constantly *becomes* an individual with a character and disposition that defies description and cannot be accurately measured, but that clearly makes one say: "Here goes a real Jew."

Learning and doing, believing and being, further interact to form an inextricably interwoven whole. One learns to do *mitzvos*, and it is a *mitzvah* to learn. Learning and doing, in turn, create the Jew that *is*, with a certain *hashkafah*, with certain traits, general behavior, and disposition. This inner self then has a "mental set," an inner program of thinking, feeling, and responding that is Jewish in the fullest sense of the word. For example, the proper *hashkafah*, based on *emunah* and *bitachon*, faith and the true belief that all is ordained from Above, will protect one from unreasonable envy of his more fortunate friend, will make him less competitive and more pleasant towards others and towards himself. And if, *chas veshalom*, harm befalls him, he will not turn sour, nor burn with envy, nor engage in wild competitiveness. He will turn inward, reflect upon his deeds, and attempt to better things by doing more *mitzvos* or learning more, or *becoming* a better Jew — indeed, a better person. As a rewarding by-product, he will enjoy better health, physically and emotionally.[1]

The *Mishnah*[2] describes this mix of learning, doing, and being, and labels it as *kinyan Torah*, the acquisition of Torah. Its product is an individual who not only *is*, but constantly *becomes* and grows. (In the *yeshivishe* vernacular, it would be said that such a person constantly *"shteigs."*) The matrix unfolds, and here is listening and understanding, reverence, humility, joy, friendship, serving one's master, purity, patience, goodness of heart, satisfaction, loving G-d and one's fellow man, loving righteousness and correctness, empathy, learning to learn and learning to do — and much more.

For the sake of operational definition, then, we may speak of *limud haTorah* (learning), *mitzvah* (doing), *hashkafah* (beliefs), and, in large part as a result of the above, *middos* (feeling, disposition, and being). While it is not for us to valuate the importance of our various duties as Jews in the fullest sense of the word, it is clear that without *middos* all else is hollow and, *chas veshalom*, meaningless. As the Yiddish saying goes: "*Du host oisgelernt Shas,*

---

1. See Chapter 32, "Musings of an Orthodox Psychotherapist." See also *Rambam's Peirush HaMishnayos*, Peah 1:1, and *Imrei Shefer* on *Shiluach Hakan, Ki Seitzei* 22:7. Concerning physical health, note that stress does kill, *chas veshalom*. See *Malbim, Bereishis* 2:17.
2. *Avos* 6:6,7.

vos hot Shas dir oisgelernt? (You have studied Torah, but what has Torah taught you?)"

Middos, the Inner Jew: Its Import and Definition

The significance of *middos* is clearly spelled out by our Sages in the Talmud.[3] Describing the rare individual for whom there is no hope or forgiveness, neither in genuine repentance nor in the power of the holy day of Yom Kippur, nor in suffering, they state:

> "… he who has read Torah *(she'korei)* and has studied Torah *(v'shoneh)*, and has served his masters *(umeshamesh talmidei chachamim)*, yet his being and behavior is dishonest and he fails to be pleasant towards his fellow man. What does society say of him? 'Woe to him who has studied Torah, woe to his parents … and to his master … Behold how repulsive is his behavior and how despicable are his ways.' "

This, our *chachamim* point out, is *chillul Hashem,* profaning the Holy Name. Learning and doing without *middos* becomes a defect, for not only has the individual who does so failed to "become," he has also caused others to speak badly of G-d and of our holy Torah.

How does one define and measure the "inner Jew," the Jewish character par excellence? Obviously, different masters and various schools will stress certain traits and qualities. Yet no one will argue against the statement that they include items such as true faith, optimism, patience, tolerance, humility, modesty, honesty, impulse control, empathy, generosity, sensitivity towards the needs of others, and general satisfaction with G-d's bounty and with one's state, while ever searching for spiritual and social growth. In addition, all of the above should be optimally weighted, depending upon a variety of factors unique for a particular moment or occasion. This precisely describes what is meant by the word *middos* — measures, and by the concept of having *middos*: measuring and weighing, feeling, thinking, and doing as befits a *mensch* and a Jew, in proper proportion as the situation demands.

---

3. *Yoma* 86a.

The Burning Question

If there is such a thing as a national *cheshbon hanefesh*, an honest accounting of our state of Jewishness, is it not clear that though we are experiencing a renaissance of Torah learning — as evidenced by a proliferation of *shiurim*, learning programs, Torah tapes, Judaica, and *Daf Yomi* celebrations — *middos* lag far behind? Though there is ever growing attention to the fulfillment of *mitzvos* in a most exacting fashion — as attested to by the publication and use of a host of charts, tables and measurements, and *mitzvah* primers — *middos* have suffered from gross inattention. There are individuals who study Torah, observe the *mitzvos*, give charity, and are honest;[4] yet their general demeanor is somehow unpleasant. They are impatient, curt with other people, simply "not nice." In addition, there is a kind of uptightness, a blend of anxiety and depression — not exactly in a clinical, pathological way, yet displaying a lack of the calm confidence inherent in one possessing *emunah* and *bitachon*. And ironically, though there is a significant increase in *maasim tovim* — private, public, and semi-public efforts to help our less fortunate brethren — there is an uncomfortable feeling that our disposition towards our fellow man, the *seiver panim yafos*,[5] has not kept pace. Something is missing, a certain lack in being a *mensch* and a *Yid*, the Torah way. The "inner Jew," the *"baal middos"* as portrayed by the giants of *Mussar* and *Chassidus*, has yet to emerge.

No Laughing Matter

"Men lacht fun dem naar, ober der naar is meiner." One pokes

---

4. In spite of recent "exposures" — even by our own well-meaning but, in my opinion, misguided friends. Jews, even Orthodox ones, unfortunately have their share of mental ills and emotional maladjustments. But Torah Jews who beat their wives are still rare. Those who do drugs or take to drink are still few and far between. The divorce rate is still relatively low, and the same holds true for stealing and cheating. Yes, when such perpetrators are exposed, it unfortunately makes headlines, "good copy," and *chillul Hashem*. And it should not. "Figures do not lie, but one can lie with figures." My Torah colleagues and I, who probably see more religious patients in a week than outsiders see in a year, will attest to that.

5. *Avos* 1:15, the admonition to be ever friendly towards others.

fun at the fool — but if I am the fool, or my relative is, then the joke is on me and the pain is my own. We strive to be *frum*, and the word needs no explanation, yet we chuckle and nod our heads in a kind of reluctant acknowledgment when we hear the sad joke repeated once again: "What does the acronym F-R-U-M stand for? *Feil Rishus Und Meshugas* — Much evil and insanity." Sadly enough, even among our very own, we have come to wink at this "hollow" Jew, as if it is acceptable to be a not-nice person as long as one is *frum*. That must not be.

Yet it is clear that the principal goal of the Torah Jew is to be a *mensch*, an individual free of moral depravity and full of goodness. His life should be governed by *bitachon* and *emunah*, trust and faith, and devoid of superstitious, unreasonable fears and *meshugasen*,[6] those subtle quirks of behavior that are wrong, irrational, and simply not Jewish.

The negative "twins" — unpleasantness towards others, and *meshugasen* within — are not simply coincidental. Both elements are created by the same pathology.[7] In its most rudimentary definition, mental health is the manner in which an individual relates towards himself and towards others. Thus, the satisfied, optimistic *baal emunah u'bitachon* smiles with a sense of secure well-being and envelopes others into his happy orbit. He is connected, and doubly so: with the *Ribbono Shel Olam* and with mankind. Conversely, the pathological F-R-U-M fellow holds on to *Yiddishkeit* with *shtick* (such as by singling out certain *mitzvos* or customs and practicing them to the extreme while neglecting others, and neglecting his obligations to his spouse, to his children, and to his fellow Jew), not with a Torah grip, and moves away or against people — again, not in a Torah way.

Thus the way man acts towards others is primarily determined by the way he feels — towards life, towards himself, and towards the world around him, or, to put it differently, by his state of *emu-*

---

6. *"Tamim ti'hiyeh im Hashem Elokecha* — Be wholeheartedly [trusting] in Hashem" (*Devarim* 18:13). See *Rashi*: "Walk with Him with simple faith. Depend on Him. Do not speculate [and overly worry] about the future."

7. The saying in Yiddish is: *"Er iz nit mit alemen* — He [the disturbed individual] is not [put] together." More literally, he is alone, not with others. Much of psychopathology is a regression, a withdrawal from others. His remedy, conversely, is in good part restoring relationships with others as well as with himself.

nah and *bitachon.* Fortunately, however, these "twins" — unpleasantness towards others and disturbed inner feelings — have another side, a positive, remedial, and therapeutic one: namely, the way one acts, so does one feel.

A person is feeling miserable. What is a good "fix"? One can ingest drugs — street drugs or medically prescribed ones, or get drunk or stuff one's face with fats or carbohydrates. One can brood and wallow in self-pity, drown oneself in work, or take out one's frustrations on others, perhaps by abusing one's spouse or children.

A true Torah *mensch* does otherwise. He reaches out and helps (or at least is pleasant to) his fellow, and, lo and behold, he feels more pleasant within! This maneuver is, of course, more difficult, but oh, how much better and more permanent! Sadly enough, we find individuals who are forced by their professions or businesses to wear a smile during the day, and they feel pretty okay. Yet when they come home or go to *shul,* when the professional smile is no longer required, they "let it all hang out," thus effecting a short-term quick fix, but long-term losses: losses in relationships, losses by fostering an inner pathology, losses in failing to become Jews and *menschen,* and losses by failing to develop a lifetime psychotherapeutic "fix" — relating and loving.

The focus, then, should be on a certain group of *middos,* inherent traits, that make the man, namely, his deep inner feelings which govern his disposition and, consequently, his behavior towards his fellow man. The focus should shift away from high-profile, measurable deeds such as charity or honesty, and concentrate on the subtleness of being pleasant with others and with oneself, on being calm, trusting, and confident. (Yes, confident — not as an arrogant *baal gaavah,* but with the deserved confidence of one who knows he is host to a Divine *neshamah* [soul], and that he is a *tzelem Elokim.*)

If we see that Torah is studied and *mitzvos* are observed, yet these vital traits are stunted or inadequately developed, then there is obviously something wrong. One need not cite chapter and verse of the abundance of admonitions in both the Written and Oral Laws to behave decently and to have faith, the essential twins that govern an individual's disposition.

We thus must ask ourselves several vital questions: Why is it relatively easier to learn like a Jew and do *mitzvos* like a Jew, than to be and behave like a Jew? Why are *middos* so vulnerable to erosion, while Jewish learning and doing *mitzvos* are relatively immune to deterioration? What occurs in a Jewish life or what fails to take place that affects *middos* adversely?

These painful issues are not really new. The *Netziv*,[8] in the introduction to *Bereishis* in his work *Haamek Davar*, bemoans the state of affairs at the time of the destruction of the Second Holy Temple. In his words, "[People were] righteous, pious, and students of Torah, but they were not *yesharim*, correct in their everyday lives. Consequently, they suspected those who differed with their view, developing baseless hatreds, thus bringing about the destruction of the Holy Temple."

In contradistinction, the *Netziv* continues, the *Avos*,[9] besides being righteous, pious and lovers of G-d in the extreme, were also *yesharim*, correct and proper. He goes on to cite chapter and verse showing how they dealt with everyone, even with barbaric idolaters, with love and concern. Not so the scholars at the time of the Second Temple. Similarly, we note the problem of *middos* with remain Rabbi Akiva's students.[10] The question remains: Why have *middos*, so clearly exemplified by our *Avos*, declined in the days of their children?

Personality Development: to Be A Jew — Torah She'biksav, Torah She'be'al Peh, and Shimush Chachamim

The giants of *Mussar* wrestled with the question of why Torah failed to specifically legislate laws of *middos*.[11] Why, for example, is there not an *assei*, a positive commandment, to be pleasant, to be optimistic? Or why is there not a *lo saaseh* — a specific prohibition command — not to be angry or lacking faith? To the behavioral scientist this is not a real question. What we are dealing with here is *feelings*. And feelings cannot be simply altered or modified with

---

8. R' Naftali Tzvi Yehudah Berlin of Volozhin.
9. Forefathers (Avraham, Yitzchak, and Yaakov).
10. Talmud *Yevamos* 62b.
11. Viz. R' Chaim Vital in *Shaar HaKedushah*, Chapter 2.

cognitive, rational thought. That is why it does not help at all to tell one not to be depressed or not to be angry — no matter how many rational arguments one can muster. Nor can the obsessive-compulsive individual comply with the most revered *rebbe's* edict to desist from acting out his compulsivity dressed up as super-religiosity. For to *do* and to *act* can be legislated or, with heroic willpower, self-imposed. But to *be*, to be disposed and to feel, cannot be ordered. One's temperament cannot be legislated, it has to be developed. We may wear masks and act upon the stage of life — but how does one *become* and *be?*[12]

Without resorting to a crash course in the psychology of personality, it is clear that personality development takes place within the context of certain social-emotional settings. First there is the "word," a value system, a set of rules, tales of heroes and history from which to learn. Then there is society, living human beings who keep alive and ever fresh the tenor of the system, the subtleties and finer nuances, and adapt and develop them as the vicissitudes of life demand. And then there are special and intimate relationships. These relationships create human feelings and a oneness between learner and master that enable the individual to identify with and introject the cultural system as exemplified by his or her human "transmitter." Such a relationship is the final but crucial leg of the bridge that spans the history, the culture, the nuances and overtones, the oneness and the sense of belonging. Most importantly, it creates the necessary inner feelings — it literally makes the man. For whether we like it or not, man *is* and is programmed *to do*, far more as a function of feeling than as a result of thought.

Without attempting to explain the real whys and wherefores of Torah, be it *biksav* (written), *be'al peh* (verbal), or *shimush talmidei chachamim* (relational), it is clear that it embodies the very tools of personality development. Though Torah demands of us to develop a personality verily parallel to that of our Creator,[13] and a character

---

12. See *Minyan HaMitzvos L'HaRambam, lo saaseh,* 58, the *mitzvah* "not to fear." The *Raavad* takes exception. Even the *Rambam* is explained to mean that one should develop faith and fearlessness, not simply be fearless.
13. See *Talmud Shabbos* 133b, "As the A-mighty is merciful and compassionate, so are you to be likewise."

of the highest order, it has, as articulated in the *Mishnah* in *Avos*, built in the very mechanisms that shape, mold, construct, and, if necessary, reconstruct.

First there is *Torah She'biksav*, the word, the rules, the value system, and the tales of our heroes, the *yesharim* of which the *Netziv* speaks. Then there is *Torah She'be'al Peh*, the living Torah. To those initiated, it needs no description. For those who have not partaken, it may be a most difficult concept to understand: how, through *Torah She'be'al Peh* there come alive not only the Talmudic sages such as Abaye and Rava, but also the *yesharim* Avraham, Yitzchak, and Yaakov, and all the giants of Torah through the ages — until we are verily sitting with the latter-day teachers, with R' Akiva Eiger and R' Chaim Brisker, listening and discussing, learning and living Torah.

Finally, there is the *rebbe*, the teacher — our exposure to, and our involvement and relationship with, the *chacham*, the master, that enables the student to grasp the myriad of nuances of the Jewish spirit and character, so elusive and intangible, yet so crucial. And as this *rebbe* participates in bringing alive our *yesharim*, he transmits to the student not only what they said, but how they said it: the manner of the *yesharim*, their pleasant demeanor, their style, their true faith, their love and patience, and much more. In addition, an intimacy develops between *rebbe* and student. The *shimush talmidei chachamim* develops that vital relatedness, the feeling and desire to identify with and *become* like his *rebbe*, the Jewish character par excellence.[14] And when necessary, because of the very special relationship, the *rebbe* becomes the therapeutic agent, to heal and reconstruct.[15] Now we can return to our *gemara* in *Yoma* and more specifically see all of the above. To be condemned for failing to be a Jew is he who has: read (*korei*) *Torah She'biksav*, studied (*v'shoneh*) *Torah She'be'al Peh*, and interacted with (*umeshamesh talmidei chachamim*) his *rebbes*, for he had the opportunity to be that Jew, the Jewish character par excellence, and he has failed. Moreover, because he outwardly appears to be the learning-doing Jew, without *being* the correct and proper Jew, he also creates a *chillul Hashem*.

---

14. To see to what lengths some of our Sages went in *shimush chachamim*, see *Talmud Berachos* 62a.
15. See Talmud *Kiddushin* 30b.

Our Sages thus speak of three items that should have molded a person into a Torah *mensch*, but somehow failed to do so: delving into the Written Law, studying *Mishnah*, and serving and interacting with the masters of Torah. We can use these three categories of endeavor — reading, studying and serving masters — as a format of sorts to describe how a person can develop a Torah-guided personality befitting a *Yid* and a *mensch*.

"Korei": to Read Torah

We all read, but what do we really read?

We all have many experiences, but why do we dream about some and not about others? Obviously some things impress us while others do not. Similarly, some admonitions are readily accepted, while others are glossed over, for many reasons. For example, one sees, hears, and is impressed with something, and is likely to act upon it when it "fits" — that is, when it is consonant with the way we behave or want to behave. We do not notice, or wish to learn, or allow ourselves to be impressed with, items that will evoke feelings of guilt, or make demands of us that we cannot act upon, or do not wish to act upon. The question, then, is: Do we really read? Are we impressed with, and are we ready to act upon, Torah demands that call for feeling, being, and becoming, as we do for demands for doing? Are Torah demands, such as *"Lo sisna es achicha bilvavecha"* (not to hate), or, *"Lo saarotz bifneihem"* (do not be afraid [of your enemies]), of any less import, *chas ve-shalom*, then saying the *Shema*, or wearing *tefillin*?

Do we excuse ourselves by claiming: "I cannot help it if I *feel* nervous or angry or hateful. But, yes, I can *do* things, and *do* them well"? Then, all too frequently, such action-based *mitzvos* can easily become compensatory devices for proper feelings. Yes, I can be "perfect" by spending an inordinate amount of time to get every word of the *Shema* just right, or to have the *tefillin* centered just perfectly. Or, I can take pains to "enlighten" fellow *mispallelim* (people who are praying) regarding relatively minor customs — all at the expense of other *mitzvos* of feeling, being, and acting as a Torah *Yid* should.

Certainly we are to do *mitzvos*. And doing, besides being right, in and of itself, creates proper feelings. When compulsivity sets in, however, and these *mitzvos* fail to create the desired disposition and character, something is wrong. Moreover, when doing develops a flavor of blind perfectionism and becomes *mitzvos anashim melumadah* — habitual deeds without feeling or concern regarding the total Torah *mensch* — something needs to be done.

Not only do the Torah's commands call for specific actions, but they prescribe ways of thinking and feeling.[16] And if Torah prescribes it, it obviously can be done. The fact that it is more difficult to affect one's inner self and become a Torah *mensch* than to do an action-oriented *mitzvah*, obviously does not make the former less important than the latter.

The task then before us — individuals, parents and educators — is to read *all* of Torah, to have well-defined, clear, and explicit goals of what the Torah *mensch* is to be, and then go about striving for it.

"V'shoneh": to Study Mishnah — Torah She'be'al Peh, the Oral Law

It can be said that our behavior not only brings about that which one wishes to produce, it also becomes part and parcel of that individual's personality. For example, when one laughs, he not only raises his mood for the moment, but he also sets the stage to laugh at another occasion. Simply put, we are what we do, and we "become" because of what we do.

---

16. Let us note, for example, that Torah demands of us to be joyous on Yom Tov, to be sad on Tishah b'Av, to be solemn on Yom Kippur. And, more specifically, to feel on Pesach night *k'ilu hu yatza miMitzrayim,* as if each individual himself escaped from Egypt. The Torah further expects of us to manipulate our feelings. For example, an individual is, *chas veshalom,* mourning the loss of a parent. Now it is Yom Tov or Shabbos, and he must interrupt his mourning and invoke joy to the extent *halachah* prescribes. Or, even while in mourning, he learns of an inheritance and he is required to recite *Shehecheyanu,* a *berachah* requiring an expression of gratitude and happiness.

If the Torah asks for it, obviously it is possible. *Rambam* (*Minyan HaMitzvos, lo saaseh,* 58) counts as a command the admonition *v'al taartzu,* not to be afraid (of your enemies). Obviously it can be done, not by "throwing a switch" or simply deciding to do so, but by working on the inner man through faith, belief, and trust in Hashem — and in our fellow man.

Learning *Torah She'be'al Peh* is an exercise and an immersion in spirituality, creative thinking, and emotional and social growth. The very fact that it is the Word of G-d creates a spiritual setting that uplifts the individual, making by comparison the daily hassles and the many everyday conflicts petty and relatively unimportant. It dilutes the pain of the daily grind by uplifting us to a higher sphere of living.

The fact that learning Talmud takes place in a social setting, with a *chavrusa*, a partner, and a *chaburah*, a group, creates an opportunity to relate, to strive — and to compete *not* to best the other, but to join in a kind of race to understand the word of G-d and to resolve conflicts. The Talmud frequently reminds us and relates to us the love and respect the scholars had to one another in spite of real disagreements concerning Torah law and tradition. So does learning with a *chavrusa* create love and caring while there is competition to understand and to grow. It thus teaches us that competition, perhaps a natural human trait, can be used not *against* the other, but to *join* others in order to grow intellectually, socially, and spiritually. Thus, it has been said that learning that does not lead to love of others is not true Torah learning.

Additionally, learning and researching creates an inquisitiveness, a striving to understand G-d, His Words, and the many fine nuances of the practical *mitzvos* as well as those which "make" man and improve him. Thus, as with *Torah She'biksav*, we need to be impressed not only with *halachah*, the law, but also with what *aggadah* has to say. *Aggadah* is that portion of the Talmud that teaches subtly and indirectly, but powerfully so, what the Torah *mensch* is to *be*, in addition to what he is to *do*. In addition, there can and must be spiritual and human growth simply by one's immersion in the *yam haTalmud*, the Talmudic ocean, wherein one is totally enveloped in God's thoughts — thinking, analyzing, and feeling the majesty of His holy words; conversing with the saints and scholars of generations ago,[17] and being occupied not with temporary and mundane matters, but with something enduring, something holy. Exactly how this works may be beyond us, but students of Talmud will confirm that this is so.

---

17. See Chapter 2, "To Be a Teacher," and Chapter 3, "For Love of Learning." See also Jacob Mermelstein, "Learning to Love Learning," *The Mesifta Chronicle* (Mesifta of Long Beach, N.Y., 1988).

Some such learnings are closer to the surface. For example, our Sages say that the tractate *Eruvin* teaches us to care for our neighbor. Does not tractate *Berachos* also teach gratitude? Or *Nazir*, temperance without austerity? One could go on. Yet, like all else, this needs to be pointed out. Do we say to ourselves and to our students, "Wow, look at this! What does it tell us, teach us? How does it make us better, sweeter, softer?" When studying *Berachos*, contemplate the importance of gratitude and taking nothing for granted: "Thank you, G-d; thank you, fellow man; thank you, spouse or child or parent!" What would assuming such a habit make of us? Grumpy complainers and nervous wrecks? Or, more likely, loving, caring, sweet "people's people," endowed with calm confidence and feelings of security, possessing *bitachon*, trust in the *Ribbono Shel Olam*, and in mankind? Such is the power of *Torah She'be'al Peh.*

Shimush Talmidei Chachamim — Serving and Interacting With Torah Scholars[18]

To begin with, Torah scholars teach us, emphasize, and point out in Torah and in Talmud precisely such teachings that produce the Torah *mensch*. Yet they do much more.

A man walked into my office — *farbissen*, grumpy, uptight and bristling. After dumping on me all his complaints against his wife, his children, and his business partner, he went on: "And what does the *Ribbono Shel Olam* want of me? More learning, more *davening*, more *tzedakah*, and more *mitzvos*. What about me?"

I offered him a cup of coffee, and went about developing a rela-

---

18. Many titles have been given to our era. It has been called the age of anxiety, the age of "me first," the age of "anything goes," and so on. All of these, at least in part, are true. May I add, "the age of the guru." Very briefly: Value systems have been lost to such an extent that man no longer knows who he is and what life is all about; so, enter the "guru," who "knows." Obviously, there are destructive gurus who exploit, and there are insane gurus who seduce people to join their insanity. And then there are gurus who may mean well, but who do little else but "make nice." Doing so might make our sufferer feel better temporarily, but nothing really changes.

There are also good "gurus," pardon the term. These are individuals who have the ability to make people feel good by their ability to relate to them, and not sit in judgment. However, there must also be material to be mastered, value systems to be learned, and changes to be expected.

tionship with him. At a much later time, I reminded him of his comments and said to him, "My friend, we are tuned in to the same *Ribbono Shel Olam, baruch Hashem.* Yet I heard the *Ribbono Shel Olam, kaveyachol,* very differently. I heard, *'Kind leben,* dear child, I am happy with your learning and *davening.* But when you learn your *daf,* the daily page of Talmud, look into these commentaries, and you will understand better, enjoy it more and become closer to the Word of G-d. When you *daven,* try to infuse your words with more *kavanah* (concentration), and your prayers will have far more meaning to Me and to you ... And here are a number of *mitzvos* you may have forgotten about. They may be a little difficult at times, and having fun and doing nothing might seem more pleasurable. But think about after... After the deed, after the *mitzvah* or after wasting time, how does it feel? Consider the gain and the loss. So, because I love you,[19] do it, and you will love the result. As far as your spouse, your children, and your business partner are concerned, consider the fact that because of them you do not feel alone. You are important to them. Yes, there is a cost — to consider their needs and to cater to them. But how about the gain? By being pleasant to them, you will feel pleasant and become a habitually pleasant person!'"

Two people can be learning the identical words of G-d, yet integrate them into their thinking-feeling-doing system in such two diametrically opposing manners. Clearly it was not the words that differed, it was the delivery system which reflects the kind of person the parent or the *rebbe* is, the kind of Jew he is, and the kind of *mensch* he is.

Middos: Vulnerable and Susceptible

Because *middos* are developed and cannot be legislated, and because they come about through relationships and social-emotional states, they are highly vulnerable to social factors and susceptible to emotional ills. First and foremost is the fact that, consciously or otherwise, man learns from his fellow man.[20] The Yiddish saying

---

19. "*Ratzah HaKadosh Baruch Hu l'zakos es Yisrael ...*" (*Makkos* 23b). Torah and *mitzvos* were given to mankind because of G-d's love for us.
20. See *Mishlei* 27:19, "*Kamayim hapanim lapanim.*"

goes: *"Asoi vie ess kristelt sich, asoi Yidelt sich."* The Jew learns from the world around him and, in turn, reflects society's state of affairs. With modern life, there has been ever increasing contact with society at large. Interestingly enough, this contact became greater with the advent of *"haskalah,"* the so-called enlightenment which attempted to undermine *Yiddishkeit,* and the beginning of the *Mussar* movement, our defense against *haskalah.* All of this occurred at the very same time that the decline of human values and *menschlichkeit* was taking place,[21] producing the bitter fruit that we are eating of today.[22]

Furthermore, because of the effect of emotions on *middos,* adversity erodes the inner character.[23] Jews have suffered and are suffering — physically, socially, and spiritually. There are assaults from the outer world, overt and covert anti-Semitism. There are and there have been assaults from within — Hellenism, *haskalah,* assimilation, and reform. And there are assaults from the *yeitzer hara,* our very inner selves. With the modern world open before us lacking the protection, the insulation, of the ghetto or *shtetl,* there is conflict: to remain fully insulated or, *chas veshalom,* taste some of the forbidden, or at least dangerous, fruits?

Finally — and here one must step with great caution and trepidation — is it possible that our great fervor to learn ever more, and do *mitzvos* in a most exacting fashion, without at the very same time attending adequately to the inner Jew, has created a dangerous imbalance?[24] Have we become infected by the modern world's preoccupation with productivity and materialism and blind competitiveness? Thus learning and doing *mitzvos* have become

---

21. *Mori v'Rebbi, HaGaon* R' Yaakov Kamenetsky, spoke of certain junctures of modern life when humanity took a sharp turn downhill. In this personal communication, he unfortunately did not explain exactly why this came about. One may speculate that technological growth without attendant spiritual growth enabled man to distance himself from his fellow man. In war, man could kill long distance — technology was the issue, not feeling. Thus, Nazis were able to speak of efficiency in exterminating organisms and save themselves from having to feel that they were dealing with humans, and hurting their fellow man.

22. The deterioration of human values, the breakdown of social institutions, the decline of morality we are witnessing today, is self-evident.

23. See *Rashi, Bereishis* 41:2. *Lehavdil,* it is clear that psychopathy or raw evil is the result of severe emotional trauma.

24. Viz., see *Talmud Beitzah* 15b. Great attention to one *mitzvah* may make one neglect another, even greater one.

"acquisitions" for which one competes at the expense of others.[25] Have yeshivas, perhaps inadvertently, looked for the teacher who is the greatest scholar, who can produce, and who has the best techniques to make his students learn, while neglecting to examine the teacher's own *middos*, or his concern with the inner *"mensch"*? Similarly, have teachers taught exclusively what Hillel and Shammai *said*, without at the very same time reflecting upon the *middos* they possessed and taught?[26] (Such an omission effectively demonstrates to the students the relative unimportance of *middos*.) Have yeshivas preferred such "experts" over others, less skilled, but who, because of their own proper inner selves, would implant *middos* into their students?

Absorbing the Teacher With the Lesson

How does one behold the fine nuances, the intangibles, the sweetness of Torah and the sweetness of just being sweet? It is of course the *talmid chacham*, the *rebbe*, and the *shimush talmidei chachamim* — the serving and intimate interacting with these great people — that teach those overtones and undertones of loving and caring for the word of G-d and for His creations, our fellow man.

Exactly how? Firstly, by their very own demeanor, their sweetness, their friendship towards their fellow man and *kaveyachol* towards G-d, their inner peace, their *emunah* and *bitachon*, their mannerisms, their goodness and the myriad of subtle nuances that makes one into a person about whom it is said: "Blessed are he, his parents, and his teachers."[27] Exposure to such people creates others in their mold. Lectures, admonishments, and threats do not perform the task; experiencing interaction with good people makes other people good in the same manner.

---

25. One must very carefully distinguish here between destructive competitiveness, and *"kinas sofrim tarbeh chochmah* — proper competitiveness develops greater learning"* (*Bava Basra* 21a). Proper competitiveness includes the vital *"Ess vahev besufah"* (Talmud *Kiddushin* 30b) — competitiveness couched in love, competing in the search for truth, not for personal glory.
26. Viz. *Talmud Beitzah* 16a; *Avos* 1:12,13,14,15; *Eruvin* 13b.
27. *Yoma* 86a.

In addition, such a teacher will teach Torah with a sweetness, exuding the Torah attitude that he has within. He does so even as he generalizes, such as: *"U'vacharta bachayim.*[28] Behold, *tei'era kinderlach*, here, beloved children, is Torah and the gift of life. Choose, I beg of you, the good life." Furthermore, in teaching and translating the words of the positive protagonists in Torah (such as the *Avos*, our forefathers), the heroes of Torah, this *rebbe* uses words and nuances that capture the essence of the commandments and conveys them — not with harshness nor dictatorship, but with love and as an offering, a gift. In the process of teaching, such a *rebbe* will bring alive the *yesharim* — their ways, their beliefs, their *menschlichkeit* and goodness, the inner Jewish soul — and transplant them into his students.

For example, when teaching children about Avraham's instructions to Sarah and Yishmael to serve the visiting angels, does the *rebbe* verbally act out Avraham's sweetness: "Beloved wife and beloved son, here is an opportunity to participate in the beautiful *mitzvah* of *hachnasas orchim*. Please help me prepare the following refreshments"? Or, does the *rebbe* act out Avraham in an autocratic way, commanding his wife and son to "Go, fetch, and do!"?[29]

When a student asks less than brilliant questions, does the *rebbe* demonstrate patience and tolerance, qualities the student himself should acquire in order to be a *yashar*, a proper Jew? *HaGaon* R' Avraham Kalmanowitz, in his *hesped* of *Mori v'Rebbi*, R' Shlomo Heiman, *zt"l*, recalled that whenever a student asked a valueless question, R' Heiman would transform the meaningless question into a valuable and sensible query so that the student should not feel foolish.

The implications for parents, *rebbes*, and teachers should be awesome. For what are we really teaching? Similarly, it should behoove every one of us to introspect and examine more closely our own doings. Additionally, because of *areivus*, the responsibil-

---

28. *Devarim* 30:19; see *Rashi*.
29. Psychopathology is frequently the result of hypocrisy and double standards that children see in their parents and teachers. Thus, the parent who acts with warmth to outsiders, such as guests, while turning around with harshness, demanding of his spouse or child to serve him/her, sends a mixed pathological message with possibly dire consequences.

ity every Jew has for his brother, and the fact that man affects man by his being and by his behavior, one not only "makes" himself, he also "makes" his fellow — into a pleasant individual or into an unpleasant one. Thus we may say that Torah learning and Torah life is, among much else, a process that shapes an individual and verily creates him and/or modifies him and brings about such dispositions of which we speak.[30] As such, Torah is (if we may use the term) reconstructive therapy par excellence.[31] It takes man to make man; and the transmitter of Torah — parent, teacher or *rebbe* — by his being and in his manner of relating with the student/child, teaches far more than by his preaching or even doing.[32]

Achieving Balance

The imbalance created by increased emphasis on "doing" coupled with decreased emphasis on "being" has another dangerous side effect. It makes it all too easy to slip into the dangerous practice of using Torah[33] to denigrate others whose religious styles differ. As the *Netziv* points out, to *act* like a Jewish zealot, to follow one's brand of piety to the extreme, without *being* the Jewish character par excellence, lends itself to gratuitous hatred

---

30. See the introduction to *Bereishis* by the *Haamek Davar*.
31. *"Sam chayim"* (*Eruvin* 54a). Torah is a perfect medication. See also *Rambam's Peirush HaMishnayos, Peah* 1:1, also *Imrei Shefer* on *Shiluach HaKan — Ki Seitzei* i22:7. Also, *Malbim* on *Parashas Bereishis* 2:17.
32. With the reader's permission, a homiletic thought: G-d said, "Let us make man" (*Bereishis* 1:26, see *Rashi* and *Ramban*). G-d creates man, his body, his brain, and a certain temperament. Yet the man's personality is shaped to a great extent by his interpersonal life, particularly that of his early childhood. "The child is the father of man," the saying goes. We are what we experience.
Thus, *HaKadosh Baruch Hu, kaveyachol,* asks of every one of us, "*Naaseh Adam —* come help Me make man." Relate to him, help him, teach him to become the kind of man I, *HaKadosh Baruch Hu,* want him to be — a Torah *mensch,* to serve Hashem, to serve mankind and lead a happier and better life himself (see J. Mermelstein, loc. cit.).
33. Psychologists speak of the "superego" in the service of the "id." To ventilate one's own rage or deal with one's own inadequacy, one finds a way to act in an evil manner while cloaked in the mantle of nobility. A famous example is the role of Inquisitors, ostensibly motivated by their fervor for the true (sic) faith, but clearly being inhuman sadists. Another example would be individuals charged with punishing evil-doers, who delight in their opportunity to legally hurt others, far more than in doing justice.

and endless strife,[34] all ostensibly in the name of being religious.[35]

What is to be done? The first step would be to expend at least as much effort for the souls of our children, their *middos* and *hashkafah*, as we do for our businesses and other possessions. Then we should search far and wide for genuine individuals who, by their own makeup, are therapeutic personalities and create for their students corrective emotional experiences. Our great *roshei yeshivah* should set up Boards of Examiners to evaluate *rebbes* and teachers, not primarily or solely for their scholarship and techniques, but no less for their own *middos* and *hashkafah*, and their *menschlichkeit*. These teachers would then teach Torah in the fullest sense of the word: learning, doing, and *being* the *baalei middos* that Torah demands of us. *Middos* would not need to be taught; *middos* would be in the air of the classroom, breathed in and absorbed by the students as they observe the teacher's personal behavior and the way he brings alive the ways of the *yesharim*.

I conclude with a personal note. One is what he is by virtue of what he has been exposed to, what has impressed him and how all this has been integrated. Though man may be a victim of his experiences, he is still responsible for his being and his behavior, because man has choice. Even the Nuremberg Trials, after World War II, confirmed this. *Kal v'chomer*, how true this is of the belief system of the Torah Jew. It thus behooves man to give credit to others for the good he has learned from them, and to assume responsibility for the bad within himself so as to become a better person.

As it does for everyone else, this holds true for me. I was fortunate to have had some outstanding teachers. My very first one was my mother, *a"h*. Among much else, I saw, I experienced, I lived, and I heard constantly, "*Vehevei mekabel es kol haadam beseiver panim yafos* — Receive everyone with a cheerful disposition."[36] At times, this

---

34. Even superficial perusal of the Jewish scene or a sampling of Jewish gossip clearly shows us how Torah and *Yiddishkeit* is used to besmirch others. *Vedai lechakima*.

35. The sad jest obviously holds: "Strife in the name of G-d will endure." Namely, *frumkeit* lends itself to fighting others, and prevails ad infinitum, because one "justifies" fighting for a worthy cause.

36. *Avos* 1:15. It is not for us to understand our Sages, much less, *chas veshalom*, to judge them. It may seem that *Shammai HaZakein* was a stern and demanding individual. If so, that was his *shitah*, his Torah point of view. Yet it was he who also practiced and lived by this dictum, "to receive everyone with a cheerful disposition."

may surely be very, very difficult, but if we have the admonition before us, if we constantly review it, practice it and see the reward, oh, how good it is![37]

---

37. Vienna, where we lived, was a transit town for emigrants from Poland and Russia. Thus, having *orchim,* guests at the Shabbos table, was the norm. When I excused myself for inadequately conversing with these *orchim,* because of my shyness, my mother, *a"h,* said, "Your shyness, your personal difficulty in conversing with strangers, is no excuse for having our guests feel uncomfortable or, *chalilah,* unwanted. It is your job to overcome your shyness, and do what you are supposed to do." And of course, doing just that is, or can be, a powerful remedy for shyness or feeling alone.

Chapter Thirty

Living by the Word

A Brief Encounter, a Telling Exchange

*I*t was hot, it was humid, and I was late. Wearing my dark Shabbos suit and black hat, *shvitzing* as I ran to *shul,* I encountered this fellow sauntering along, clad in shorts and a tee-shirt. Unencumbered by any headgear, his tousled hair was brushed ever so lightly by the occasional tiny breeze. "Good morning," I said. Stopping momentarily, he looked at me and replied, *"Shabbat shalom."*

Something rankled in my head. Since when does a "Good morning" beget a *"Shabbat shalom"*? But no time for that now. On to *shul.*

When we humans do something, there are invariably a number of reasons for our actions.[1] Unless one is a psychoanalyst, however,

---

1. Behavioral science believes that all behavior is multi-determined: that is, whatever one does comes about for more than one reason — some minor, some major. When giving *tzedakah,* for example, the major determinant, ideally, is to do G-d's will. Yet, there may be others, good, bad, conscious, or subconscious: perhaps a soft heart, guilt,

it is not always useful or desirable to analyze everything we do or experience. Yet this simple incident activated enough neurons in my brain to get me thinking.

On the surface, here were two human beings who, based upon each one's perception of the other, acted appropriately and correctly. I saw an apparently nonreligious Jew and wished him a good morning. He saw a "black-hatter" and said, *"Shabbat shalom."* So why was I troubled?

Was it the recent turmoil in the neighboring village of Hewlett Bay Park, a nonreligious neighborhood, where a girls Yeshivah High School was to open — *and we were not wanted?* Many "reasons" were cited for this, possibly some genuine, some less so, and some obviously prejudicial: additional traffic, rising noise levels, tumbling real-estate values. Other "reasons" given: "They" (the Orthodox) keep to themselves; "they" do not become part of the community or "add" to the social structure. "They" look down upon "us," taking over, coercing "us" to close our stores on Saturday. "They" patronize only their own *(shomrei Shabbos).*

My problem: What message did I send that fellow, and what message did he return to me? What messages are we *Yidden, bnei Torah* (and *menschen*) supposed to send to others, and what messages do we thereby attract ourselves? Is *their* opinion of the "black-hatters" totally due to *their* prejudice, or are we ourselves at least in part responsible for their attitude? What about words and language in general? Do we study sufficiently what our words do to others?[2] Additionally, or parenthetically, are we doing enough "selling" of *Yiddishkeit?* That is, besides our obligation to do *kiruv,* to actively attempt to bring our brethren back to *Yiddishkeit,* do we do

---

pride, gaining esteem from others, a needed charitable deduction from the IRS, or embarrassment. *Lehavdil, Rabbeinu Bechaya* explains: *"Ki adam ein tzaddik ba'aretz asher ya'aseh tov v'lo yecheta"* (*Koheles* 7:20) — that all good behavior has some bad components. Indeed, at times, the bad "helps" the good to come about. Thus the notion *"bishnei yitzrecha,"* one must serve G-d both with the *yeitzer tov* and with the *yeitzer hara* (*Berachos* 54a).

2. In this respect, Torah demands of every Torah *Yid* to be a behavioral scientist par excellence. Thus the *Tanna* in *Avos* (4:23) teaches: "Do not attempt to make amends at the moment of your fellow's rage — do not face him at the time of his downfall." Good intentions are not good enough. Study and learn what your words and your behavior do to others.

so also incidentally — but potentially powerfully so — by our behavior: our *menschlichkeit* and our spirituality?[3]

Of Risks and Possible Gains

This brings me back to my encounter, my "Good morning" and his *"Shabbat Shalom"* and the overlay of messages. Should I have risked saying "Good Shabbos" to him, implanting a feeling in him that I recognize him as a fellow Jew? After all, what is the great risk — a dirty look?

What about the possible gains? It would be naive to fantasize that my risking a "Good Shabbos" and engaging him in a mini-encounter, instead of offering a *pareve* "Good morning," would have him rush home, don a *yarmulke* and suit, and proceed to *shul.* Yet there might have been a windfall of other possibilities.

Could a hearty "Good Shabbos" have generated within him a *tzip beim hartzen,* an extra heartbeat, saying, "Yes, I too am a Jew. There is a Shabbos.[4] There is something to *Yiddishkeit."* Additionally, would I have unconsciously, but powerfully so, implanted in him a feeling that "I am a Jew, I must attempt to act like a Jew"?[5] Might such a "Good Shabbos," coupled with a genuine smile, have dispelled the notion that the "black-hatters" look down

---

3. In order to sell there must be buyers — and indeed there are. With the social fabric unraveling and value systems virtually nonexistent, there is a reawakening to return to old value systems, responsibility, and spirituality. Recent best-sellers in psychology and human behavior are *Care of the Soul* (Thomas Moore) and *The Road Less Traveled* (M. Scott Peck).

4. Anyone who lived in Williamsburg in the 40s and 50s will surely remember Reb Chaim Gelb, *a"h,* who was responsible for the closing down on Shabbos of practically all stores on Lee Avenue which had previously been open on Shabbos. His style was to walk in and say, "Good Shabbos." There was a message that worked!

5. See the fascinating *gemara* (*Bava Metzia* 85a) which tells how the simple act of bestowing an exalted title upon a wayward youth relabeled him and brought him back to *Yiddishkeit* and propriety. (This incident is discussed in Chapter 2, "To Be a Teacher.")

Lehavdil, there has been a series of research studies proving that teachers who had been intentionally misinformed regarding their students' true intellectual weaknesses, elicited relatively superior performance — simply because of inflated expectations. What a powerful tool: "You label me a Jew, I am a Jew. Consequently, I must act like a Jew."

Common sense supports this. We say to our child, "You are a good child, therefore you will act accordingly." This is a labeling technique which works, if it is genuine. Man lives up to the expectations others have of him.

upon their nonreligious brethren as outsiders and different, i.e., bad? Consequently, there might have been a *kiddush Hashem*, a glorification of G-d's Holy Name.

Finally, might I have exercised myself — and taught my fellow man — the great power of a *gut vort*, a kind word? Would I have practiced and demonstrated, by use of words, the great mandate of *"Ve'ahavta lerei'acha kamocha"* — loving one's fellow man?

The Power of Language: The Word and Life

The crowd below is divided. "Don't jump!" some shout. Others gleefully yell, "Jump!" And the man perched above, about to end his life — what does he hear and what does he feel? What is the real meaning of the crowd's words? Do they really care? Or is he (as he feels he has always been) a sideshow, a worthless nonentity, quickly to be forgotten when this is all over?

Suddenly one man detaches himself from the crowd, endangers his own life, and climbs along the windowsill slowly and carefully, until the would-be suicide spots him and stops in his tracks. The would-be rescuer says something — exactly what we'll never know, because there is no script. But lo and behold — a life is saved! How? Again, we'll never know, but we may speculate. Perhaps the lonely, desperate man "heard" a message and felt, "I am important enough for this one man to risk his life for me." Perhaps it was the effort of the man from the crowd which did it. Or perhaps that man said something that sparked a positive feeling, a meaning to life, and hope. Yes, the human word extended life to another human being.

"Maves v'chayim b'yad halashon — The human tongue rules over life and over death."[6] And it does so in more ways than one. There is life as in living and breathing, as opposed to, *chas veshalom*, physical death. There is life as in "being alive," enjoying a lively mood, feeling the joy of living, as opposed to mere existence, listlessness, unhappiness, and depression. Then there is life as emotional balm, the injection of a good feeling, a psychological band-aid, as opposed to verbal barbs, hurts, and "salt upon one's wounds."

---

6. *Mishlei* 18:21.

The Word and Life — as in Breathing and Living

There are many scenarios similar to the one above, of the man poised to jump off the ledge. They may be less dramatic, perhaps, yet they are real enough.

The physician has, *chas veshalom,* bad news. The patient is very ill, but what about hope? Will he rally all his physical and psychic resources, take his medication faithfully, practice supportive health habits to build up his immune system, and possibly survive? Or will he give up, physically and mentally, and through the by-now-proven mind-body connection "help" to destroy himself? That, to a large degree, is up to the physician and the "message" he is sending.[7]

Or the man sees a *rebbe* or *rosh yeshivah,* and the *rebbe* gives him a *berachah.* The *rebbe* himself truly believes, and a life is saved. But how? A miracle, a *berachah* of a *tzaddik,* yes — and/or, additionally, a lifesaving device G-d has built into our immune system: hope, mind over matter, a will to live. Call it what you like — it really works. *Maves v'chayim b'yad halashon* — the human word can save a life and maintain a life.

The Word and Life — as in Mood and Joy

How does man feel about himself? Is self-esteem a function of possessing money, power, good looks, intelligence, or one's vocation? All of the above, you will say. Not really. For there are those who ostensibly have a lot going for them, but inwardly feel empty. What, then, is mood, feeling, self-esteem, and human emotion?

---

7. *"Tov she'berofim leGehinnom* — The best among physicians deserves *Gehinnom* [the severest of punishments](*Kiddushin 82a).*" Why? The most common explanation is that *tov* numerically equals 17. That is, the good (i.e., conceited) physician does not subscribe to one of the 18 *berachos* in *Shemoneh Esrei,* namely *"Refa'einu* — G-d heal us." He thinks he can do so with his own scientific expertise. Now, not every disbeliever automatically deserves *Gehinnom.* But the "best" physician does because he virtually can kill his patient. Medical science often has nothing to offer, yet *emunah,* faith and hope, does — even scientifically so. Certainly to the Torah Jew, *emunah* does heal.

What awesome power in the word, the attitude, and the message of hope! And the totally scientific, conceited physician denies his patient this hope because he does not possess it himself.

In a most simplistic way, one can say that self-esteem, mood, courage, and drive are derivatives of messages one sends to oneself and receives from others. Such messages, of course, can be and usually are colored and distorted — at times for the good, and at times causing harm. These messages are sent, at times clearly: *"You are good,"* or *"You are bad,"* but more frequently in a subtle way: *"You are noticed,"* or *"You are ignored."* And the messages one sends to oneself — these too are projections of what one believes others think of him.[8]

One example should suffice. Look around in *shul*, in school, or wherever people gather. Why is one an outsider, slinking off by himself when school is over or *davening* has ended? He is shy, you will say. This is probably true — but what are we doing about it? Do we take the easy way out and rationalize: This fellow likes to keep to himself, he has nothing to say (which really means: "I don't enjoy talking to him")? Or do we use the tongue that the *Ribbono Shel Olam* has given us to inject life into this fellow? "Hi! *Shalom aleichem*! What is your name? What do you do? How are you [genuinely]? What do you think about the *rav's derashah*?" Or *(lehavdil)*, "We need another man on our baseball team!"

A smile, a word, a warm handshake, a mini-encounter, or drawing an isolate into a social circle, can give life to our fellow man. Giving him a message: "You are one of us, you belong, you are wanted and you are needed, you are a *mensch tz'vishen menschen*, a fellow human being contributing to others your social self."

The Word and Life — as in Healing and Hurting

Various *mitzvos* enjoy greater or less popularity, in ways unrelated to their significance. One popular *mitzvah* is *nichum aveilim*, visiting and comforting mourners during *shivah*, the first week of mourning. People travel great distances to do their duty, and if unable to come,

---

8. Numerous research projects have proven that body build does relate to personality, success in life, and emotional status. These are obviously not functions of something within, e.g., an extra muscle making a leader, or a pair of glasses a scholarly bookworm. Rather, it is the ingestion of a view of oneself originating from others, e.g., "I am what others say I am."

offer a profusion of excuses. Obviously, besides the great *mitzvah,* there is much more. Yet people frequently ask: "What is one to say to the mourner? What real comfort could one offer?"[9] To begin with (and to continually bear in mind), it behooves the Torah Jew to consult the *Shulchan Aruch,*[10] which tells us not to speak until the mourner himself opens the conversation. What follows, then, should be a function of the "fifth *Shulchan Aruch*": good sense based upon thought, feeling, sensitivity, and our responsibility to be therapists for our fellow man.[11]

We have much to achieve by not speaking to the mourner. To begin with, we do no harm, which is the primary duty of every healer of body and healer of mind. We also send the mourner vital messages. Our presence, our genuine empathy, our demeanor, speaks volumes: "You are not alone. I care. I understand, or at least try to. You have sustained a loss of a loved one; in a small way my presence and that of others should fill the void and repair the loss." Then, of course, you acknowledge what the mourner says. You catch the spilling of his heart, you provide an opportunity for the healing power of catharsis, and you offer genuine empathy.

Other Times for Mourning

In real life, even under the best of circumstances, every human being has periods of mourning and loss: loss of health or wealth, loss of self-esteem, loss of self-control, and regrets. People may suffer injuries to their pride, worries that are real or exaggerated, depressions and anxieties.

Do we stop, feel with the sufferer, think, and then do or say something that is helpful? Do we listen — genuinely so — and say nothing, yet provide empathy and an opportunity for catharsis, permitting him *"aropzuredden fun zein hartz"* — to get things off his chest? Or do we rush in blindly, speak, and cause far more harm than good?

---

9. One is frequently saddened by perhaps well-meaning, but misguided, visitors who, in order to distract the mourner, create a social get-together rather than true *nichum aveilim.*
10. *Yoreh De'ah* 376:1; also, Talmud *Moed Katan* 28b.
11. See note 2.

"You are depressed? Look, the sun is shining, you have your health and your wealth and wonderful children. What should the poor people of India say?"

Or, "You worry about this? You are crazy! This is far-fetched and very unlikely to happen!"

The results? The depressed and the anxious continue to feel the way they do, and you have added a little salt on their wounds, for now they are not only depressed and anxious, but also fools — and crazy ones, at that. Rationally, you do make sense. But emotionally you have not helped; you have added to the hurt.

"You are 38 and not married. You are too picky," you, the all-knowing oracle, say. Actually, you really have no idea whatsoever why the person is unmarried in spite of a wish to be wed. Yet you have added additional pain to the single person by playing "Let's blame the sufferer."

"You were mugged. I am sorry. Where, when? Two o'clock at night walking alone in that bad neighborhood? No wonder!" So what did you accomplish? You told the sufferer that he himself is to blame for his loss. Great therapy!

Why, where, when? Could have ... should have ... Tell me ... I'll tell you, I know it all. What are we doing with our tongues? Helping? Or, *chas veshalom*, hurting?

On the Positive Side

On the positive side, do we use sufficiently our *maves v'chayim* tongues to provide emotional nutrients to our loved ones, to our friends, to our neighbors, and to the world as a whole? Do we seek out opportunities[12] to bestow such messages, emotional nutrients, band-aids, and pleasure pills upon others?

Do we say "thank you" sufficiently and create opportunities to do so? "Thank you for the piece of chicken ... Thank you for being here ... Thank you for your smile ... Thank you, stranger, for populating my neighborhood, so that I feel less alone ..." (and of course, "Thank you, *Ribbono Shel Olam*" — but that is something I do for myself).

---

12. "*Machshevos adam ve'tachbulosav* — G-d judges man's thoughts and his machinations, his scheming for good as well as for bad" (*Yamim Nora'im* liturgy).

Are we big enough to say, "I am sorry," when we have actually hurt others, or even when inadvertently and through distortion another human being feels hurt? Finally, do we say, "I care about you ... I love you ... You matter ...You are a *tzelem Elokim* — made in G-d's image"?

Learning to Use Our Tongues to Heal

Assuming one has neither a pathological need to hurt others by being an angry, hurtful, aggressive human being, nor a need to boost his ego by enjoying the pain of others *(mis'chabed beklon chaveiro),*[13] what is the training program for developing a life-sustaining tongue?

To begin with, one disciplines himself to pause, think carefully, and speak to those in pain only if he is quite sure that his words will diminish the hurt rather than aggravate it. "Well, one has to say something" is not true — even when the sufferer *asks* for a response. Your genuine listening ear, your demeanor of empathy, are already at work. Most certainly, do not attempt to teach one at the time of his pain — one does not teach his fellow to swim while he is drowning.

Time and again we resolve to watch our tongues, yet we fail. Why? Man is a creature of habit. Doing something even once[14] sets the stage for it to happen again. Certainly then, it is difficult to change a long-term habit. Yet, it can be done.

Needed is a constant alert in order to reprogram one's verbal

---

13. *Yerushalmi Chagigah* 2a.
14. Note *Bereishis* 27:19, "*Anochi Eisav bechorecha.*" *Rashi* emphasizes that Yaakov's words to Yitzchak can be construed so that no untruth was said, namely, "I am Yaakov. Eisav is your firstborn." Why this verbal gymnastic? Upon Rivkah's orders, Yaakov was to lie to Yitzchak. I suggest: Yes, Yitzchak was to hear an untruth, but Yaakov's tongue should not lie — in order not to change him and alter him. Similarly, after Avraham *Avinu* told Avimelech that his wife, Sarah, was his sister, he later explained, "Moreover she is indeed my sister' " (*Bereishis* 20:12). Really, she was the daughter of Avraham's brother, but through the dictum "grandchildren are as one's children," Sarah, the granddaughter of Avraham's father, was also the "daughter" of his father — hence, Avraham's "sister." Although he had deceived Avimelech, his lips did not speak untruth.
Every behavior conditions and sets the stage for subsequent similar behavior. Thus, *mitzvah goreres mitzvah, v'aveirah goreres aveirah* — any deed determines the deed to follow, good or bad.

habits. So you try, but *ess leigt zich nit oif de tzung*, the tongue is simply not conditioned *not* to speak, or to speak positively. What then?

Think what you did when you wanted to expand your vocabulary. You found the word or phrase, and sought out opportunities to use it. Here, too, seek out opportunities, attempt all kinds of *tachbulos*[15] — strategies, schemes, plots and projects — to implant into yourself the habit of *lashon tov*, a good tongue.

But suppose one is a person of few words, shy — in part, genetically so?[16] There is still hope. If one programs his heart — not merely trains, but conditions it[17] — then his mouth will follow suit. This person can depend upon the promise of "*haba letaher mesayin oso* — he who attempts to mend his ways can count upon G-d's help."[18]

This is our task: constant vigilance, reprogramming our feelings and our thoughts — and soliciting G-d's help to succeed.

---

15. See note 12.
16. There is evidence that a certain amount of shyness is genetically inherited. *Lehavdil*, note "*umeiHashem ma'aneh lashon* — verbal facility is a gift of G-d" (*Mishlei* 16:1).
17. "*L'adam ma'archei leiv* — it is up to man to condition his heart" (*Mishlei*, ibid.).
18. *Shabbos* 104a.

Chapter Thirty-one

Piety, Psychopathology, and Parent Power

A Torah of Life ... and Emotional Stability

linicians who serve the Orthodox Jewish community are frequently called upon to concern themselves with matters regarding which it is not quite clear whether they are within the province of psychopathology or are really religious issues where guidance or resolution should be sought from appropriate religious authorities. Such matters become particularly thorny when they are enveloped within interpersonal conflicts, such as between parents and children or husband and wife, because at those times other confounding factors also operate to becloud the real issues. Less frequently, one also encounters situations where an individual finds himself behaving in certain ways ostensibly because of religious conviction, yet somehow he himself senses an overlay of psychopathology of which he wants to rid himself.

In proceeding to deal with such matters, extreme caution is in order for more than one reason. To begin with, merely speaking of Torah-true Jews and mental-health problems in one breath may give our detractors added ammunition in their notion that being a *shomer Torah u'mitzvos* (observant Jew) does not make one into a better human being, but to the contrary, that there exists *(chas veshalom)* a correlation between *chareidus* (piety) and maladjustment. This idea, of course, is not a particularly new or novel one. Anti-Semites, Jewish and non-Jewish, had "discovered" the "Evil Jew" ages ago. Similarly, well-known clinicians in the mental-health field, past and present, have confused their otherwise correct clinical observations with wild metapsychological speculations or personal biases to conclude that "religion is a neurosis," or at least contributes to mental ill health.[1] To the contrary, it has been clearly demonstrated elsewhere[2] that, holding other variables constant, true and normative Torah life indeed correlates with positive mental health.

The fact that certain individuals who are ostensibly *shomrei Torah u'mitzvos* do manifest antisocial behaviors cannot shake our axiomatic belief that our *Toras chaim*[3] provides us with a tried and tested blueprint for impulse controls and for social and emotional adjustment, and prescriptions for positive mental health. It merely says that, imperfect as we surely all are, such individuals are not truly *shomrei Torah u'mitzvos*, or are perhaps "partial" ones who conveniently forsake certain portions of the *Shulchan Aruch*, or fall prey to the demands of the ever active *yeitzer hara* (evil inclination).

---

1. Viz., W.D. Criddle, "Guidelines for Challenging Irrational Beliefs," *Rational Living*, 1974, pp. 8-13. Also Albert Ellis, *Humanistic Psychotherapy: The Rational Emotive Approach* (New York: Science House, 1970), pp. 24-25. Similarly, Sigmund Freud, *passim*. For his overall view on religion, see Ernest Jones, *The Life and Works of Sigmund Freud* (New York: Basic Books, 1962), pp. 349-374.

2. Jacob Mermelstein, "Halachic Values and the Clinical Practice of Psychotherapy," *Intercom* 16:2, pp. 4-9.

3. *"V'chai bahem"* (*Yoma* 85b), fulfillment of commandments cannot be contradictory to life or health.

Similarly, those suffering from anxieties and depression have either been exposed to excessive trauma or have failed to integrate *emunah* (faith, trust) and other Torah prescriptions into their lives, which would have permitted them to benefit from their protective mechanisms. To the Torah-true Jew, *"V'chai bahem —* and you shall live by them" is unequivocal assurance that *mitzvah* observance furthers physical, social, and emotional well-being.

Yet even among our very own it has become permissible, indeed fashionable, to speak of *"frumies"* or of being *"meshuga frum,"* as if piety does somehow relate with psychopathology. Here, of course, as in the case of all behavior, an individual views that which he practices as "normal," while the practices of others, particularly if extreme, are seen as abnormal, or *meshuga*. In the hands of *kallim* (superficial *mitzvah* observers) this notion is exceedingly dangerous, since it permits them to all too readily label any or all honest piety as pathology.

Moreover, in cases of parent-child conflicts, the problem is compounded by the question of to what extent parents have a right, indeed an obligation, to have a say in their child's behavior. Specifically, one must ask what is parenting and guiding — and what is simply fighting, interfering, or engaging in pathological power struggles.

Finally, in "matters of the heart," it is well-nigh impossible to truly sort out inner motivation in oneself or in others, or the proportion of the mixture that determines behavior. It thus has to be dealt with within the dictum of *shemitoch shelo lishmah ba lishmah*[4] — whether deeds performed because of impure motivation will lead eventually to pure and proper deeds and motivation.

Disentangling the Threads

Awesome and complex though all this is, an attempt must be made to disentangle the threads of piety, pathology, and interpersonal power struggles from each other, trusting that what is said here will not be misconstrued or misused by the reader. We begin with some typical situations, remembering that specific variations

---

4. *Pesachim* 50b and *Berachos* 17a; see also notes 5, 6, 7.

should not be that important once principles are seen. Similarly, descriptions of extremes are for purposes of illustration, though the nature of the situation would hold even for less radical cases.

Take, for example, the ("modern") Orthodox parent who harasses his son because he refuses to leave his yeshivah in order to learn how to earn a livelihood. Conversely, the son refuses to leave the yeshivah, and has "no time at all" for his father or his family, because it would interfere with his learning. In addition, he "demands" total support, financially or otherwise, from parents, spouse, or in-laws, no matter what the cost. The task here is to find answers to several complex questions: Is this father insensitive to the child's needs? Is he dictatorial? Is he misguided in his religious perspective? Is he engaging in a power struggle? Or: Is he genuinely concerned about his son's welfare but has somehow failed to maintain the kind of relationship in which viewpoints of parents and children are not that discordant, and such matters are dealt with amicably? Conversely, is this son truly committed to learning, or does he remain in the yeshivah in order to thwart his father, to cop out of life's responsibilities (including true Torah behavior and learning), or to engage in a power struggle with his father which he can win — because he has "Torah on his side"? The basic questions here would be whether we are dealing with genuine, if misguided, individuals, where relatively superficial family counseling is in order, whether more severe psychopathology reigns, or whether interpersonal power struggles are taking place.

On a simpler level, there is the father whose *chareidus* (piety) puts his child out of reach of ordinary pleasures and parent-child interaction. There is no time to waste on talk or play, no family trips or picnics, certainly no concerts or museum visits, and *(lehavdil)* no interaction even within the context of learning, *davening*, or the *rebbe's tish*. The child is clinically disturbed, and one hypothesizes that inadequate parenting is the culprit. Here one would want to know whether the father's forbidding posture is due to real piety, or whether it is the result of his own authoritarian upbringing, latent hostility, schizoid withdrawal, oedipal problems, or other neurotic mechanisms. In the case of the former, help should be forthcoming in terms of insight into what is happening, and guidance toward adequate parenting within the framework of that father's piety. In the case of the latter, more intensive treatment is called for in dealing with the pathology which is now evident.

The Areas of Overlapping Causes

More complex are the intrapersonal conflicts where piety and pathology may run into each other, making it difficult to discern whether one is dealing with true — if extreme — piety *(dikduk b'mitzvos)* or with psychopathology (compulsivity) cloaked in religious fervor. For example, the woman who harasses her household weeks before Pesach to remove all traces of *chametz* may do so because of one reason or a combination of several, namely:

(a) *Chametz* is forbidden in even the minutest amounts — thus this is true piety.

(b) The lady is generally anxious, and compulsively checks and double checks — thus her religious practices (and Pesach cleaning) are in line with her general (anxious) behavior.

(c) This individual has a more specific anxiety-related syndrome, relating to cleanliness — thus her meticulous Pesach cleaning is in line with this specific compulsivity.

(d) Harassing one's family for Pesach is an "excellent opportunity" to be hostile in a safe fashion (superego in the service of the id); or, here is a chance to control others, to be heard, or to satisfy other neurotic needs.

One may readily recognize determinant (a) as obviously religious behavior. Determinants (b) and also (c), if part and parcel of a persistent structure, can similarly be expressions of true *mitzvah* observance. Thus, the Chazon Ish reportedly commented that the Brisker Rav's great piety and, for example, his frequent repeating of words during *Krias Shema* were in line with his general attention to detail, worry, and need for certainty in important matters. Contrary to frequently cited interpretations of this incident, Rabbi Shemaryahu Karelitz, nephew of the Chazon Ish, assured me in a personal communication that this remark did not *chas veshalom* imply criticism; it clearly shows the importance of the *mitzvah* in that it generates anxiety and is dealt with in *that* individual's habitual (normal, i.e., usual) anxious fashion. Yet the intent and purpose of the behavior is the *mitzvah*.

On the other hand, totally neurotic motivations, as in determinant (d), have little, if anything, to do with *mitzvah,* and can indeed lead to *aveirah.*[5] First, as with all compulsivity, there is the "all or nothing" possibility — total attention to relative nonessentials and neglect of essentials.[6] Moreover, if the repetition of words (in the *Shema*) is carried to a pathological extreme, back and forth, it may no longer be *Krias Shema* — reading the *Shema* — but a caricature of the *mitzvah,* a reading of words. Moreover, performing a *mitzvah* in such distorted form may interfere with *tefillah b'tzibur,* with learning, even with providing for one's family and general human existence. The essential test, then, would be to determine whether this particular manifestation of piety adds to one's total religious behavior or detracts from it.[7] More fundamentally, one must consider the intent of Torah life and *mitzvah* observance — the joy coming from an introjected beloved Torah, the *simchah shel mitzvah* — as opposed to

---

5. Note, for example, *mitzvos shehechziku bo kusiim* etc. (*Berachos* 47b). *Kusiim,* who adopted certain *mitzvos,* observed these to the extreme, while totally neglecting all others. According to some authorities, they embraced Judaism (at least parts of it) because of fear and superstition (*geirei aroyos hayu*). Thus their observance had nothing to do with *mitzvah* observance; it was simply a neurotic (superstitious) device to ward off fear. Halachically, they were not considered to be Jews.

6. Another example of the "all or nothing" phenomenon also occurs with certain *baalei teshuvah* (individuals newly and rather suddenly enthused with Torah), some of whom manifest compulsive traits. Have these individuals truly developed a love for Torah — but in their "enthusiasm" (and relative ignorance) accepted it in a compulsive fashion? Or have these individuals sought an arena for their compulsivity and believe to have found it in Torah with its rituals, exacting demands, and authority consciousness? As one such individual put it to me: "Fantastic! No doubts, no unknowns, no need for decisions — Torah even tells us which shoe to put on first and which to lace first!" In either case, the therapist is frequently called upon to sustain their Torah behavior, yet free them from the attendant compulsivity — a difficult, and at times almost impossible, task. One patient, after a successful analysis, put it this way: "I now seem to have less of a religious experience — but I believe I am doing more what the *Ribbono Shel Olam* really wants." Thus, such *baalei teshuvah* may well reach great heights in their fervor — but may also lose all of it if the primary determinant is compulsivity, and other devices are found to serve their psychological needs.

Yet another example is the *yeshivah bachur* whose extreme fervor in learning, both in terms of intensity and time (frequently against the advice of his *rosh yeshivah*), culminates in total nonlearning once he leaves the yeshivah and/or his compulsivity invests itself in other matters.

7. Note the *Ran* in *Pesachim* 50b on the question of *"Shemitoch shelo lishmah ba lishmah."* He concludes that though at certain times, *mitzvah* observance predicated upon improper motivation will eventually lead to proper motivation and should thus be encouraged, at other times it should be harshly discouraged. He says, or can be understood as saying, that the former dictum obtains when, for example, selfish motivations operate, which help to get an individual started *(bishnei yitzrecha),* but once initiated they become

performance out of neurotic fear[8] with attendant bitterness and impatience. Similarly, one must ask: Is one's *mitzvah* observance with feeling (warmth, closeness to Hashem) — or does it appear as automated, repetitive, compulsive, magical behavior (*mitzvas anashim melumadah*)?[9] And what is the outcome? Does the *mitzvah* performer become a better person himself, and more loving toward others, or is he bitter, angry with himself, and controlling others, belittling them and using his "superior" *mitzvah* observance to cast down his fellow man?[10]

Practically, then, to distinguish true, if extreme, piety from compulsive psychopathology, one may use an intrapersonal as well as an interpersonal approach. In the former mode, one may ask whether an individual's particular piety is correct from a Torah point of view and consonant with that individual's total Torah behavior.[11] Concerning interpersonal life, one must discern the extent to which a particular brand of extreme piety lends itself to, or better yet, is propelled by, psychological ploys to control or harm others.[12]

---

part and parcel of him — a new personality. (Compare Allport's notion of "Functional Autonomy": C.W. Allport in Calvin S. Hall and Gardner Lindsey, *Theories of Personality* [New York: John Wiley and Sons, Inc., 1957], pp. 257-293.) On the other hand, when the *shelo lishmah* has an "anti-Torah" determinant, a life of its own, such as an evil intention, this type of observance will not lead to *lishmah*. It must be condemned. In the same way, when a person's observance is totally motivated by neurotic-compulsive propellants, it will not lead to *lishmah* without intensive therapeutic intervention. In the words of the *Ran*, "There are many kinds of *shelo lishmah*." See also *Tosfos, Berachos* 17a.

Concerning Torah behavior shaping personality for the better, see also Jacob Mermelstein in *Intercom* 17:1, pp. 31-36.

8. See *Tosfos, Gittin* 55b, on the matter of "*Ashrei adam mefached tamid,*" also *Maharsha.* Only fear concerning *dikduk b'mitzvos*, Torah learning, or other *reality* factors should be encouraged. On the other hand, baseless fear (neurotic anxiety) or anticipating harm is deemed as sinful (see also *Berachos* 60a). Also, *Rashi (Devarim* 18:13), on the *pasuk*: "*Tamim tihye im Hashem Elokecha* — Be simple (wholesome) with your G-d," makes it clear that one must refrain from anticipating anxiety, from overplanning, and from superstition. Rather, one should be simple, perfect (*tamim*), and put his trust in Hashem.

9. *Yeshayahu* 29:13.

10. See the *Shaarei Teshuvah* 1:18 on the *pasuk* in *Mishlei* (28:12) regarding how the righteous find good in people as opposed to the wicked who search out the errors in people in order to cast them down. He says: "*Hatzaddikim mefa'arim umechabdim bnei adam* — The righteous praise and honor others." See also note 30.

11. In a very general sense, perhaps the point made by Reb Yisrael Salanter, referring to the *gemara Chulin* 105a, that religious practice should have some uniformity, could be applied — albeit with great caution.

12. *Yatza secharo behefseido* — one loses more than one gains. (Free interpretation of *Avos* 5:14.)

Concerning religious behaviors which generate parent-child conflicts, one must first dismiss out of hand issues that are clearly battles of wills and use *Yiddishkeit* as a battleground, but have in reality nothing to do with guiding our youth, or with *chinuch*. For example, there is the parent who has failed in the education process of his child and hounds him instead — or, conversely, the child who defies a parent — on whether the boy's hair is too long or short, or the girl's dresses too immodest or overly modest. Such a situation will deteriorate into a power struggle and accomplish nothing but polarization and hate. Parents argue that they have a "right" to impose their brand of *Yiddishkeit* upon their children, and, conversely, children claim to have a "right" to lead their own lives. There may be merit in both "rights," or even in the issues involved. Yet, when the struggle goes on regardless of adverse results, and is continued ad infinitum — this is clearly a struggle, a power play. The bitter result, the "war" that is lost to all, is the proof of the nature of the battles. Needless to say, there is also the *aveirah* of *lifnei iver*,[13] causing the child not only to continue the wrong (or the extreme right), but to disrespect the parent in the process.

The Positive Use of Authority

This brings us to the ever complex matter of authority vested in parents and teachers,[14] and how this authority is to be exercised. Here, careful distinction must be made between true authority on the one hand, and authoritarianism and permissiveness on the other. Like most extreme and opposite psychological phenomena, authoritarianism (dictatorship) and permissiveness essentially stem from the very same root — an inadequate parent or teacher. The incompetent authority, unable to reach the child (learner) through modeling and a loving relationship,[15] makes

---

13. "Do not place a stumbling before the blind" (*Vayikra* 19:14), referring to any action that can ensnare another in a misdeed. Thus one must avoid overly harsh treatment of one's child lest it incite him to act disrespectfully.
14. Viz., "*Es Hashem Elokecha tira*" — *lerabos talmidei chachamim* (*Pesachim* 22b). "Fear of G-d" should be extended to include awe of one's teacher.
15. See text of Jacob Mermelstein's address, "Torah Insight in Educational Psychology," delivered at AOJT forum, "Torah Sources for a System of Pedagogy," in "Proceedings of AOJT Professional Conference," *AOJT News*, Nov. 1974, 9:2, pp. 55-57; also Chapter 11, "To Be a Parent: The Whole and the Sum of Its Parts."

harsh, arbitrary rules,[16] or gives up entirely and fosters permissiveness. Both extremes are invoked to simplify life for the authority, but in actuality cause havoc and severe intra- and interpersonal disturbances. This is a far cry, and qualitatively very different, from child rearing that is based upon strength of conviction *and* authority, *but* in an ever-loving, relating fashion.

Proper child rearing uses authority (there are values and standards for behavior), love, approval, and direction. As a result, the child's conscience is developed to the point of self-direction, which now rewards itself (feeling good) and punishes itself (feeling guilty); yet, all of it is enveloped in unconditional love. Authority is viewed with both love and awe, and will be sustained through this balance (really, reverence). On the other hand, authoritarianism produces extreme negativism and defiance, or overt compliance (to the extreme, because of mortal fear), but with latent rage. Permissiveness usually brings about chaos and nihilism, a life void of meaning and substance.

Wise parents and teachers ever so carefully proceed according to the situation and the child with whom they are dealing. In exercising their authority, they subscribe to a general value system, such as the concept of reward and punishment, the value of time, and the need for achievement. But they individualize their exhortations. They never, for example, indiscriminately wield admonitions such as, "*Men vett mohnen* — you'll have to account for that," to the child already beset with overwhelming guilt, or, "*A shod die zeit, men darf shteigen* — must not waste time, one must strive," to the student already racing along far beyond his mental or emotional capacities. Whether the arbitrary, ever-hounding dispensers of such admonitions — frequently so-called educators who should know better — are destructive compulsives themselves or simply use poor judgment, the result is the same: The child/adolescent suffers, and is likely to become a compulsive himself.

---

16. Note the dictum, *"Al yatil adam eimah yeseirah be'soch beiso* — One should not be excessively harsh and authoritarian" (*Gittin* 6b). Similarly, the notion, "*Le'olam yehei smol docheh veyamin mekarev* — One should repel with one's left, while drawing near with one's right," indicating that the exercise of authority is to be within a caring and loving relationship (*Sotah* 47a).

The Disciplined Jew in a Compulsive Society

Because all of this affects a substantial portion of the population, it is essential to discover the source of this particular syndrome (compulsivity), and ways and means to bring about relief to those already affected. Basically, emotional disturbances come about because of various factors, some of which are intrafamily relationships, particular child-rearing practices, values espoused by one's social group, and environmental factors inherent in society at large.[17] It is generally agreed that today's striving middle class, if and when afflicted with psychopathology, tends to "favor" the obsessive-compulsive syndromes.[18]

Even in the absence of clinical symptomatology there is a proclivity towards the development of compulsive personalities who are "driven" and must succeed at all costs, who are highly conforming, overly inhibited, and rigid. They are excessively exacting, highly value self-control, and tend to repress and intellectualize feelings. To bring this about, child-rearing practices are highly controlling, with an overinvolvement colored with both anger and anxiety.

The overly striving, compulsive, rigid, frigid, and unloving Orthodox Jew, then, *does not* reflect Jewish values. It is rather the Jew living within a particular social group which produces compulsives. This social group espouses values which may *sound* Jewish (like chicken soup) but, if anything, are akin to materialism, authoritarianism, or phony Victorianism. Briefly, these values equate happiness with material success, regard safety as more important than joy, value brain power to the exclusion of emotion, stress the repression of feelings, and make shame an experience to be avoided at all costs. Child rearing takes place within the context of arbitrary dogma where being a parent is a "job" — making sure the child is always "safe" and striving toward success (i.e., education, money, power, fame). And the child is controlled with "love," which becomes conditional — "if you

---

17. See Marvin K. Opler, "Cultural Determinants of Mental Disorders," in *Handbook of Clinical Psychology*, Benjamin B. Wolman, ed., (New York: McGraw Hill, 1965), p. 240.
18. See Henry P. Laughlin, *The Neuroses* (Washington: Butterworths, 1967), pp. 244-45.

are good." In essence, then, we "accept" the child's intellect and reinforce it — but we reject him as a feeling, sensing, loving human being. As a result, the child fights the parental intrusion, and at the very same time incorporates these values, some intact and some with his very own neurotic modifications — a form of neurotic compromise.

It is no wonder that ostensible Torah behavior is all too frequently flavored by compulsivity, yet nonetheless is defended as a special brand of piety or *dikduk b'mitzvos*. Torah does teach values that should bring about desirable behavior, but the control of one's behavior should result from the internalization of such values. It should not result from blind repression, authoritarianism, and dogma, leaving intact undesirable tendencies, ever ready to explode whenever control is loosened or becomes unbearable.

Needless to say, materialism, or achievement and the pursuit of knowledge unaccompanied by commensurate action,[19] is not appreciated. The entire body of *Torah She'be'al Peh* (the Oral Law), and the knowledge open to all of us should lead us to obedience that does not flow merely from blind dogma. Moreover, while one should strive toward the highest perfection, a concept such as "*ad she'yado maga'as* — [one's responsibility extends] as far as one can reach"[20] clearly indicates that there are limits to what one is expected to achieve.[21] In fact, we are warned, "*Al tehi tzaddik harbei* — Man should not be overly righteous."[22] If one goes to unwarranted extremes in one particular virtue, one may in the process fall prey to other weaknesses.[23]

Similarly, on the question of blind repression of impulses and hypocrisy, neither of them are encouraged. The *yeitzer hara* has a

19. *Avos* 3:12, also 3:22.
20. *Shulchan Aruch Orach Chaim* 433.
21. See *Avos* 2:21; "*Lo alecha hamelachah ligmor* — Yours is not to complete the task." Also see the *Sfas Emes* on the *pasuk* and *Rashi* in *Bereishis* 1:1 saying that though G-d's design was for perfection in man, it is simultaneously decreed that perfection is impossible.
22. *Midrash Rabbah, Bamidbar* 21:6.
23. See the *Or HaChayim* on "*Af ki omar*" (*Bereishis* 3:1), how it is the *yeitzer hara* who is all forbidding in order to heighten lust and have man give up Torah altogether. This notion has also been voiced by the Chafetz Chaim on "*Vehaser Satan milfaneinu ume'achareinu.*" See also "*Lo dayoch mah she'asrah Torah*" (*Talmud Yerushalmi, Nedarim* 9a).

place in this world, albeit to be controlled and channeled.[24] By the same token, human behavior, in *all* its aspects, is dealt with honestly and frankly without hypocritical shame.[25] *Chazal,* in the context of Torah study, do not shrink from discussing frankly most intimate matters,[26] yet condemn lewdness with utter harshness.[27] The power of unwanted or excessive impulses is recognized, yet is to be dealt with not through massive repression, but by therapeutic sublimation and displacement.[28] There is no room for phoniness, nor for false modesty. Rabbi Aharon Kotler, *zt"l,* in a personal communication, spoke out against skipping "delicate" *parshios,* lest our children be "disturbed." Honest Torah learning by healthy individuals, he said, cannot possibly harm our young.

Nonetheless, though qualitatively quite different, honest piety and compulsive pedantry are easily confused because of certain superficial similarities[29] and also because certain practitioners of piety in public positions themselves contaminate their *Yiddishkeit* with compulsivity.[30]

---

24. E.g. *Yoma* 69b — the need for the *yeitzer hara* to propel life (note similarity to the concept of the "id"). See also *Mishlei* 25:21, the comments of the Gaon, how the *yeitzer hara* facilitates the good deed *(Mosh'cheihu lebeis hamidrash* — Have him participate in the *mitzvah).*
25. E.g. *Berachos* 62a — how one is to learn *all* of human behavior including proper toilet practices, because *"Torah hi ve'lilmod ani tzarich* — It is teaching, and I must learn it."
26. E.g. *Bava Metzia* 84a — sexual behavior is discussed without shame or false modesty.
27. E.g. *Shabbos* 33A — *"Hakol yodin* — The Sages harshly condemn those who prattle about private conduct.
28. See *Succah* 52a and 52b concerning how one's drives can be displaced and sublimated. Note in particular *Maharsha.* Similarly, see *Yoma* 78b as to how aggressive drives can be dealt with. *"Kol de'asrah lanu Torah* — All that is forbidden [can be practiced elsewhere in an acceptable fashion]" *(Chullin* 109b) — may also be a form of how Torah itself provides for displacement and sublimation of one's desires.
29. See Sigmund Freud, "Obsessive Acts and Religious Practices" (first published in 1907), in *Collected Papers,* Vol. 2 (New York: Basic Books, 1959), pp. 25-85. While Freud obviously had no understanding of Torah, and wrongly used pseudoscience to "explain Torah," he does not equate compulsivity with religiosity. In his words "... equally obvious are the differences (between religion and compulsivity) some of which are so startling that they make the comparison into a sacrilege ... an obsessional neurosis furnishes a tragicomic travesty of a private religion" (pp. 27-28).
30. See note 10. It is a sad comment to find some latter-day "preachers" who harass their fellow Jews through fault finding, belittling, and harsh denunciations — all in the name of *Yiddishkeit.* In contradistinction, for example, Rabbi Avraham Kalmanowitz, *zt"l,* in his *hesped* on *Rebbi u'Mori* Rabbi Shlomo Heiman, *zt"l,* lauded the *niftar* (deceased) for building and elevating his students gratuitously, finding and inventing rationales to make even errors sound good and worthy of discussion.

Deprogramming the Compulsive

What is to be done? Obviously, as a preventative measure, sound knowledge of what Torah life is all about (including the proverbial "fifth *Shulchan Aruch*"), proper child-rearing practices, and sound values, beliefs, and attitudes that save one from psychopathology should be encouraged. For those who have already "caught the bug," the road to adjustment is quite difficult. In part, this is due to the fact that compulsive behavior "looks good" and is socially valued[31] — to strive, to be correct, to control oneself, etc.; and in part because it serves powerful neurotic needs.

Offhand, the most obvious approach would be to "tell" the individual, to explain the errors of his ways to him, to consult a *gadol*, a *rosh yeshivah*, a *rebbe*, to show him the halachically proper way. Unfortunately, such intellectual-educational approaches are rarely useful. Indeed, the compulsive will simply label that *gadol* as being "not *frum* enough." This is so because, while our compulsive may respect the *gadol* in other matters, he cannot accept any challenges to his compulsivity because of the powerful neurotic needs it serves. In addition, because of intellectualization, that individual somehow knows it all, knows it better, and will out-argue anyone who stands in his way. Thus, any amelioration of the symptoms can come about only by dealing with his underlying neurotic needs and by breaking through and establishing emotional contact[32] that overrides intellectualization and rational power struggles.

Those who undertake to deal with such matters must have sufficient knowledge to recognize the difference between honest piety, no matter how extreme, and compulsivity; be thoroughly versed in the very many specific practices of particular groups; and remain ever ready to consult the *gadol* when true Torah behavior and compulsivity overlap. Therapists subscribing to the modern dynamic methods — dealing with both underlying determinants as well as with current everyday behavior — must also be well versed to counter chapter and verse (Torah and Talmud) that patients cite out of context to support their compulsivity.

---

31. Henry P. Laughlin, *ibid.*, n. 17.
32. Reb Yisrael Salanter always stressed that the study of *mussar* should be *be'hispaalus* — creating feelings and emotionality to make such learning effective. Also note the "*rebbe's tish*" — how rational teaching is to be enveloped in feelings generated through camaraderie.

On a rational level then, perhaps, a somewhat new view of Torah and its demands of man must be developed in the mind of the patient. For example, the value of man in "being" (every man a *tzelem Elokim*) as opposed to "doing," may free him from his driven behavior and the exaggerated need to produce. And by carefully distinguishing between *teshuvah* and constructive guilt *(sheviras halev)*, and destructive guilt *(atzvus)*, Torah behavior will be freed from unwarranted (neurotic) fear and equally incapacitating guilt.

Emotionally, contact between patient (or *talmid*) and therapist (or the *rebbe*) is essential, for the real wounds that produce psychopathology come from these emotional sources.[33] Thus *shimush* — education through service, modeling, and interpersonal contact — is a highly useful therapeutic device. Here the teacher (be it the *rebbe* or the therapist), himself living the Torah way (and using the "fifth *Shulchan Aruch*"), reaches the individual on a rational as well as an emotional level, helping him adjust his rational thought by enveloping all such learning and growth within a caring, emotional relationship.[34]

---

33. See R. Hoen-Saric, ("Emotions and Psychotherapies," *American Journal of Psychotherapy* 31:1, pp. 88-94) who says that "... of greater importance than the technique seems to be the therapist's ability to reach the patient emotionally and to provide a corrective experience with a cognitive as well as emotional reorganization."

34. *Mori v'Rebbi*, Rabbi Yaakov Kamenetsky, when approached by his *talmidim* in the *beis hamidrash*, always rose, smiled, and somehow exuded an aura of a relationship of caring, in dealing with people, in responding to their rational (Talmudic) questions, and in attempting to be of help in any matter. Similar modes of dealing with people were, of course, the stock in trade of countless *rebbes*, where *ahavas Yisrael* was *the* instrument of choice to bring about relief, to have one modify behavior, to correct the transgressor and to be used in dealing with people in general. Those in our generation who had the *zechus* to know the Kapitznitzer Rebbe, *zt"l*, saw in him the personification of all this — and how his demeanor brought about change. He once said to me: "*Zu machen Yidden, gib ihm a glezzele tea, freg ihm wie er fielt — und dernoch sog: 'Mein kind, host du gelegt tefillin heint?'*" To bring individuals closer to *Yiddishkeit*, first give him a gift, be his friend, *and only then* suggest that he mend his ways.

Chapter Thirty-two

Musings of an Orthodox Psychotherapist

The following article is abstracted from a paper presented to a professional forum sponsored by the Behavioral Science and Mental Health Section of the Association of Orthodox Jewish Scientists, and subsequently published in *Intercom.* In releasing these remarks to the public at large, I ask my readers to be aware of the limited scope of what is attempted here. Specifically, I ask the reader to bear in mind what is being said, and why — and what is not said, suggested, or implied.

The paper was presented in response to the needs of some of my colleagues who, as Torah-observant individuals, expressed difficulty in maintaining their integrity as *bnei Torah* while practicing their profession, because of an alleged antagonism between Torah and scientific psychotherapy. It was to them that I originally addressed myself, attempting to share my beliefs and methods. In addition, I endeavored to show how Torah can indeed be a source for insight and method in dealing with human difficulties. At the very same time, in no way is it implied that this is "Torah Psychology," or "Torah Psychotherapy."

While there certainly is a Torah view of man as well as Torah psychotherapeutic approaches to deal with the *"choleh hanefesh,"* I have not found a way these can be taught or learned in the traditional manner. Moreover, while certain giants of the schools of *Chassidus* or *Mussar* were unquestionably "psychotherapists" par excellence, their methods cannot be simply handed over for others to practice. This is so, I believe, because of the vital, yet highly elusive "personal equation" operating in all therapies. While generally agreed upon to be a crucial factor, the therapist's personality is still insufficiently recognized as perhaps *the* therapy more than anything else. It has been scientifically established that a particular drug has a different potency when prescribed by one physician than when the identical drug is prescribed by another doctor. How much more so does this hold for human thoughts, feelings, and words! Therein lies our difficulty. Therapy must be genuine. One cannot take the words and all the intangibles of one therapist and simply implant them into another. The therapist and his therapy must fit. Thus, for example, the very words or ideas of a Reb Yisrael Salanter, which were balm in his hands, could well become poisonous barbs in the hands of another.

Concerning "adjustment," I wish to emphasize that, because of Torah concepts such as *mesiras nefesh, olam haba, yesurim shel ahavah,* etc., there can be no thought of comparing what "adjustment" means to the man in the street and what it means to a *maamin* (believing Jew). What is attempted here is to demonstrate that the aim of both Torah and all therapies is toward adjustment, whatever that may mean, including the all-important social adjustment.

In reading *out* of Torah useful insights and methodology, one must be cautioned against the danger of reading *in*. To assure that, the "reader" has to be a sufficient *ben Torah* to begin with. A sad example of this can be found in certain "kosher" *Chumashim* where *mefarshim* are seen as "reading in" — that is, seeking to have their opinion read as the Word of G-d.

Concerning *tochachah*, an attempt is made to demonstrate that the popular notion that *tochachah* is harsh while psychotherapy is all-loving and kind does not hold. To the contrary, the need for love, relationship, and acceptance of the sufferer resides in both. Deliberately omitted are other rules in *tochachah*, such as "*ad shemakeh oso*" — to admonish the sinner even when physical conflict or strife might ensue. Thus one cannot possibly view *tochachah* and therapy as identical methods, but we may abstract principles of the former and apply them to the latter. In this respect — relevant to all of us, *bnei Torah*, and *bnei Torah* therapists — there is the following painful question: Why, when viewing murder being committed, do we intervene (or at least think to do so) *ad shemakeh oso*, even though we are endangering ourselves physically, while we are able to view our neighbors' *chillul Shabbos* with little more than a sigh? Obviously, then, this is our problem, our inadequacy — be it as Torah-observant Jews or as Torah-observant therapists. We may perhaps find some measure of comfort in the *gemara* (*Arakin* 16b) where it is concluded that in our generation we are neither able to take *tochachah* nor equipped to administer it.

৵ৎ ৵ৎ

One approaches the task of spelling out the practice of psychotherapy within the framework of *halachah* with a great deal of reluctance and ambivalence. The reluctance is due to the dearth of halachic material pertaining to the psychotherapeutic process, as well as to the well-known difficulty in defining psychotherapy to suit all schools. And the ambivalence comes about because of two diametrically opposite notions that come to mind. On the one hand, one could argue that halachic relevancy is no different for an individual who practices psychotherapy than for one who practices law or medicine, one who teaches, or for that matter, any Torah Jew who interacts with another human being professionally or as a private citizen. Yet, one must admit that the very nature of psychotherapy — the doctor-patient intimacy, the shaping and modifying of behavior, and the total involvement in the life of another — puts the therapist in a position wherein he must deal with the patient's behavior relevant to *halachah*, and is in a position to evoke in the patient behavior that is halachically correct. This awesome realization makes it incumbent upon us to have an ongoing *cheshbon hanefesh*, constant self-examination, of what we are, or should be, doing to affect our patients as Torah Jews, as well as psychotherapists.

To do this, I propose to "listen" to myself with the well-known "third ear" and share with you some theoretical foundations and practical applications that enable me to practice psychotherapy as a Torah Jew. I hasten to add that these notions and practices are not meant to be definitive as far as psychotherapy is concerned, and much less are they meant to be halachic pronouncements. They are simply descriptive of what I believe, think, and do — correctly or incorrectly — remaining ready to exchange them for better formulations from authoritative sources.

Theoretical Formulations

My beliefs can be posited in the form of a number of axioms with self-evident corollaries.

1. All knowledge presently known to man, or to be discovered by man, is already stated in Torah.[1] Corollary to this axiom is the belief that there can be no conflict between Torah and science or behavioral science.

2. Torah precepts cannot be harmful to man.[2] Corollary to this axiom is that the practice of *mitzvos* to the extent that it harms life (physically or emotionally) is not Torah behavior.[3]

3. Besides being *"gezeiros haMelech,"* dictums of the A-mighty, *mitzvos* are also instruments to assure us the "good life." They are

---

1. *Ramban*, Introduction to *Chumash*.
2. *"V'chai bahem"* — commandments cannot be contradictory to life or health (*Yoma* 85b). See also *Rambam, Hilchos Kiddush HaChodesh* 19:16.
3. We will concede that there are some situations where Torah demands of man to suffer unhappiness. It is our belief, however, that such unhappiness is only apparent. In truth, it too is for our ultimate good.
(See the *SMAG Esin, Siman* 17, where he differs with the *Rambam* in his *Minyan HaMitzvos*. To him there is a *mitzvah* of *tziduk hadin*, the notion that the present suffering is for our ultimate good. His source is the *pasuk* in *Eikev* 8:5: "You shall know within your heart that just as man chastises his son, so does Hashem.")

adaptive in our interpersonal dealings, leading to emotional and physical well-being.[4]

Corollary to this is that one can, and must, find in Torah adaptive behavior patterns that are applicable to our everyday lives. These can be the prototypes for positive mental health and psychotherapy.

The knowledge contained in Torah can be perceived as a series of layers that have various degrees of complexity and relevancy to us in our everyday lives. This body of wisdom ranges from the deepest level, dealing with the mysteries of life and of Creation, through the sciences,[5] to the uppermost level revealed to us: items relating to human behavior.

Relevant to us as scientists and Torah Jews is the need to refrain from attempting to conciliate Torah with science. Such apologetic exercises are irreverent to Torah, and doomed to failure anyway. Rather, we must unequivocally believe that all of science is subservient to and accounted for in Torah, though only singular giants, such as Shlomo *HaMelech*, had access to it.[6] As far as we are concerned with human behavior, moreover, there is a gold mine of insights close to the surface level which can and must be mined. These insights can be gleaned from various sources. Thus there is "Torah,"[7] the narrative part of the larger concept of Torah, which also teaches historical lessons relevant today,[8] and dictums of behavior more clearly formulated in *Aggadah*, *Avos*, and *Kesuvim*

---

4. See *Rambam's Peirush HaMishnayos, Pe'ah* 1:1, where it is explained that the *peiros*, the fruits of observance, are the good life in this world. Also note on the *mitzvah* of *shiluach hakan* (*Ki Seitzei* 22:7) the comments of *Ramban, K'sav Sofer* and *Imrei Shefer*, concerning the development of traits and personality. Similarly the notion that "*Hakin'ah, v'hataavah, v'hakavod motziin es ha'adam min ha'olam* — jealousy, lust, and glory remove a man from the world" (*Avos* 4:28) coincides with the correlates found between personality types and psychosomatic diseases.

See also *Moreh Nevuchim, chelek* 3, *perek* 27, as he explains the *pasuk* in *Va'eschanan* (*Devarim* 6:24): "*He has commanded us ... for our well-being ... so that man should live* — in peace and harmony in a society that is well ordered."

5. *Ramban*, op. cit.

6. Ibid.

7. Note, for example, *Avodah Zarah* 9a, "two thousand years of Torah" in reference to Avraham's teaching in Haran: "*hanefesh asher asah b'Charan*," see the *Targum*. Apparently this teaching of "Torah" is proper human behavior, belief, ethics, etc. Note this definition of "Torah", i.e., "human behavior," also in *Ramban*, ibid.

8. Viz., the concept of "*Maaseh avos siman l'banim* — what occurs to our forefathers has significance for the children." (See *Ramban, Bereishis* 12:6; also *Tanchuma, Lech Lecha* 9.)

such as *Mishlei* or *Koheles*. And then, there is the subtle and hidden, yet all-powerful, word in *d'rush, mussar*, and *chassidus* spelled out in part by commentaries, and continually a living well of wisdom. All of us surely have a vast repertoire of psychoanalytic formulations, personal clinical observations, and research findings which, to our amazement, are found in Torah.

Because of our ignorance and inabilities, many such insights in Torah remain out of reach until illuminated by a *gadol*, or, *lehavdil*, they become visible to us through the "glasses" or tools of behavioral science. These "glasses" then help us find, equate, and validate our discoveries in Torah teachings. Yet, all lenses do is magnify and make visible; where one looks and how one looks, and how findings are interpreted, is up to the observer. Thus when one looks for contradictions, he will find them also.[9]

We may, and perhaps should, use science to find truth already in Torah. The scientific method, the hypothetical and the tentative, the morsels of knowledge based upon probability or upon theory may be validated through fact — the holy Torah. It must not be used to *chas veshalom* contradict Torah or create doubt in Torah.

Practical Applications

In formulating a rudimentary "theory" or approach to therapeutic intervention endemic to all schools of psychotherapy, we fashion a highly simplified model of the patient, his interaction with others, and the function of the therapist. The disturbed individual views himself as acting "correctly," but misunderstood by others and mistreated, and thus unable to trust people or life itself. Society, on the other hand, does not understand the neurotic because his behavior and his views are inconsistent, self-defeating, and usually do not make sense. Society is also unwilling to tolerate disturbed behavior, partially because of our own transference reactions and in part due to the neurotic's secondary gain, such as controlling others, and his emotional blackmail. The therapist enters the picture and does the following:

---

9. *"Yesharim darchei Hashem, tzaddikim yeilchu bam, u'poshim yikashlu bam"* — one finds what he seeks (see *Nazir* 23a).

a. He tolerates the patient, because he is relatively free of pathology himself;

b. he penetrates the patient's world, relates to him, and attempts to understand his thinking in spite of its idiosyncrasy (Chessick's investigative approach);[10]

c. the therapist respects the patient and develops a caring relationship (Chessick's supportive approach);

d. he carefully controls transference and counter-transference, and handles dependency and secondary-gain phenomena that invariably crop up in therapy; and

e. having mastered the "good life" himself and possessing healthy adaptive behavior patterns, he helps the patient to view the world the way the therapist does, and thus act in a more adaptive fashion.

We find a parallel in Torah within the context of *"hochei'ach tochi'ach."*[11] Superficially, *"hochei'ach tochi'ach* — chastise your fellow man," connotes a punitive judgmental approach. Careful inspection of this *mitzvah,* however, reveals to us *"hochei'ach tochi'ach"* as a psychotherapeutic exercise. Using the therapeutic model described above we find:

1. *Mochi'ach,* the one who does the correcting, lives himself a mature ethical life, and is relatively free of pathology (items a-e).[12]

2. The transgressor "disturbs" society. Like society, the *mochi'ach* is in danger of coming to hate the sinner. The function of *hochei'ach tochi'ach* — teaching, chastisement, and admonition — is invoked so that brotherly love may be restored (item c).[13] The entire process thus is enveloped within a caring relationship,[14] re-

---

10. Richard D. Chessick, *How Psychotherapy Heals* (New York: Science House, 1969).
11. *Kedoshim* 19:17.
12. *K'shot atzmecha* (*Sanhedrin* 19a). Also note prior admonition to the Torah Jew (i.e., *mochi'ach*) to be correct toward G-d, toward his parents, to be giving, to be honest, to be kind: op. cit. 19:3-16.
13. Op. cit. 19:17-18. See also *Sefer HaChinuch, Mitzvah 23a:* "The basis of this *mitzvah* is to foster peace and goodwill among men."
14. Note, for example, that Avraham chastised Avimelech only after friendly relations were established, and this resulted in mutual caring *(Bereishis* 21:25). Note also *Zohar, Reya Mahemna, Parashas Kedoshim,* concerning the role of love in attempting *tochachah.* Referring to *Mishlei* (3:12) he says: "Man must learn from G-d, to admonish with love." Also see the gemara *(Bava Metzia* 85a) about how our *Chachamim* practiced *tochachah* — not by harsh judgment, but by giving respect and praise to the sinner, raising his self-concept rather than destroying it. On this topic, see Chapter 2, "To Be a Teacher."

stricting its practice to those who have a fair chance of affecting the "sufferer."[15]

3. The *mochi'ach*, the therapeutic individual, seeks to understand the sufferer and his life (item b), and has no personal gain from this interaction (item d).[16]

Thus our therapist as well as our *mochi'ach* act therapeutically by virtue of their own maturity, by their ability to deal with the disturbed, and by their honest intentions to be helpful. They do not sit in judgment, but genuinely seek to love the sufferer-transgressor. And they apply their method judiciously, carefully controlling what to tell, how to tell, and when to tell. For in this timing lies largely success or failure. From the therapist, it demands therapeutic acumen, and from the *mochi'ach*, wisdom in knowing when to speak and when to keep silent,[17] sound knowledge of *halachah*, and a readiness to consult with a *gadol* when in doubt. The Torah Jew who also conducts psychotherapy practices *hochei'ach tochi'ach*, i.e., psychotherapy, utilizing all of his skills gleaned from many sources, yet with but one aim — to help the sufferer-transgressor. His obligation as *mochi'ach* is basically the same as it is to the layman. Because of his expertise, however, he applies this practice with greater precision and should be held more accountable for his failures. The essential goal of *tochachah*-therapy is to help the sufferer become a *"mensch"* — a productive, moral human being. The Torah Jew who is a therapist has identical goals for the religious patient as well as for the nonreligious; he has a clear percept of what proper human behavior is for the Jew and for the gentile. How and when interpretations are made or teaching is invoked is another matter, depending upon therapeutic contingencies and probabilities of success.

The Therapist and His Values

While we do not know exactly how and why psychotherapy

---

15. See *Magen Avraham* (*Orach Chaim*, 238) citing the *Sefer Chassidim*: "Only those who are familiar with the transgressor and have a chance to affect him."
16. See *Rambam, Hilchos Dei'os*, 6:7: "Inform him that this is all for his good, and be gentle at all times."
17. Just as it is a *mitzvah* to tell one that which he will listen to, thus it is a *mitzvah* to remain silent whenever we will not be heard (*Yevamos* 65b).

works, we do know that the therapist's personality is a crucial factor in the process. Thus, it is generally no longer fashionable to simply view the therapist as a nonentity, a blank, a mirror upon which the patient projects his transferences and his fantasies. The therapist is a person, with a personality and with a set of values. To facilitate therapy, he may attempt to suspend his own "being" in order to enter the world of the patient, or to allow transference to take place. Yet, in the final analysis, by design[18] or by accident, the therapist's personality and his value system come through. Even the most disturbed patient[19] catches on to the therapist's life patterns regardless of the therapist's efforts to be neutral and anonymous. This comes about by the therapist's own unconscious slips that betray him, and/or by the "detective work" patients do about their therapists.

The therapist's value system — his beliefs, opinions and attitudes — and his personality have roots not only in what he had learned about psychotherapy. They have come about through his own experiences, upbringing, and genetic endowment. In the case of a Torah Jew, they are also heavily loaded with Torah values and learning. The therapist thus meets his patient as a "whole person," including his personality and his value system. It is thus naive to consider the possibility of interacting with patients as therapists devoid of whatever Torah is in us.

Moreover, the notion of remaining neutral and "therapeutic" toward our patient, i.e., helping him adjust to *his* thing, is antitherapeutic, if not outright destructive. The idea, for example, of helping the homosexual adjust to his homosexuality[20] is analogous

---

18. Note, for example, Shands formulation of psychotherapy: The patient's defense is a way of maintaining familiar, yet maladaptive, ways of processing data. Psychotherapy facilitates data processing, using language found useful by the therapist's school or persuasion. The therapist changes descriptions of the patient to agree with those of the therapist, which are more adaptational, explain the world, are more accurate and consistent (H. Shands, *Thinking and Psychotherapy* [Cambridge, Mass.: Harvard University Press, 1960]).
19. In my experience, children, psychotics, and borderlines are particularly astute in "reading" and knowing all about us. I suspect this is due to their fixation at the preverbal level that connects with the unconscious of others.
20. In 1973, the American Psychiatric Association removed homosexuality from its official listing of mental illnesses. This was undoubtedly a political move motivated by the social climate prevalent at that time and (sadly) taught to the youngsters in public school as "alternative lifestyles." Four years later most of the psychiatrists who originally voted for the exclusion of homosexuality as an illness disagreed with their original vote. Not so very long ago seekers of freedom in Russia were "diagnosed" as "social deviates." Undoubtedly, to the Nazis sadism was similarly "normal."

to a physician complying with his patient's requests to give him pep by prescribing amphetamines or enlarging parts of one's anatomy by injecting a foreign and dangerous substance. Why then not cut off one's leg if it gets in his way? Indeed, the popularity of certain hedonistic psychotherapists today is undoubtedly due to the fact that they give the patient what he wants. This is not the way of honest therapy, nor is it the Torah way.

Moreover, there is the vital issue of "meaning," the existential dilemma, the nonbeing, the apathy, that plagues so many of our patients. Out of contact with social institutions that had given meaning to life in the past, at odds with one's family (and by extension, one's heritage), the patient searches for meaning. If not the therapist, who is to show the way? And if the therapist is fortunate to possess a value system grounded in Torah, it is incumbent upon him to share it with his patients. To the religious, he may extend his perception of Torah-life free of compulsions or destructive guilt; to the nonreligious, he may point the way towards "meaning" to be found in Jewishness; and to the gentile he may illustrate meaning or adaptive behavior the therapist believes in — including that which he has found in Torah.

The therapist who is a Torah Jew is by no means a proselytizer. But his therapy is based upon his personality which, in turn, is grounded in Torah. Thus his Torah is a factor. Why not be aware of it and use it constructively?

Chapter Thirty-three

Mood and Marriage, and Spiritual Growth

hen *Bnei Yisrael* came to the *Beis HaMikdash* on the festivals, the *Kohanim* would roll up the *paroches,* the curtain (of the Sanctuary), and show them the *Keruvim* above the *Aron HaKodesh,* which were embracing. The *Kohanim* would proclaim: "Behold your love before G-d is as the love of man and woman." When the gentile enemy broke into the *Heichal,* the Holy Sanctuary, and saw these *Keruvim* joined in a loving embrace, they took them out to the marketplace and (derisively) called out: "These Jews should be involved in such matters?!" and they debased them.[1]

The Nobel Laureate was making his acceptance speech. (His name, his specialty, and the year are unimportant.) The content of

---

1. *Yoma* 54a-b.

that speech stayed in my memory because, instead of discussing his field of expertise (for accomplishments in which, after all, he did win this prestigious award), he commented about what the *Ribbono Shel Olam, kaveyachol,* "failed" to do. "Man," he said, "is equipped with a magnificent brain, and similarly, with a marvelous body. But he is weak in the area of emotions. G-d [*kaveyachol*] has failed to endow him with the proper emotions to allow him to be happy at all times and to further social living and well-being."

We will comment on these remarks with the words of *Chazal* who pointedly describe the person who is uneducated regarding a specific topic. Not only did this one fail to study and to introspect, he also failed to do the simple reading. Torah indeed has much to say about moods, about feelings and emotions, about the joys and miseries of life, and, mostly, about loving relationships, which are the essence of moods and of one's emotional and social life.

Moreover, whereas intellectual capabilities and physical endowments are basically fixed at birth, and whereas experience and nurturing play a relatively minor role, man's emotional makeup is mostly the result of man's own doing. It is the sum total of his experiences and the way he perceives these experiences and relationships: relationships with others, with himself, with the universe, and with his Creator.

Thus, one can say with confidence: Man, equipped with two "givens" — a brain and a body — creates himself through his emotions (that is, his relationships — real or so perceived). Even the hermit on his desert island "relates," albeit negatively: "I want (or I need) to be away from people."

How can one achieve the ideal — a way of life, lived in the Torah manner?

Responding to Another's Needs

As with all things which inspire man to seek, work, and achieve, there must be a need. That need is implanted in man from the beginning of his existence on earth. The Torah describes the most important feature of man, his emotional essence, in the following concise but powerful fashion: "It is not good for man to be alone."[2] Man needs a fellow, a companion, a helpmate — a psychologist might say, a therapeutic agent — at times to relieve stress of everyday life by relaxing, and at times entertaining[3] to make it joyous. And how is all this to come about? Again, our holy Torah teaches us: *"E'eseh lo eizer kenegdo —* I will create for him a helpmate, woman." And more specifically, *"Vehayu levasar echad —* they shall become as one."[4]

How do two individuals come to be one? *Rashi* explains that the *basar echad,* the one flesh, refers to the ensuing offspring, the child "composed" genetically of father and mother. *Ramban* argues with this somehow concrete notion of oneness. After all, he says, this oneness resides also in the animal world who jointly have oneness in their offspring. Because of this argument, *Ramban* elevates the notion of *basar echad* into a social-emotional one. Namely, he says, unlike the animal who "uses" his mate, only to readily exchange it for another without any emotional qualms,[5] man and woman cling together as one, as if they are joined, with a chronic need for one another.[6] All of this is implanted into the very nature of man.

Extrapolating from *Ramban,* who adds to the physical also the emotional-social, the feeling, the caring, and the loving dimension, we may furthermore expand downward and upward. Downward, we explain *Rashi* and deflect *Ramban's* objection: Yes, the animal too has oneness with his/her mate in their offspring. Yet there is a

---

2. *Bereishis* 2:18. In Yiddish, we describe a disturbed person by saying, *"Er is nit mit alemen,"* which, in a play on words, also means he is not with others, but alone.

3. See *Taanis* 22a, where the Talmud points to two jugglers or entertainers — who entertain people and make peace among them — as typical of *bnei olam haba,* assured to deserve a seat in the future world, i.e., Paradise. Obviously, joy, calm, happiness, and the simple smile bring peace within and with others.

4. *Bereishis* 2:24.

5. As far as we know, animals live by instinct. A bird builds a nest for the young not because of feeling, but because a hormone is released which activates nest building. Thus what is truly human and exclusively human is a person's emotions — and the related soul.

6. See Reuven Margulies in his pamphlet *Olelos, Bemishor* (Jerusalem: Mossad HaRav Kook, 5707), who demonstrates that: 1. The ideal Torah marriage is one man to one woman. 2. When prominent men took additional wives, it was done only because of compelling and noble reasons. 3. In Talmudic times, it was the norm (normal in terms of usual and in terms of optimal) for Talmudic scholars to have but one wife.

crucial difference: Because the *basar echad* notion, the emotional-social-loving one, already resides in the parent, the child — who is the result, the outcome, of such loving emotional oneness — now has within him not only the physical *basar echad*, but also the emotional-social-loving one. Born out of love, he is poised and programmed to become a social-emotional-loving human being.

Moving upward, *Ramban* tells us what there is to be in this *basar echad*. It is up to us, however, to make this happen. How? It is simple and it is difficult — but the fruits are ever so sweet.

To live with another human being, to be at peace with another human being, and to enjoy another human being, one needs to develop a sensitivity for that fellow human. One needs to develop patience, tolerance, and consideration. One must learn to give up one's own needs and wishes for another, to postpone gratification, and much more. And what gain is to be had for all this? The gain is wonderful. We enjoy the emotional oneness with the other, the feelings, the love, the triumph over the existential fear of being alone, the ever-ready help one can expect, the emotional band-aids and healing that come from the other.

Becoming and Gaining

Yet even more important, by becoming patient, tolerant, considerate towards the other; by giving up one's needs for another and by learning to postpone gratification, that individual "becomes." He becomes a better human being, a patient one, a considerate one, a loving one. The saying goes: "Parents raise children, and children raise parents." As the parent must develop patience and tolerance for the child, he himself *becomes* — a patient and tolerant human being. How much more so it is for man and woman. Man makes man — and man makes himself.[7]

---

7. "*Naaseh Adam* — let us make man" (*Bereishis* 1:26). See *Rashi* and *Ramban*. In other discussions I had added to this. Not only the *Ribbono Shel Olam* and His court *(Rashi)*, not only the *Ribbono Shel Olam* and the earth create man. It is also man who creates man. An individual's words, his demeanor, and his deep inner feeling can make his fellow man or break him, *chas veshalom*. Thus the *Ribbono Shel Olam* appeals to each and every one of us: "Make man!" Love him, care for him, and "make him." Now I want to add the following: The *Ribbono Shel Olam* appeals to every one of us: "Make man!" Make *yourself* into a better and real human-emotional-spiritual being by relating and caring for the other.

Best of all, in this entire process, no one actually loses anything. There are no losers, only winners. We can best illustrate this with the well-known tale which bears repeating. The story goes as follows: Two brothers, one married with children and one single, were partners on a farm. The harvest over, they divided the crop fairly and evenly. That night, the elder of the two could not sleep. "After all," he said to himself, "I have a large family to look after me, unlike my unmarried brother who must fend for himself." So he got up and moved part of his crop across the fence to his brother's side. The single brother likewise could not sleep. "Why should my brother, who has to feed a large family, not have a greater share of the partnership?" So he too moved some of his crop to the other side. In the morning, each one of them marveled at how his own quantity of the crop remained the same. Unbeknown to one another, the brothers repeated the process until one night they met while each was carrying a portion of the harvest to the other. Astonished, they halted, they shuddered, they cried for joy, and they embraced, for they now were confronted with the ultimate love they had for one another. And that is where *HaKadosh Baruch Hu* decided to build the *mizbei'ach*, the altar, the instrument of giving, the place for love and peace and harmony. For these brothers demonstrated that by giving, one loses nothing, but gains — feelings of love and relatedness, and the ensuing warmth and joy.

Moving Upwards and Closer

Moving upward should have no limit. The *basar echad* "makes" man himself. It "makes" an engram, a kind of indelible mark, in the individual's psyche to "become" an emotional-social human being. It makes a loving relationship, a marriage, a home, and it makes likewise his/her spouse into that sensitive, caring human being. "*Kamayim hapanim lapanim*" — man mirrors and apes his fellow man, the wise king Solomon teaches.[8] Yet there is ever more: the ultimate — man's closeness to his Creator, the *Ribbono Shel Olam*. How is that?

---

8. *Mishlei* 27:19.

Again, we take the prototype the Torah prescribes, the relationship between man and woman. In fact, Torah clearly describes in numerous instances that the relationship between G-d and man is as the relationship between man and woman.[9] The *gemara* cited in the beginning is just one of many examples. How exactly does this work?

The Talmud tells us that when a marriage breaks up, the *mizbei'ach* cries.[10] What is the purpose of the *mizbei'ach* within the *Beis HaMikdash?* The obvious answer is that it is the place for our *korbanos.* And what is a *korban?* According to the common dictionary, it is a sacrifice. We may now say that when husband and wife are unable to sacrifice for one another, the marriage deteriorates and ends in divorce. Consequently, the *mizbei'ach* cries, for who will bring *korbanos,* sacrifices, to the altar when people are unwilling to sacrifice for one another?

This notion may sound right, but it is wrong both conceptually and practically. It is a mistranslation due to the paucity of language to express feelings, *and* due to a loss of correct conceptualization when one is not ever so careful in translating a Torah word — or, really, a unique Torah concept — into a foreign tongue.[11]

Conceptually, a *korban* is not a sacrifice. As Rabbi Shamshon Raphael Hirsch points out,[12] a sacrifice needs not only a giver who extends himself excessively, but also a receiver who benefits from this sacrifice. The *Ribbono Shel Olam, kaveyachol,* receives nothing, for all is His. It is the one who offers the *korban* who effects a change, and a major one at that. The word *korban,* Rabbi Hirsch points out, stems from the root *karev,* to come near. The one who offers the *korbanos,* by his deed, by his giving excessively and joyfully, draws near and bonds spiritually with the *Ribbono Shel Olam.*

Transposed to a practical husband-wife level, the word "sacrifice" engenders notions of burdens, of chores, of something forced, and something beyond reasonableness. Surely, files of marriage counselors are replete with tales of both husbands and wives relating how much each saw him- or herself as sacrificing, doing,

---

9. E.g., *"Tz'enah ur'enah bnos Tzion"* (*Shir HaShirim* 3:11).
10. *Gittin* 90b.
11. See Chapter 34, "Language, Concept Formation, and *Hashkafah."*
12. Hirsch *Chumash, Vayikra,* introduction to *korban.*

giving in, and giving up so much. As a result, each one feels cheated and exploited. Do these people lie? Not necessarily. Selective memory is at work here, along with the idea that "What *I* want is normal, while what the other one wants is unreasonable. It is I who is always sacrificing and giving." That is when giving the *korban* is a sacrifice.

This is not so when giving is the joy of bonding, when giving is an opportunity for psychological growth and personality development by developing sensitivity for others, tolerance and patience, and postponing gratification — or even doing without. When all of this is practiced by both husband and wife, and neither one counts who does or gives, chances are excellent that like our two brothers, both husband and wife end up with the same,[13] plus the individual personality development, *and* the great love and bond — the true *basar echad*.

Thus one gives and is always a winner, getting closer to the other, to one's spouse, to one's fellow man and to oneself — the new and ever better inner man who is sensitive to others, giving, loving, and tolerant — and always growing.

Now what about us mortals and the *Ribbono Shel Olam*? If to bring a *korban* is to draw near, to bond, how can one entertain such thoughts of bonding with Hashem, insignificant as man is? David *HaMelech*, the sweet singer of Israel, tells us: "*Vatechasreihu m'at mei'Elokim*[14] — man is but slightly less than angels"[15] — or, *kaveyachol*, even G-d. But how? Because we bond and become, *kaveyachol*, like Hashem. "*Ma Hu chanun verachum af ata hehyei chanun verachum* — Just as G-d is all-merciful and compassionate, so you become merciful and compassionate"[16] by bonding and becoming the true *tzelem Elokim*, as G-d intended us to be — living in this world, but bonding upwards to be close to Hashem, imitating the traits of Hashem, and, *kaveyachol*, becoming like Hashem.

---

13. "*Ayn haberachah metzuyah ella badavar hasamui min ha'ayin*"(*Taanis* 8b). Don't look, don't count, for true blessing to take place. *Lehavdil*, statistically, when one deals with large numbers, without counting or accounting, things somehow equalize. This holds true for flipping heads or tails with a coin as well as determining who does what or who gives up or who gains or loses.
14. *Tehillim* 8:6.
15. See *mefarshim*.
16. *Shabbos* 133b.

Furthermore, we must remember the notion of *"middah keneged middah"* — Hashem *Yisbarach* reciprocates. As the *Tanna* teaches: *"Asei retzono kirtzonecha, kedei sheyaaseh retzoncha kirtzono"*[17] — "You, mortal man, grow, become, bond, and thus naturally do as G-d wishes, so He too will do your wishes and fill your needs." That was the message of the *Kohanim* on the festivals as they revealed the embracing *Keruvim*.

Now what goes wrong, why do relationships sour, why do marriages fall apart? And what did the enemy see in the *Keruvim*, and how did they debase all that?

Avodah Zarah, and Using Others

It should be quite obvious to even the casual observer[18] that while there are religions that attempt to elevate man — that is, they teach him to give, to be charitable, to give up base instinctual drives, not to do what the villain in man wants to do — there are others, such as *avodah zarah*, idol worship, that do the very opposite. They "permit" and encourage man to do that which normal, decent humans would abhor — to sacrifice one's children, behave promiscuously, and perform ritual murder, to list but a few examples. Even the religions meant to elevate man usually fail. How many wars were fought or murders committed in the name of religion?[19] How many cruelties have our people suffered — Inquisitions, Crusades, forcible conversion — in the name of some god of goodness? Such gods then were *used* to serve the "worshipers," to permit them to do what common decency would forbid.

A similar phenomenon occurs in those marriages and relationships wherein others are there to be *used* — physically, socially,

---

17. *Avos* 2:4.
18. See also *Chasam Sofer, passim.*
19. How sad it is when even in the Torah world, Jews — as individuals, or in factions, or as men vs. women — abuse one another in the name of *Yiddishkeit*. How true is, sadly, the cynic's interpretation of *"kol machlokes shehi leshem Shamayim sofah lehiskayem"* (*Avos* 5:20) — that wars are endless when each contender cloaks himself in the mantle of G-d's righteousness. Psychologists call this the superego in the service of the id; in this case, our "noble" behavior is driven by selfishness and evil — or *meshugas*.

and emotionally; or those wherein others are convenient targets for man's perversions or cruelties, or just to ventilate the inner angers of everyday life.

If one believes that people are objects to be used, then one need not grow at all. Why be sensitive to the other's feelings when the other exists merely to be used — like the proverbial chicken we "love" — to slaughter, to pluck, to broil, and to consume? To the contrary, sensitivity for others would interfere with one's base desires. Social psychologists explain cannibalism in the following manner: Civilized man distinguishes between man and animal. Cannibals simply move that border, saying, "All of *my* villagers are human, all others are animals and thus may be slaughtered and eaten." The Nazis, *yimach shemam*, did the very same to the Jews. Jews, they said, are *"ungeziefer"* (the German word for vermin), which must be exterminated. It's all in the label; it's that simple.

Thus, when we popularize that "men are from Mars and women are from Venus," we state that we have nothing in common, that men and women are not fellow humans to bond and to "become." When the media speak of the war between the sexes, the message comes through that the purpose of marriage is to win wars, subjugate, use or abuse, exploit, and defeat others. Similarly, the cry for women's liberation indicates that women must have been treated as, or felt like, second-class citizens.

When the embrace is the *use* of the other's body, we become users. When the media speaks of love primarily in the physical sense, and clothing is designed to reinforce this notion; when one sees the other as a physical object to use for one's personal pleasure — we are speaking of using, not of relating.

That is what the gentile enemy saw in the embrace of the *Keruvim*, because that was their perception of *avodah zarah*, of human relationships, and of marriage. They assumed that like their idols, which were made to serve the individual, other humans, in particular one's spouse, exist for the same purpose. That is not the Torah way. *Derachehah darchei noam* — Torah way is the sweet way — for everyone. Torah forbids using certain species of *hadassim* because they are used to poison animals.[20] *Kal v'chomer*, then, nothing is permissi-

---

20. *Succah* 32b.

ble for one's use if it may inadvertently hurt another, certainly so when one gains at the expense of one's spouse.

Achieving the Ultimate Bond

The original need for man not to be alone creates a need for another. To make this need become reality and forge a permanent bond, each spouse needs to grow internally in sensitivity, caring, and similar traits. Thus, each one "becomes" a better human being, constantly growing socially and emotionally. The ensuing *basar echad*, this emotional-social-physical oneness with one's *zivug*, destined one, now produces the child, a result of this caring and bonding. Now this offspring is programmed to likewise bond, and "become" a better person, giving up his or her own needs and growing internally, socially and spiritually.

All of this facilitates and enables one to achieve the ultimate bond, the spiritual one, the *karev* in *korban* — to come near and become, *kaveyachol*, like Hashem in *middos*, noble traits, in spirituality, in values which are real and which are permanent. We are like the ladder in Yaakov's dream: "*mutzav artzah, verosho magia hashamaymah* — set earthward, and its top reached heavenward."[21] We live in this world but strive upward to "become" ever better, ever more spiritual.

Power, Harmony, and Torah

However, when another type of power comes into play; when power is to dominate, to use or abuse; when power becomes a selfish variable to take care of oneself, then a different process operates. This is a process of unhappiness, of disagreement, of arguments, of heartache — the ultimate result of which is to become ever more alone. No, worse than that — it is to be alone and to live with the enemy.

For sure, there is power that is good. Children have power to make parents more patient, tolerant, and giving. Individuals have

---

21. *Bereishis* 28:12.

power to create good feelings in others. Spouses have the ultimate power to make one another feel like the most important person in the world.[22] Individuals have demonstrated that they have power to save a potential suicide's life by merely showing that they care — genuinely. So does the good therapist — professional or layman, *rav*, *rebbi*, *rosh yeshivah*, or anyone who genuinely cares.

But, you will ask, after all is said and done, who is the "boss"? To begin with, we just don't like the word "boss." As a verb, it means to dominate, to use — and it engenders a notion of power, of the powerful and the powerless. We will, however, agree with the title "head of household," the designation printed below one's signature on an American tax-return form. But that is not a boss at all. That is the one who is responsible. Yes, Torah does obligate man to provide for his spouse, to care for her, to entertain her, to love and — even more — respect her.[23] But it is the woman who has the power to create the mood, the joy, and the ambiance to the extent that *Chazal* proclaim: "He who lives without a wife, lives without joy, without happiness, without blessing, without goodness."[24]

Yet you will ask, "Who decides? Who has the final say?" Picture the harmonious home where one can hear the following: "This, my child, you ask Daddy; and this, you ask Mommy. And this, Mommy and Daddy will discuss and let you know."

Finally, there are simply decisions which reflect the Torah way. *"Azoi tut a Yid* — This a Torah Jew does, or does not, do." There is *halachah*, Jewish law, and *minhag*, Jewish custom. How many times have I heard *Mori v'Rebbi HaGaon* Rabbi Yaakov Kamenetsky, while learning *Yoreh De'ah*, ritual law, in his home, say, *"De she'eilah fregt men bei der Rebbetzin* — This question we must ask the *rebbetzin*,"

---

22. "Eyn ish meis ella l'ishto," Talmud *Sanhedrin* 22b. Ultimately a man's death (or life) is relevant only to his wife. It was already hours after the *levayah* of *Mori v'Rebbi HaGaon* Rabbi Shlomo Heiman, *zt"l*. We, his *talmidim*, were sitting with the *rebbetzin*, *tibadel l'chayim*. There were no tears left, only the bitter void. The *rebbetzin* forced us to leave and go home, and she commented: "Yes, my children, you have someplace to go to, but for me there is no place and no one." At that time, all of us must have thought only of the *rebbetzin's* loss. But in retrospect, there obviously was the far, far more important gain of having had one another as a true *basar echad*.
23. *Sanhedrin* 76b.
24. *Yevamos* 62b.

who knows the *mesorah*, the custom, from her mother, who knew it from her mother, and so on back through the generations.

When the decision maker is the Torah, or good sense, or the personal competency of one or the other; when harmony is more important than raw power, there are no bosses and there is no need for bosses. The only "boss," then, the only power that directs, is the one which promotes loving, caring, joy, and harmony — spiritual, social, emotional, physical, and practical.

Identification With Others

Differences which come between a couple will, in a successful marriage, fade, if not disappear altogether. How? It is frequently said, at times in jest, how happily-married couples get to look alike. And there is some objective evidence that this indeed is so. Obviously, the shape of one's nose or ears does not change, nor do physical dimensions or mental abilities. What is likely to change and "regress to the mean," that is, get closer to a "middle" both can live with, are beliefs and attitudes, minor mannerisms and opinions, as all of these "rub off" on one another.

Notice similarly how one can easily identify a *yeshivah bachur* of a particular yeshivah, or a *talmid* or *chassid* of a particular *Rebbe*, by the "walk" and the "talk," by the special *"shuckel"* (fervent swaying) during *davening* or while learning. These mannerisms are a language and an identification with another or others who come to think alike, feel alike, and then act alike. Love, caring, and relating melt down individual rigidities, and, ensconced in the joy of the relationship, individuals truly come to think and feel as one. Have you ever stepped into the hallway towards the end of a wedding reception, in search of your spouse, to suggest that it's time to leave? And, lo and behold, there is your spouse, coming to meet you and to make a similar suggestion! Mental telepathy? Not necessarily so. But you have come to think and feel alike — and now act alike to get your coats and leave.

To seal this idea with a *d'var Torah*,[25] the reader is referred to

---

25. *"Lo yipater adam mei'chaveiro . . . ella mitoch d'var halachah* — One should take leave of his friend only while discussing a Torah thought" (*Berachos* 31a).

Rashi who quotes the Talmud concerning Yosef *HaTzaddik's* response to the overtures of Potiphar's wife.[26] "... And one sage says that yes, Yosef was about to sin. He was saved from sinning as he beheld the face of Yaakov, his father." Did Yosef *HaTzaddik* have a hallucination? *Chas veshalom,* certainly not. Now look back at an earlier *Rashi*[27] where the relationship between father and son was discussed. We will take the *darshan's* (preacher's) liberty and roll three explanations into one: Yosef was "Yaakov's bright son," with whom his father shared all he had learned in the yeshivos of Shem and Ever, and they looked alike. Looked alike? Consider our discussion. The *rebbi,* Yaakov, and the son/*talmid,* Yosef, interacted, studied, discussed, and related — to the point of thinking, feeling, and looking alike. Thus the face of Yaakov, his beliefs, his feelings, his totality was imprinted upon Yosef, the son. And when Yosef beheld the face of his father, it was the face *within* him, the introjected father/teacher/*rebbi* — the conscience, if you wish — that curbed the impending immoral impulse.

The true apprehension of every caring parent — "Do you know where your children are?" — has become a popular theme in the mass media. Yet the concern is real. How does a parent really know or feel secure about the child's whereabouts? Where is he? What company is he keeping? What is he about to do in the face of temptation? How strong is the conscience or how powerful are the impulses? Security, then, lies in the relationship, in the implant of the parent within the child — just like the bonding of the couple — and, *kaveyachol,* the bonding to the *Ribbono Shel Olam.*

---

26. *Bereishis* 39:11.
27. *Ibid* 37:3.

Chapter Thirty-four

Language, Concept Formation, and Hashkafah

he Talmud relates: "The Emperor Ptolemy ordered five Talmudic sages to translate the holy Torah into the Greek tongue." And the Talmud declares: "For our people, that day was as tragic as the day they worshiped the Golden Calf."[1]

That not only hurts (because we are ever more dependent on translations and elucidations), but it puzzles.

We have before us many wonderful works from ArtScroll, Feldheim, and other English-language publishers, prepared by authors, translators, and elucidators of caliber. They are preceded by works written by Hirsch in German, by *Rambam*, the *Kuzari*, and others in

---

1. *Soferim* 1:8.

Arabic, and the *Me'am Loez* in Ladino. To be sure, there exists a vast Torah literature written in other languages. What, then, is the great tragedy of Torah in Greek? True, we cannot and need not comprehend the depth of every *aggadah* (the non-halachic portions of Talmud). Yet some understanding of this Talmudic statement is in order.

Obviously, the tragedy the Talmud mentions cannot be the product of the simple translation of words from the Hebrew. To the contrary, translating and elucidating in one's native tongue helps one understand the text, and in general furthers Torah learning and comprehension.[2]

It thus follows that the tragedy we are speaking of lies elsewhere. Can we learn what this calamity is? Can we learn to avoid it? Conversely, can we learn to do the very opposite and be ever more successful?

Language, Thought, and Concept Formation

Let us begin by asking: What is it about words, what is it about language — about *lashon hakodesh* (the holy tongue), and conversely, about foreign language — that is so crucial?

We begin with the obvious. Words do far more than describe matter, and language is not simply a means of communication among people. Language and the ability to speak shapes man and represents the very essence of that man, and that of his particular social group. That this is so will be demonstrated shortly, but its principle is found — like all else[3] — in Torah. Torah describes man, his creation, and his very being in terms of language: *"V'hayah ha'adam l'nefesh chayah"* — the holy spirit that Hashem breathed into man created the *nefesh chayah*, which the *Targum* translates as "speaking man."[4]

---

2. In the days when the Day School movement was conflicted concerning teaching *Ivrit b'Ivrit* (Hebrew into Hebrew), and even concerning teaching Torah in Yiddish, our *gedolim* always emphasized the importance of comprehension, regardless of language (personal communications from Rabbi Yaakov Kamenetsky, *zt"l*). See also the many approbations to the ArtScroll literature.

3. See *Ramban, Introduction to Chumash.* Shlomo HaMelech learned all the wisdom there is from Torah, for all is within Torah (*"Hafoch bah vahafoch bah, d'cholah vah* — Delve in it [the Torah] and continue to delve in it [the Torah], for everything is in it" [*Avos 5:26*]).

4. *Bereishis* 2:7.

In a different context, the *Malbim* elaborates and describes "speaking man" in the following manner: "... man at birth, physically the weakest of all creatures ..., yet the power of language embedded in his very being is the epitome and the ultimate creation *Hashem Yisbarach* displayed in His world."[5]

What is language and how are words coined? Language and words are clearly, as the *Ran* puts it, the result of consensus of each nation or social group.[6]

Rabbi Shamshon Raphael Hirsch furthermore points to the mental content, to the conceptualizations and the uniqueness of both language and the thoughts it represents. He says "... the formation of words and sentences which is brought about by spiritual, mental agreement of the way that things and their relations are looked at."[7]

Now, what about us, our people, and the Torah language, *lashon hakodesh*? Do we look at things and conceptualize them in a certain manner because that is what we are?

Yes, certainly. If *Yidden* are *rachmanim* — sensitive, and feeling for others[8] — their concepts of *tzedakah* (charity) are consonant with that set of mental traits. But there is more. Because the Torah was given in *lashon hakodesh*,[9] it follows that the *Ribbono Shel Olam's* words contained the very characteristics that they are meant to represent. Thus when *Rashi*, quoting the *Toras Kohanim*, tells us: "Every *mitzvah* given at Sinai included its rules and details,"[10] we may well add: "It also included the proper thoughts, feelings, and attitudes belonging to it."

Putting all this, *lehavdil*, in psycholinguistic terms, we can say the following:

1. **Words denote:** A word (or a sentence) names objects, describes activities, feelings, values, ideas, and notions.

---

5. *Tehillim* 8:3.
6. *Nedarim* 2a.
7. *Bereishis* 11:1. Note also the many other instances where Rabbi Hirsch, *zt"l*, clarifies words which cannot be translated. For example, note the word *korban* (sacrifice), where the English translation is totally inadequate (*Vayikra* 1:1). Also, concerning *tum'ah* (uncleanliness), see *Malbim, Parashas Chukas*.
8. *"Kol mi she'eino merachem* ... whoever is uncaring and insensitive of others [is not a descendant of Avraham]" (*Beitzah* 32b).
9. *Bereishis Rabbah* 18:6.
10. *Vayikra* 25:1.

2. **Words are concepts:** Each word also describes a group or a class of things. Take, for example, the word *house*. To the average American, its shape — square, round, or oblong — may be irrelevant, but it needs to contain individual sleeping quarters, cooking space, and a living-dining area in order to be defined as a *house*. It is not a *room* nor a *shopping center*.

3. **Concepts are relatively unique for each individual and for a social group:** In our example, to a citizen of an impoverished third-world country, a room or a hut may very well qualify as a *house*. Similarly, what is viewed as being *rich* by one individual or a particular social group may be considered quite *poor* elsewhere. And so on.

Consider, now, more complex concepts and the words that represent them, such as *life, love, happiness, believing, giving,* or *learning.* How much more so does each individual or group have a unique understanding of these concepts, and attach unique characteristics and values to them.[11]

Furthermore, once established, these words would then reinforce the concepts (i.e., the characteristics) of the notion they represent. Now, if a word represents complex thoughts, feelings, and spiritual attitudes, it follows that, in turn, the word would trigger and evoke within us the very thoughts, feelings, and attitudes of the concept it represents. For example, we classify a group of insects as "spiders." In turn, the word or the thought "spider," or the picture of a spider, may evoke within us a feeling of disgust to the point of sensing a spider crawling up our backs. However, when one's environment undergoes changes, or when translations are used too casually, one's conceptualizations are likely also changing. Suppose our spider-phobic individual decides to learn all about spiders, to study and collect them; then all these erstwhile feelings would very likely change. Spiders will disgust him no longer, but probably interest and fascinate him.

Similarly, we learn a language, and come to think in that language. Is there not clearly a likelihood that as our language

---

11. See Jacob Mermelstein, "An Investigation Concerning the Meaning of Synonyms and Antonyms of Words Denoting Time, Size, and Amount for Children and Adults" (unpublished thesis, Rutgers University, 1964) for a fuller discussion of words and their meaning.

changes, so may our erstwhile conceptualizations — the original way we thought about things, the distinct characteristics we had attached to these notions — change as well?

We can bring this closer to home with our example of tzedakah. We speak of tzedakah, and we translate the word (i.e., the concept) as "charity." But what does this word — or concept — really mean? Several years ago, The New York Times published the income-tax returns of several prominent Americans, including those of some of our presidents, with the amount of "charity" they contributed. To the average Torah Jew committed to the mitzvah of maaser (tithing), the relatively high ratio of the reported incomes to the amount of charity given must have seemed ludicrous. So much for the numbers.

What about the meaning of the act? Tzedakah is just what it says: tzedek, the just action to take. As one businessman told me, he receives a check, and automatically 10 percent goes into his tzedakah account. It is more than an obligation, more than a mitzvah. It is the thing one does, period. The word "charity," on the other hand, connotes giving out of goodness of heart and nobility: the very act, as well as the amount, are things to be controlled by the giver.

Let us return to our example of a Torah Jew who has been giving tzedakah for many years. Assume he has been obliged by circumstances to move out of his Torah neighborhood, and he makes friends with his gentile neighbors on the new block. They speak of many things, including "charity." Numbers are mentioned, and are labeled as "charity." Is there not clearly a danger that after a while our Torah Yid may come to think of tzedakah as charity, in the way his neighbors do — both in terms of amount and in terms of its being a voluntary deed — rather than as something one must simply do, and do so in a fairly well prescribed fashion?

The danger of words and the thoughts they evoke within us is indicated in Torah. "Abed t'abdoon ..."[12] — one must destroy the places of idol worship to the extent of altering their names, lest their erstwhile names evoke respect rather than disgust.[13]

It should be clear, then, that when we say, "Men darf trachten vee a Yid — One needs to think like a Torah Jew," we must add

12. Devarim 12:3.
13. Avodah Zarah 77a.

that one also needs to speak in the manner of a Torah *Yid* — to reinforce the concepts, the original mind-set, the very quality of each and every Torah notion, the attendant feelings and attitudes, the full meaning of each word and what it represents. It thus follows that we need to be ever wary of translating words, because translation is not solely another form of communication. The word translated may very well bring along distinct connotations and spiritual meanings. There is a danger here, indeed.

Thus, man uses words freely without giving thought to their precise meanings. Yet by his use of words he reinforces the meanings, the concepts, and the attitudes he has learned to associate with them. The science of psycholinguistics studies all of this and clearly demonstrates the profound effect of words having different meanings to different people — and how this affects the very nature of their existence. This should be clear to anyone who remembers the American-Russian debates in the United Nations.

Most amazingly, both representatives of their respective countries espoused the notion of "democracy." Yet the meaning of this word, the concept of the way of life that word represents, the myriad of ways each brand of "democracy" affects the lives of every citizen differed to an extent that would take volumes to describe. Yet the very word "democracy" was identical and was used to defend systems ranging from one connoting freedom to the extreme to the other connoting restrictions to the extreme.

The study of words and their meaning is really not that new. Already we find Rabbi Shamshon Raphael Hirsch explaining the words *chartoomei Mitzrayim* not as popularly translated — as the magicians or soothsayers — but rather, as those versed in hieroglyphics — that is, the scholars and students of the meaning of words and symbols. Nonetheless, the crucial difference these meanings have in our everyday lives, and particularly in our lives as Torah Jews, needs to be borne in mind constantly.

I have demonstrated elsewhere[14] that much of everyday conflict may arise simply by misunderstanding the meaning of words. For example, mother and child agree for the child to be home "around" 11 o'clock. To the mother, this phrase may mean

---

14. See footnote 11.

anytime between 10:45 and 11:15. To the child, however, both because he wants to stay out late, and because of a child's tendency to see time and space in extremes (the past is ages ago, and tomorrow equals never), "around 11 o'clock" may well be extended close to 12 o'clock.

Certainly then, Torah concepts are unique to Torah *Yidden*, and translating them, or coming to "read" and interpret them as our gentile neighbors do, represents danger to the extreme. Coming back to the notion of freedom, while the world around us, the most tolerant and understanding, would label the laws of *kashrus* or Shabbos as restrictive, we see them in the very opposite way — as connoting freedom: freedom from lust, freedom from the *yeitzer hara*, freedom from the desire to do what one wants to do, always. As *Chazal* put it succinctly: "*Ein lecha ben chorin ella mi sh'oseik baTorah* — The only freedom (from want) belongs to those who live the Torah way."[15]

Behavioral scientists differ concerning the issue of whether psychological traits are genetically passed on from generation to generation. To the Torah Jew there is no question that they are.[16]

We now draw two conclusions: (1) The Jew is born with a unique personality, with Torah traits dating back to Avraham *Avinu*, our father Avraham, and, (2) Torah language reinforces and maintains these concepts, all of which create the Torah *hashkafah* we speak of.

Yet there is more. *Rambam*, in his *Peirush HaMishnayos* to *Chagigah*,[17] states: "There are certain concepts that are chiseled into the souls of the spiritually accomplished, but when the attempt is made to put these concepts into words or to strike an analogy that would convey them, the meaning is subtly altered and lost."

All this should caution us to have *emunas Chachamim*, the total trust and belief in our sages and elders who have the gift of understanding true Torah concepts. Furthermore, we must hold onto the very words and concepts and the myriad facets of Torah life as understood by our parents and teachers, and passed on to us. Finally,

---

15. *Avos* 6b.
16. See footnote 8.
17. *Chagigah* 11b.

we must be ever on the alert to subtle changes that may occur when we mingle with others and adopt their words — and thus their meaning — that may well be alien to us.[18]

---

18. The serious reader is referred to Matityahu Clark's *Etymological Dictionary of Biblical Hebrew* (Jerusalem: Feldheim Publishers, 1999). In addition to collating the many words *HaRav* Shamshon Raphael Hirsch analyzed for us, Rabbi Clark makes a strong argument concerning the danger of using foreign languages to find meanings of words in Torah — much of what this essay is all about.